Feminist Groupwork

D0289205

Gender and Psychology

Series editor: Sue Wilkinson

This international series provides a forum for the growing body of distinctively psychological research focused on gender issues. While work on the psychology of women, particularly that adopting a feminist perspective, will be central, the series will also reflect other emergent trends in the field of gender. It will encourage contributions which are critical of the mainstream of androcentric or 'gender-neutral' psychology and also innovative in their suggested alternatives.

The books will explore topics where gender is central, such as social and sexual relationships, employment, health and illness, and the development of gender identity. Issues of theory and methodology raised by the study of gender in psychology will also be addressed.

The objective is to present research on gender in the context of its broader implications for psychology. These implications include the need to develop theories and methods appropriate to studying the experience of women as well as men, and working towards a psychology which reflects the experiences and concerns of both sexes.

The series will appeal to students of psychology, women's studies and gender studies and to professionals concerned with gender issues in their practice, as well as to the general reader with an interest in gender and psychology.

Sue Wilkinson is principal lecturer and head of the psychology section at Coventry Polytechnic.

Also in this series

Subjectivity and Method in Psychology
Wendy Hollway

Feminists and Psychological Practice
edited by Erica Burman

Feminist Groupwork

Sandra Butler and Claire Wintram

SAGE Publications
London • Newbury Park • New Delhi

© Sandra Butler and Claire Wintram 1991

First published 1991
Reprinted 1992

All rights reserved. No part of this publication may be
reproduced, stored in a retrieval system, transmitted or
utilized in any form or by any means, electronic,
mechanical, photocopying, recording or otherwise, without
permission in writing from the Publishers.

 SAGE Publications Ltd
6 Bonhill Street
London EC2A 4PU

SAGE Publications Inc
2455 Teller Road
Newbury Park, California 91320

SAGE Publications India Pvt Ltd
32, M-Block Market
Greater Kailash – I
New Delhi 110 048

British Library Cataloguing in Publication Data

Butler, Sandra
   Feminist groupwork. – (Gender and psychology)
   I. Title   II. Williams, Claire   III. Series
   305.42

   ISBN 0-8039-8209-7
   ISBN 0-8039-8210-0 pbk

Library of Congress catalog card number 91-53085

Typeset by AKM Associates (UK) Ltd, Southall, London
Printed and bound in Great Britain by
Biddles Ltd, Guildford and King's Lynn

305.42
B986
1991

Contents

METHODIST COLLEGE LIBRARY
Fayetteville, N.C.

FALLING FALLING DOWN DOWN
MURKY WATER, LET ME DROWN
SINKING AND CRYING
SCREAMING OF DIEING
IS THIS ME NO NOT ME
I'M DARK I'M ANGRY
RED AND FLAMING
SEETHING BLAMING
WHERE ARE YOU WHO AM I
NOW I'M LOW NOT HIGH
WHAT IS GOOD OR BAD
I KNOW THAT I AM SAD
IN A TURMOIL
LIKE A COIL
NOW I'M CHURNING
FULL OF YEARNING
FEELINGS FOUND FEELINGS LOST
CREEPING LIKE A FROST

(Glenys Dacey –
women's group member)

We dedicate this book to all the
women we worked with, who shared with
us their pain and sadness, their
triumphs and their joy.

Acknowledgements

First of all, we would like to express our gratitude to Glenys Dacey for allowing us to use her poignant poems in the text.

Secondly, we would like to acknowledge the major influence on our work with women in groups, namely Sheila Ernst and Lucy Goodison's book *In Our Own Hands* (Women's Press, 1981). The games and exercises in this book are an endless source of inspiration. We would like to thank the Women's Press for permission to quote from the book.

Thirdly, we would like to thank Ian Buehring, Neil Fox and George Mossman for their tireless work and support during the construction of this book.

Introduction:
The Way In

Our knowledge of women working collectively is only now painstakingly being pieced together by writers, researchers and historians, with a commitment to rectifying the inaccurate and misleading picture created for us by white male historians and publishers (Lewis, 1981; Rowbotham, 1973). Current right-wing opinion would have us believe that we live in a 'post-feminist' era, that all our battles for female equality have been fought and won. In this book we hope to expose the falsehoods on which this ideology is based by revealing the struggles that women in groups go through in their attempts to recognize and deal with their experiences of oppression. This book exists as a microcosm of feminist organizing and plays one small part in the world stage of women's collective action.

Our personal and professional experiences have shown us that women brought together can offer each other support, validation and strength, and a growing sense of personal awareness, in a way that is difficult to achieve otherwise. As generic social workers within two County Council Social Services Departments, one of us operated in a rural area and the other an inner-city area; the nature of our geographical locations therefore threw up a whole range of different social problems, although core elements of social and material deprivation remained. Our social work responsibilities involved crisis and short-term work, with services largely provided on a reactive basis to persons or families in positions of extreme vulnerability, with whom work was undertaken to a point of resolution of problems, or, as was more often the case, the recognition of states to be endured.

Throughout these interactions we were acutely aware that on most occasions the person in the family we were likely to end up representing, advising and remonstrating with was female. Inevitably, she was in a caring role. Just as often she was likely to be experiencing fear, isolation and loneliness. However, given the impoverished climate within which statutory social work operates, there is little scope for innovatory or preventive work which attempts to get beyond palliative measures to a more proactive stance, promoting social and political change. It was within this atmosphere that we established and sustained two community-based women's groups with the aim of breaking down and offering alternatives to these experiences. We wished also to construct and maintain for the women concerned a view of themselves based in their own thoughts and feelings, and not those of others. We knew that such an approach was far more likely to reinforce the positive elements of their life-styles and experience than anything we could offer as individuals.

Within the context of the women's groups themselves, we co-worked the inner-city group for a period of six months and, in addition, one of us sustained a group for recently bereaved women, where group members were drawn from council housing estates, inner-city terraced housing and a private owner-occupier housing estate. Subsequently the inner-city group ran for three years; group members were drawn from a council housing estate and a terraced housing environment. The group ended on a formal basis after that time, but supportive friendships were sustained beyond this. The rural women's group was established and ran for three years with a co-worker from the same social services office; in that time, we saw a range of women move through the group and beyond, with the women's group itself making significant links with other groups in the area, and becoming more active on a political front. After the withdrawal of the workers, the women's group became self-sustaining without any professional involvement, although group members had recourse to professional contact, on their terms, when and if they wanted.

Fear, isolation and loneliness lay at the root of the experiences of many of the women with whom we were involved over the years. These three factors intertwined, forming their own perfect prism. The *fear* results from the threat of, or the actual occurrence of, physical, sexual and psychological violence. *Isolation* is caused by material constraints, such as lack of transport, money and child-care facilities, which all restrict mobility. There is no real contact with other people. Each woman convinces herself that she is the only one to know what she is feeling and experiencing. The *loneliness* that arises from such circumstances needs little elaboration, especially when a woman is told often enough that she is a failure, receiving little if any positive reinforcement for the endless domestic labour and low-paid work she may perform. Feelings of unreality, of going or of being mad, are all common amongst people divorced from any point of reference. Solitude, in such circumstances, breeds powerlessness.

Our understanding of feminism in the context of the groups is based on the structure of consciousness-raising groups of earlier stages of the Second Wave Women's Movement (Ehrenreich and English, 1979, p. 206). As white women working in a middle-class professional milieu we personally had reaped the benefits sown by such groups. Our own participation in women's groups, and the knowledge and wisdom gained from other women in reading or discussion, left us with the conviction that collectivity amongst women is a major tool in the process of deconstructing masculinist oppression, and reconstructing an alternative, personally significant reality. No woman, in any circumstances, can achieve this on her own without reference to the experience of others.

Undermining individuals and ultimately convincing them of their 'wrong thinking' is a common feature of the hierarchical structures within which most of us have to function. The arguments explaining how women remain in inferior positions, despite protestations of equality of opportunity and a true recognition of their abilities, are rehearsed elsewhere (Brook and Davis, 1985; H. Scott, 1984). As workers, we face the daily struggle of denial and dismissiveness, of the position we choose to adopt in paid work being undervalued. Yet solidarity and collectivity are exhilarating. As women, we know that we survive because of the support we receive from our sisters, whether our views coincide entirely or not, and that without this validation we would very soon suffer the distressing consequences of isolation.

Working with women from this perspective led to a far greater awareness on our part of the relentless nature of the daily struggles they faced and of the strength and resilience that kept them going. Our views of the women with whom we worked changed throughout the experience of the group process, as did our views of ourselves. We could no longer continue to define ourselves as 'professionals' divorced from the dilemmas and excitement experienced by group participants.

The stark reality of repression experienced by all women became increasingly clear in direct proportion to our involvement with the groups. We could see how our own feminist identities, confidence and anger were all harnessed and dulled by our work environment. The creeping mediocrity in our own lives enabled us to perceive much more sharply the same phenomenon in other women's experiences. Being confronted by women's pain and distress, we grew in sensitivity. We identified our own pain. Our defences against organizational pressures were so strong that we had suppressed our emotionality, just to survive. In order to get alongside women's pain and joy, we needed to shift from patronizing altruism to sharing and carrying some of the burden. Anti-oppressive practice in this context means recognizing and celebrating the humanity within each one of us. This process of our awakening throws into relief the universality of our group experiences. We can move from the specific context of a group's history to the development of key themes and arguments about groupwork which are widely applicable and transcend a localized experience.

As for the structure of the book, Chapter 1 presents our underlying philosophy, values and principles in establishing women's groups as a way of bringing women's cultural experiences out of the margins. Also, we outline our conceptual and theoretical framework, placing this within the sphere of feminist influence. Chapter 2 moves on to examine the importance of planning and preparation in feminist groupwork as a means of clarifying thinking, and follows with an outline of the importance of structuring the group programme whilst maintaining flexibility. An exploration of the role of group activities, methodology and action learning in the development of women's self-expression and collective action forms the basis of Chapter 3. In Chapter 4, we take a look at structural group relationships, and women's group dynamics and process, as a means of drawing out the necessary requirements for group identity development. By way of contrast, Chapter 5 concentrates on personal identity issues as revealed through the connections and contradictions highlighted by the content and process of group sessions. Stepping beyond the internal workings of the group, Chapter 6 examines the interface between women's groups and the environment, and the impact of members' resistance and rebellion within the personal and public spheres. Throughout all of this, we attempt to break down the culture of dominance and, instead, to locate women's experiences within the ebb and flow of personal concerns and socio-political explanations.

1
The Feminist Sphere of Influence

One of the central tenets of this chapter is that women's groups provide a basis for overcoming some of the psychological obstacles produced by occupying subordinate positions. Through the unfolding of women's lives, we will present key principles of feminist theories which have influenced us enormously and which we have used as a framework of analysis. Fundamental concepts of women's invisibility; the personal that is the political; and the oppression and empowerment of women will be explored. A discussion of women's physical isolation as well as psychological distance from each other, coupled with the violence which is meted out to them, will add weight to these feminist concepts. The deleterious effects on women's psyche of these systematic and institutional forms of oppression are then explored. Working-class women's forgotten and excluded status is highlighted further when we examine how the power of language shapes our thought patterns and our subsequent actions. By sifting through our terminology, we can acknowledge both the severely restrictive role that definitions can hold, and the ambiguity of meaning embedded within them. By focusing next on groupwork and identity issues, we will emphasize the range of changes which women's groups are capable of bringing about. Ending the chapter with an analysis of interrelationships which underpin the book, we will consider our roles as workers and people who write in connection with women's group members.

Understanding women's lives: The philosophy and principles of feminism

> The goals and strategies of feminism must be articulated with felt oppression, and with the utopian hopes, fears, wishes, aspirations of women. (Lovell, 1980, p. 87)

Our involvement with women in groups has been a privilege. It has enabled us to discern themes and recurring patterns which have affected dramatically our awareness of women's psychology. By focusing on the understandings which have informed our groupwork practice, we can provide a conceptual framework for examining the nature of women's groups. It is essential to begin on a note of caution. In the search for multiple meaning and knowledge in relation to women's experiences of groups, we should never lose sight of the argument of Stanley and Wise (1983) that theoretical intricacies can only ever be an approximation to reality. Our assumptions must be made as explicit as possible, if we are to pin-point connections and contradictions inherent in our feminist conceptual framework. Our journey begins on the road of feminist philosophical principles, proceeding via an exploration of the background and nature of women's group members' lives. Then there will be an examination of the links between group process and shifts in identity. Thirdly, we will analyse the process of feminist discovery for ourselves as women workers and authors, and the implications that this holds for our past and present relations with women's group members. We cannot leave ourselves out of the equation, nor our consciousness out of our own conceptual framework.

Feminist theories are neither monolithic nor static – it is their diversity and dynamism that are worthy of attention. Forming an integral part of our world-view, our core feminist beliefs are by no means unique; they are tried and tested, the corner-stone of feminist thought and behaviour. We voice these beliefs with commitment rather than romanticism.

Women's invisibility
There is a discernible pattern within feminist work which addresses the invisibility of women's experience and knowledge in domestic and public spheres, and redresses this injustice by reclaiming women's own history and language (Daly, 1973; Rich, 1980; Rowbotham, 1974; Spender, 1980, 1981; Stanley and Wise, 1983, to name but a few). We have already indicated that isolation and distance were at the heart of group members' experience. Autobiographical accounts of women in poverty sit uneasily with the sanitized words of professionals and academics. The social sciences lean on the massive prop of traditional research, and a woman on her experience of 'sitting under the same glass jar, stewing in my own sour air' (Plath, 1963, p. 196). By recording the hidden lives and social reality of women with whom we worked, we can generate principles for understanding and insight which may guide future practice. The relevance of feminism to the whole range of working-class women's lives has received relatively little academic attention (Ferree, 1983; Kenner, 1985; Phillips, 1987). When they have been in the spotlight it is through concentration on their roles as partners and mothers, which inevitably limits the scope of their reality.

Significant in the shaping of women's identities was their experience of isolation, being apparent on a variety of planes – physically, emotionally, psychologically. Within this theme of isolation there were differences in its meaning for women in rural and urban communities. Taking the rural community first, factors of physical or geographical distance, the general lack of public transport, dependence on lifts, weather conditions, walking, and the time involved in this, all play major parts in shaping perceptions of isolation. Life can become an exercise in organization, planning each day round the different distances to be covered and the likelihood of any lift being offered. Such factors influence the ease with which it is possible to form and sustain relationships with other women. It means that in a moment of crisis physical or geographical isolation is felt acutely. Even being able to contact someone by phone is no guarantee of their ability to respond and offer help. Within the urban community, although women may be living on the same housing estate, perhaps in adjacent streets, they may well not know each other in any real sense. They can have no idea of the other's range of experiences, their need for support and capacity to provide it. Propinquity does little initially to diminish the emotional distance and isolation the women experience.

In neither setting, therefore, are women left with any immediately identifiable reference point by which to measure and compare their experiences. Any deprivation they feel, as regards their needs being recognized and met, is explained by what they see as their own 'inadequacies'. They turn inward and on themselves for answers to questions that cannot be formulated with ease. The assumptions with which a woman has grown up and that she has taken into relationships remain unchallenged. There are no different perspectives from which she can choose, nor encouragement to test out whether things could be different. Survival exists in a vacuum.

Sometimes the exact opposite occurs, when limitations on the scope for self-expression mean that a woman's physical manifestations of feeling become more acute and open to such interpretations as 'bizarre' and 'inappropriate'. The whole notion of 'distance' underpins the experience of this dislocation. By not trusting her own reactions, a woman's responses to similar events become inconsistent or self-destructive. Feelings of self-blame and of being out of control rapidly ensue. Memories of other possible responses may be dim. The belief that she can take control of her destiny in however limited a way may never have been nurtured.

The increased visibility of *all* women therefore involves a recognition of the complexity of our responses to isolation and distance. Only then can we grapple with the differences *between* women, based on the interplay of dimensions such as race, ethnicity, age, sexuality and disability.

The personal is political

The central tenet of the contemporary Women's Movement has been a belief in the validity of personal experience as a means of understanding the nature of women's oppression. Thus, power imbalance and exploitation are lived out as much in women's personal lives as in social structures, which are themselves re-created by individual action. This argument forms the building block upon which we will construct our thoughts concerning women together in groups. It is the process of collective self-reflection and analysis which leads to a broader understanding of the political, from which women can construct their own personal meanings.

The relationship between individual consciousness and theoretical understanding of reality is not problem-free. As we will emphasize later, the recognition and identification of the links between women's daily activity and the nature of social processes can be painstaking and painful. With the realization that the distinction between the private and public, the personal and social, is blurred, there is still the barrier to overcome of so-called intellectual skills which have become socially divisive, monopolized by the superficially articulate white middle classes. This raises two crucial points for us. First, theory needs to be accessible (Stanley and Wise, 1983). Secondly, connections need to be made between existing feminist theories and our learning from the practices of women's group members.

The oppression of women

An underlying feminist assumption which permeates our thoughts, behaviour and attitudes is that patriarchy systematically oppresses women in every sphere of life. Although the mechanisms and consequences of patriarchy are experienced by women in many different ways, women's groups provide a shared means of becoming conscious of the nature of that material and ideological oppression.

Beginning from the broad sweep of this feminist principle, there are particular aspects of feminist debate which we wish to accentuate in our search for a discourse between theory and experience. The women with whom we worked had all experienced subordination not only by virtue of their gender socialization, but also in terms of intense social and economic deprivation. Initially, we were faced with a question which emerged for us as practitioners and has stayed ever since – namely, how far have the priorities and practices of the Women's Movement excluded and denied the experiences of many working-class women? If exclusion has occurred in the past, then how can working-class women in groups offer a sensitive recognition of differences between themselves as well as similarities?

These questions prevent us from falling into the trap of believing that the feminism of the Women's Movement can be presented as the consciousness of women in general. The reasons for this are twofold and concern the meaning of knowledge, as well as our understanding of culture. First, the women with whom we worked had been denied 'knowledge' because their experiences were unrecognized. In contrast, 'knowledge' which is elevated to the level of theory has social status, and becomes divisive rather than explanatory. Secondly, the cultural dispossession of working-class women has occurred because the information they offer is misused and cultural concerns are seen to be interesting, yet socially inferior. An outline of significant life factors amongst group members will serve as an illustration of the denial of their cultural experiences and the depths of their oppression.

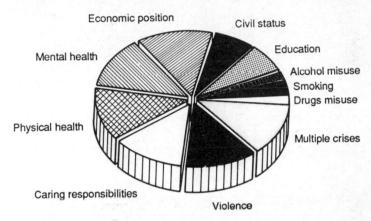

Figure 1   *Significant life factors amongst group members*

As can be seen in Figure 1, there were major and constant similarities amongst the women who attended the rural and urban women's groups, revolving around their perceptions of mental and physical health, their caring responsibilities, their experience of violence and multiple crises, and their use of alcohol, drugs and nicotine. The women also had things in common as regards their economic position and civil status. When we look at the membership of the urban and rural groups in greater depth, however, structural differences did exist between them:

1 *Economic position*: All members of the urban groups were dependent on state benefits. If any were engaged in paid work, it was sporadic and low-paid. Members of the rural groups had a mix of employment status. Whilst a significant proportion were in receipt of state benefits, women were also involved in low-paid part-time work or full-time factory work, with split or twilight shifts.

2 *Civil status*: Two women in the urban groups were married and living with their spouse, whilst the rest were cohabiting, single or divorced. The rural groups' membership consisted of married, single, divorced and cohabiting women. There were lesbian women in this group.

3 *Education*: Across all groups, women had not undertaken further or higher education, and some had left school early because of teenage pregnancy or truancy. Levels of literacy varied greatly.

4 *Physical health*: In both groups gynaecological problems were common. In addition, some members of the rural groups experienced bronchitis and chronic respiratory difficulties, as well as physical disabilities which restricted their mobility.

5 *Mental health*: A significant proportion of all women across the rural and urban groups had been involved in the psychiatric system, being labelled as schizophrenic, post-natally depressed, manic-depressive, agoraphobic, and subject to anxiety attacks. These definitions of themselves had been internalized by group members. Those women who had not received a formal medical diagnosis nevertheless felt mentally distressed at times.

6 *Caring responsibilities*: In the urban groups, all members were mothers and held the major responsibility for child-rearing. In the rural groups, the performance of caring tasks was more diverse, involving not only child-care, but also the care of elderly parents or relatives and disabled partners.

7 *Multiple crises*: All women in the urban and rural groups had to deal with multiple crises in their lives and as a result tended to live vicariously, lurching from one pressured situation to another. Crises ranged from bereavement, illness, debt, eviction and prosecution, to domestic violence.

8 *Substance abuse*: A significant proportion of women in both the urban and rural groups had misused or were abusing prescribed drugs or alcohol. The majority of women in the urban groups and half the rural groups were smokers.

9 *Experiences of violence*: Women in both the rural and urban settings had experienced a range of physical, sexual, emotional and psychological violence during their lives. These experiences kept women in positions of fear and subordination and were compounded by the psychological effects of isolation.

The difficulty of creating and sustaining social networks affects women's awareness of the need to name and discuss their own and each other's experiences of violence. The taboos surrounding this perpetuate the impression of distance. In such circumstances self-blame takes precedence and is used to explain any violent episode. Rationalizations become one of the main tools of survival. 'If only I'd tried harder, been quieter, kept my mouth shut, answered him the way he wanted me to . . . things would never have got out of hand.' In other words, do not exist at all in the way that feels right.

The psychological effects of oppression   What then is the impact of this cultural dispossession on women's psychology? The cumulative effect of the elements listed above was debilitating, so that all women identified low self-image and self-esteem as a major concern for them. Statements made by women themselves at the beginning of each series of sessions were largely constant across both settings and for each new group of participants. They focused very much on the following:

> I'm aggressive. I'm caring. I give in to any pressure. I'm impatient, I lose my temper. I'm not loving enough. I'm wicked. I'm demanding. I don't try hard enough.

At the root of these self-perceptions was their experience of oppression, represented visually by women in Figure 2. Here, the immediate pressures of children, men and families jostle with the discriminatory practices of caring professional groups such as social workers, doctors, psychiatrists, teachers, Education Welfare Officers and the police. All of this was framed by a system of economic disadvantage, stemming from government policies and lived out through women's experiences of substandard housing, Income Support and, for some, the Fraud Squad. Women lurched from one day to the next trying to juggle with inadequate resources, both financial and emotional, and with no room to move other than in a reactive fashion as they dealt with a plethora of demands.

An appraisal of mainstream psychological interpretations of women's behaviour and their terminology (Walker, 1981) readily demonstrates the ways in which socio-economic factors, compounded by paternalistic and patriarchal definitions, have been ignored as major contributory factors in women's depression, or at best conveniently put to one side (Chesler, 1972; Daly, 1978). Notions of individualism have done much to exacerbate this and to reinterpret broadly based social issues as private problems.

Here indeed is a central feature of the private problems–public issues argument (Longres and McLeod, 1980). Women's reactions to states of stress, their manifestations of distress, are pathologized as private and personal problems, bearing no relation to the social construction of motherhood or lack of resources. This interpretation has become an almost automatic response across welfare agencies, backed up by considerable theoretical weight, as mainstream psychological views perceive women to be mentally unhealthy and victims of biological determinism (Allen, 1987; Chesler, 1972; Ehrenreich and English,

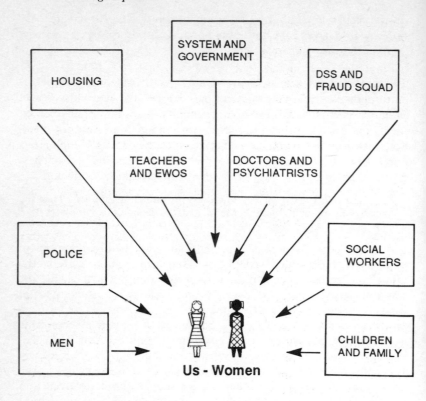

DSS   Department of Social Security
EWOS   Education Welfare Officers

Figure 2   *Women's psychology: the weights of oppression*

1979; Nairne and Smith, 1984). If this is the only explanation women
are offered by those they turn to for help, and whom they see as having
knowledge and power, then it is not surprising that such stultifying
explanations are accepted.

It is at this point that the psychiatric model is offered as a way of
dealing with these public issues (Penfold and Walker, 1984), bringing
damage in its wake. If women's health is permanently unsound
(Broverman et al., 1970), this in itself is adequate explanation for their
discomfort in the world. Broverman and her colleagues examined the
sex-role stereotypes of a group of mental health professionals, asking
them to define mentally healthy men, women and adults. The
characteristics of the mentally healthy adult corresponded closely with
those of the mentally healthy man. Women, on the other hand, were
perceived as different from the healthy adult because they were more

submissive, less adventurous, more easily influenced, more emotional and excitable in minor crises, less competitive and aggressive than their male counterparts. This constellation of factors renders women vulnerable to being labelled as neurotic and mentally disturbed because such characteristics are not perceived as mentally healthy. It becomes clearer why participants' descriptions of themselves feature statements such as 'I'm not loving enough', 'I don't try hard enough.' Responsibility is pushed back on to them to adapt their own shape to fit better into spaces in the world that do not accommodate either their needs or their skills.

Deconstructing oppression: The role of feminist theories If it is accepted that the causes of depression are inextricably bound up with patriarchy, where women are kept in compliant and subservient roles, then any shift away from this state of affairs will involve a radical overhaul of societal functioning. This is where radical feminist arguments (for instance, Firestone, 1972; Millett, 1971; Rich, 1976) come in. The omnipresence of the deep-rooted status differences between men and women sustains gender relations which are socially constructed. Liberation only occurs when women create their own value systems and world-views to counteract social injustice. Within this broad framework, socialist feminist arguments help us to recognize the social control of women's labour and the links between class inequality and sexism (Barratt, 1980; Phillips, 1987; Rowbotham, 1974, 1983). We need to be sensitive to all dimensions of social injustice and to distinguish between the widely differing structures and ideologies of women's oppression in different social groups, periods of history and social classes.

We are aware of the need to be flexible rather than rigid in our analysis of feminist ideology. It is possible to move between differing points of emphasis regarding the cause and effect of women's oppression. Whilst attempting to draw out principles for practice and understanding that can be available to women across social boundaries, we need to be equally alert to the ways the word 'women' has masqueraded for black and white, for middle and working class, for lesbian and heterosexual, for able- and non-able-bodied. This is so much the case that we can end up believing that differences are figments of our imagination, that woman is woman (Daly, 1978; Spender, 1982) and her story remains the same.

There is a danger that, in seeking to apply our groupwork theory and practice across diverse social situations, we will inadvertently end up stereotyping women on the basis of age, class, race, ethnicity, sexuality and disability. If we focus on racism, as white feminists working with white women, we must immediately recognize the ethnocentric nature of our practice and our role as white oppressors. At the same time, our analysis needs to acknowledge the arguments of those women who have accused the Women's Movement of denying the significance of race and of developing feminist theories which do not account for black women's historical and contemporary position (Carby, 1982; A. Davis, 1982; Hooks, 1982; Joseph and Lewis, 1981). The term 'black' has political significance in that it is a validation of the shared experiences of those who are marginalized on the basis of their physical characteristics and skin colour.

A particular difficulty lies in our conceptualization of patriarchal relations, because white feminists understand patriarchy to be the source of women's oppression. In contrast, women from any cultural group outside the dominant white order have come together, despite their diverse cultural experiences, to argue that men from these same cultural groups do not have the same relationship to patriarchal–capitalist hierarchies as white heterosexual men (Bryan et al., 1985; Carby, 1982). It is important for us to recognize that sexism operates independently of and simultaneously with racism (Hooks, 1982) and other forms of social inequality.

Does our use of the terminology 'working-class white women' invoke the judgement, as Packwood (1983) recognizes, that every member of this social group possesses the unenviable characteristics of coarseness, stupidity and ignorance? Does this description leave these women any opportunity for self-expression or self-definition? We have made a conscious decision to use this terminology because of women's own perceptions of their structural position. It remains to be said that the ease with which our language slips into stereotyping should alert us to the subtle and indirect, but none the less damaging and insidious, forms of oppression dressed up in the cloak of liberalism.

The empowerment of women
Having sketched the struggle which lies ahead in order to address the complexities of women's realities, we need to move beyond women's oppression into the realms of women's empowerment. We want to celebrate womanhood. By providing positive images of women we will address the following questions:

1   How can working-class white women become aware of forces maintaining their survival as well as their oppression?
2   Are such models of collaborative effort potentially transferable to other women from different socio-economic and cultural backgrounds, spurred on by the strength and inspiration of their sisters?

Women's strength and fortitude, as played out in group sessions, gave confidence for challenges, however small, to male tyranny outside the context of the group. Hence, women learnt to take power for themselves and use their energy positively. The move from the identification of shared pain to shared strength is not linear – there are pitfalls and diversions along the way. Despite the range of women's negative self-perceptions, there was always an expressed wish for change in Self, in life-style, and in the circumstances surrounding this. The hope that women identified emerged out of their resilience in dealing with adversity. Women taking power means that time is often spent in deliberating about the old order and engaging in the excitement, but also the apprehension, of the new. It is readily understandable if women opt to remain with the familiar environment of oppression, even if they are conscious that this is precisely what they are doing.

Empowerment also involves an exploration of the interstitial and spreading branches of women's diversity. Far from being fragmentary, the diversity between women is a positive asset, enriching and challenging to such an extent that horizons are widened and women's relations with each other become a force for change. To move from awareness to positive action is an overwhelming experience, the repercussions of which can be both frightening and exhilarating, but in the long-term lead to a reappraisal of the Self in its social context. Empowerment for us involves building bridges between women separated by social inequality. At the same time, we need to make as explicit as possible those individual biographies situated within a set of class, gender, sexual, race, ethnic and cultural constructions.

Framing groupwork and identity

Social groupwork in Britain has its roots in United States practice dating back to the ideologies of the post-war period, predominantly the 1960s onwards. Encounter groups, group psychotherapy and behavioural approaches all have their offshoots on this side of the Atlantic. Groupwork as sanctioned within statutory settings is likely to be constrained in nature, with workers and other participants expected to maintain distant and differentiated roles. In addition, the aims and purpose of the group must be seen to comply with the policies and philosophy of the agency. There are inevitably variations in responsiveness to workers' wishes for involvement in groupwork within different agencies. Nevertheless, groupwork with women, organized *by* women, and carried out from a feminist perspective, is likely to be seen as at least risky, and at most as a direct challenge to normative practices. There is no doubt that fear is generated when groups of women are together. The masculinist status quo is threatened even more when women organize themselves within a socio-political context of poverty and deprivation.

Definitions of 'sex', 'gender' and 'working class'
The range and depth of our contact with women who defined
themselves as working class has convinced us that the status afforded
them by virtue of their sex and class is 'social junk'. By piecing together
the fragmentation of existence, the group gives them the opportunity
to become 'social dynamite' (David, 1986; Dex and Phillipson, 1986;
H. Scott, 1984; Spitzer, 1973). The fear of this transition is symbolized
by the confused usage of the words 'sex' and 'gender'. For us, 'sex'
refers to genetically determined characteristics and is a biological term,
whereas 'gender' has a psychological and cultural basis. It is the
complex interplay of the forces of societal expectations with the prescriptions on behaviour, attitudes and roles based on sex differentiation.

Women's awareness of themselves as 'social junk' is further
characterized by their use of the term 'working class', which for
women's group members not only embodied the denial of access to
education, health care, paid employment and socio-economic status,
but also denial of their lived experiences. Their perspective does not
fall prey to the traditional practices of class analysis which have relied
heavily on masculine experience, particularly in terms of stratification
by occupation (Phillips, 1987). For them, the definition of 'working
class' from a woman-centred perspective took on the positive
connotations of identifying with their historical roots and having pride
in the continuity of family rituals and traditions, which have been
excluded from the white culture of dominance.

Definitions of 'groupwork'
Definitions have another role in providing clues about individual and
organizational attitudes and values. The assumptions which underpin
generally accepted groupwork approaches reveal that women need to
carve out their own space in what is essentially a hostile environment.
Such approaches assume that welfare agencies can 'meet needs'
effectively (Smith, 1980). The ideology of need is riddled with value
judgements (Doyal and Gough, 1984; Illich et al., 1977) and
patriarchy's own views inevitably impinge on beliefs as to what is
relevant and worthwhile. 'Needs-meeting' has become part of the
instrumental justification of groupwork and revolves around the
following approaches.

Defining felt need 'Felt needs' (George and Wilding, 1976) are
closer to the psychological concept of 'want', in that they are
'perceived needs' stemming from within and not ascribed from
without. It may be that people will only 'feel a need' if they already
know that there is a service available to satisfy it, and the limited social
horizons of women in lower income groups restrict their demands.

Defining expressed need We cannot know of the existence of a felt need unless it is translated into action, that is, it becomes an expressed need (Bradshaw, 1972). This can only be fully understood by investigating the interests of the professionals who shape these demands. When workers bring together people with similar expressed needs, it is felt that these can best be met by imparting knowledge jointly. There may not be any clear idea of how this knowledge will be used.

Defining changes in behaviour   When behavioural change is deemed appropriate, workers may hold beliefs that such changes are likely to be encouraged in a co-operative or semi-coercive fashion through group participation. The group is seen as a forum for reinforcing appropriate behaviour and for establishing and sustaining normative values.

In the groups under discussion in this book both definition and reality diverge from agency expectations and norms. By engaging in feminist groupwork, we challenged agency structures and offered an alternative paradigm of the groupwork process. The definition of 'feminist groupwork' that emerges from our experience is that of enabling women to meet and identify both their common and their diverse dissatisfactions and needs and to translate these into wants. The group process facilitates the exploration of ways in which these wants can be met. Integrated throughout is the belief that women have the right to seek power and control over their own lives, and to feel secure in challenging conventional images of themselves. The group provides scope for re-evaluation, with change emerging out of collective and individual action. The impact on participants, workers included, is great, transcending the confines of the group itself.

It is inevitable that definitions drawn up by practitioners and academics will be more narrowly based than those developed by participants themselves. If we peel off the layers of academic and agency sophistication, we are left with women's own powerful and fundamental statements. For them, the group is:

1   a source of immediate support, where the knowledge that the meeting will take place every week provides a safety net in itself;
2   a place to recognize shared experiences and the value to be derived from these;
3   a way of breaking down isolation and loneliness;
4   the source of a different perspective on personal problems;
5   a place to experience power over personal situations with the capacity to change and have an effect on these;
6   a source of friendship

Clearly, the breadth and quality of these perceptions lead us to an analysis of the principles underpinning the theory and practice of feminist groupwork.

Within the small group structure the question is not only, '*What* do groupworkers *do* in relation to women's groups and *why*?', but also, '*Why* should this feminist practice *be* as it is?'

We aim to show that:

1   Groupwork, both its practice and theory, is a value-laden enterprise. Attitudes and beliefs are *there* in workers' actions at *every* stage of the practice endeavour, whether they are aware of it or not. Feminism helps workers to make these values and theoretical principles as explicit as possible, and to share them at every stage of the group process.

2   Theory and practice are interdependent, making it possible to transfer groupwork methods and approaches to diverse situations.

3   As Mullender and Ward (1985) point out, a 'practice wisdom' of innovatory groupwork may be built up and passed on between practitioners, by word of mouth, but its impact remains localized and short-lived. Such pioneering developments need a wider audience to disseminate the practice skills, techniques and values which have emerged through trial and error. These can then be tried and tested across different professional groups, having a far wider impact for workers and their clients.

4   Groupwork practice from the worker's perspective needs to evolve from a theoretical consideration of group structure and dynamics. Whilst to some extent we will be addressing key issues surrounding groupwork *per se*, it is the *effects* and *consequences* of practice on the nature, purpose and direction of the group itself that need critical attention. How therefore can we *understand* group dynamics, as particular aspects unfold before us, spontaneously, as well as through the planning process? We shall be addressing two aspects of group theory which are especially relevant to women's groups, namely:

(a)   group identity formation and development;

(b)   individual identity development and change.

These two dimensions are by no means separate: they are dialectically related and are revealed through group structure, process and dynamics (to which we shall return in Chapters 4 and 5).

If identity is intertwined with group dynamics, it presents us with a thorny problem. There are many definitions of identity, all potentially conflicting and derived from different schools of psychological thought, but all of which attempt to understand the same fundamental processes and phenomena, namely those characteristics which differentiate one person from another. As with any theoretical concept, the thorns are potentially damaging, their structure and components changing, depending upon whose definition of reality (or, in this case, identity) is being used. Our model of identity must draw together intrapsychic and socio-political processes. This is in keeping with Breakwell (1986), who argues that identity should be treated as 'a dynamic social product, residing in psychological processes, which cannot be understood except in relation to its social context and historical perspective' (p. 9). Nowhere is this better illustrated than in the case of women's identity. Women, for the most part, are only conscious of the Self in relation to others, and hence the construction of 'Self' is largely defined by those around them.

Breakwell's model of identity, which is devised in order to examine threats to identity and coping strategies, is particularly relevant to our study because its various components can be applied and adapted to the workings of women's groups. It offers a level of theoretical understanding which captures the dynamism of group process and reflects the personal realities of group members. Drawing on various traditions of thought, Breakwell proposes that identity is structured across two planes – the content and value dimension. The *content dimension* encompasses both what has previously been considered 'social identity' (group membership, roles) and 'personal identity' (values, attitudes, cognitive style), thus abandoning a distinction between the two. Each element in the content dimension holds a positive or negative value (*value dimension*), which is constantly subject to reappraisal, in response to changes in social systems and the individual's position in relation to such systems.

Every time a women's group session takes place, each woman uses *aspects* of her identity drawn from roles and group membership (social product), which themselves possess a particular *identity value*. These values are attributed on the basis of social beliefs (social context) in interaction with previously established personal *value codes* (historical perspective). Through the process of communication in the group, the values attached to particular social roles (for example, mother, daughter, partner) may be reconstructed through each woman's social representation of her position. This may lead ultimately to changes in, or the ability to cope with, existing aspects of her identity.

No person exists in a vacuum, and intrapsychic processes are tied up in an individual's multiple encounters. Hence, an understanding of *group identity* formation and the role of *mutual identification and influence* is crucial if we are to gain a clearer picture of why women's groups come to be a source of support and strength. It is our hypothesis that within the context of a women's group, a woman's development of positive identity concepts occurs around her *individuality*. This then feeds into group identity, of which each group member forms a part, and out of this individuality comes the force of *collectivity* and *social action*.

At this stage it has only been necessary to refer to the infrastructure of our model. Central tenets of Breakwell's (1986) theoretical propositions will be used in our analysis, although we diverge from her arguments concerning threats to identity and coping strategies, to which we will return in Chapter 5. Although not written from a feminist perspective, there are parallels between Breakwell's analysis of identity and our own discoveries concerning individual and group identity whilst engaging in practice. As Wilkinson (1986, p. 21) indicates, though, it is crucial that any theory devised outside of feminism is considered critically for its value *for* women and, in addition, should not preclude the development of woman-based theory.

Our theoretical framework is a hybrid of concepts and models drawn from a whole range of sources. Each component is critically examined from a feminist baseline; if found wanting it is discarded, but if potential exists, it will be adapted for the purpose of feminism. This methodology is not without its conflicts, as theoretical principles invariably pull against each other. Our aim is to be clear which developments are made from already existing theoretical materials, and which components have been derived *directly* from practice. At the end of the day, if theory does not crystallize the intricacies of women's experiences, then it is redundant and has little place in the empowerment of women.

Framing process within feminist theory

So far we have looked at the emergent themes and properties that we hope to generate and have concentrated on the structural and ideological *content* of our theoretical world. A holistic presentation also includes an analysis of the *process* of the enterprise with which we are engaged. We need to consider our role as women workers and writers, and our relations with women's group members, both actively and retrospectively.

There has been considerable debate amongst feminists (Finch, 1984; Graham, 1984; Roberts, 1981; Stanley and Wise, 1983) about the nature of research and the risks of manipulation or abuse of women who prove to be 'fair game' for the social researcher. Women who stand at the sharp end of socio-economic disadvantage are vulnerable to exploitation by the researcher, who, in true liberal fashion, may inadvertently expose the idiosyncrasies of lives to abuse, with pleas of confidentiality and integrity of intent. These dangers fill us with dread. How can we avoid the double jeopardy – the risks of oppression of

women's group members through our role as paid workers, *and* through our commitment to unpicking the complex threads of group members' lived experiences by using the vehicle of writing? This central dilemma can be explored through the dimensions of:
  (a) woman-to-woman relations;
  (b) writer-to-woman relations;
  (c) worker-to-client relations.

Woman-to-woman relations
Above everything else, and whatever our roles, we must not lose sight of the fact that we are women working together. This provides the opportunity for enrichment and challenges, where disagreements and our own oppressive behaviour can be examined honestly and critically. By this we do not wish to imply that the developing relations between women are only significant in terms of their sentimentality and cosiness. The appeal of sisterhood is not to dismiss differences to the point where we are all walking on a straight line. Rather, the divergences of woman-to-woman relations draw out our weaknesses and vulnerabilities, our strengths and achievements, our conflicts and our potential.

Writer-to-woman relations
If we apply discussions regarding feminist research to the writing enterprise, researchers have argued on points of methodology and ethics that there is no irreducible norm with which all feminist research methods should comply (Klein, 1983). Similarly, masculinist notions of the neutrality of the researcher and the distinctions between subjectivity and objectivity have been met with considerable scepticism by feminists (Du Bois, 1983; Spender, 1980; Stanley and Wise, 1983). In order to move away from the fragmentation of women's lives from their social context, feminists have argued for a holistic approach which incorporates a range of research methods with an analysis of the dynamic interaction between researcher and researched. Stanley and Wise (1983), in particular, have stressed that all research is conducted through the consciousness of the researcher.
  In our case, there seems little point in avoiding and making invisible the complex ways in which reflexivity occurs. Our *direct* involvement with women's group members as social work practitioners (rather than as observers or participant-observers, in the research sense), meant that we were *of* and *in* the groups simultaneously. In addition, our retrospective analysis of the groups cannot be divorced from this reflexive process, because our interpretations and theoretical constructs are shaped by and through our *own* experiences of being part of the groups. We were both actors and acted upon. This might expose us to

claims of bias and triviality, as highlighted by Roberts (1981, p. 14), but the 'personal' dynamic must remain central on all fronts, both for women's group members and for ourselves. After all, theory and research activities are both value-laden and socially determined constructions.

How then can we attempt to temper the tendency towards misrepresentation once the recording of daily activities is processed through the consciousness of the researcher? We can turn to Graham (1984) for assistance, as she stresses the need for data collection and analysis to involve the direct participation of the women who are involved in the research process, which gives control to all participants and acknowledges the validity of their social context. She advocates the use of stories as a means of collecting data, where story-telling around certain themes allows the women who are providing the information to contribute to the structure of the interviews and avoid the fracturing of women's experiences.

In applying such principles to our work, it is possible for us to counteract the potential risk of exploitation. Our retrospective analysis, based as it is on the process of reflexivity, will draw upon records and reports written during the duration of the groups; written summaries and feedback from women regarding group sessions; women's personal statements made in group sessions and during the evaluation process. The sum total of these sources of information constitutes a collection of group 'biographies', which together create a picture of women's lives and give rise to patterns and themes which have emerged out of scattered, individualized statements.

The dimension of women as writers also pushes our discussion further. Lury (1987) suggests that the category of 'experience' can be seen as the primary mediating relation between reader, writer and text, between talk and action. We want to extend this to include women's group members and the representations they can make to women readers from other social arenas through *their* experiences. Having said this, these representations have been mediated through the process of writing, and our comprehension of women's lives is itself a social construction. There is no 'truth', just different ways of seeing and believing. Lury also challenges the traditional picture of the reader in opposition to the writer, and again we wish to extend this awareness to the notion of *partnership* between women as subjects, and women, like ourselves, who are 'people who sometimes write' (Morley and Warpole, 1982, p. 58). The deconstruction of the word 'writer' acts as a release from the constraints of language and artistic ability, where, rather than being seen as a gift writing becomes a skill which can be learnt. For ourselves as women who sometimes write, collectivity is also mirrored in our methods of writing, where 'we', rather than 'I' or 'she', becomes a conscious statement about women writing together, as well as women being together in groups. As Itzin (1987: p. 115) has said, 'As our writing is our thinking, it is a powerful tool in our own and everyone's liberation.'

Worker-to-woman-relations
The third facet is our relationship with women as paid workers. Because of dominant social ideologies concerning women's caring responsibilities, women frequently receive social work attention (Brook and Davis, 1985; Marchant and Wearing, 1986; Wilson, 1977) as they act as negotiators between the state and the family. In addition, women are denied access to resources on a level comparable with men (Hutter and Williams, 1981) which makes them more vulnerable to state intervention. On the other side of the table, women social workers, although cushioned from grinding poverty by virtue of their education, status and salary, are nevertheless carrying state-sanctioned caring responsibilities towards people in positions of vulnerability. 'Caring' has therefore remained predominantly the province of women, in both the family and state sectors. Women social workers also experience discrimination once in employment through the vertical and horizontal segregation which occurs in the promotion stakes and the sort of work that is valued. It is women who are the front-line workers, carrying out lower-status jobs, yet they are predominantly managed by men. It comes as no surprise, then, that the social worker–client encounter is most frequently a sex-specific one of woman to woman.

Given this context, as women social workers we took with us to group sessions a recognition of our status within the organization, whilst at the same time knowing all too well that the fact of receiving a salary each month and owning a car immediately created a difference between us and women's group members. It would have been dishonest to ask for unanimity between women by hiding our salaries and material trappings behind a call for false equality. The differences in our socio-economic positions were noted, not as a source of conflict, but as a statement of fact:

> Well, at the end of the day, we're all committed to the group, but there's one difference – you're getting paid for it and we're not.

This pertinent observation by one women's group member raises the dilemma of power relations between women. As group workers/social workers, we are invested with a degree of normative and expert power, by virtue of our roles and group members' initial perceptions, which could easily turn to exploitation. During the group's duration it is essential that these structural positions are examined and broken down as much as possible.

Our conceptual framework draws on material which is in one sense specific and localized, but the women's strength which we encountered provides dynamic material for a processual rather than a static analysis that is applicable across a range of situations. We have encapsulated the interplay between feminism, women's identity and the practice theories of groupwork. These discourses are linked dialectically to the ideological and structural implications of the writing/research process, where the personal dimension is of paramount importance. Our relationship with the women was creative, active, and our own resulting conceptualizations of the entangled world of such dynamics are constantly evolving. This is a searching and purposeful endeavour, and we hope to do justice to the women by letting them speak for themselves and by weaving their accounts into the fabric of our writing.

Women working together in groups offer more than a particular theoretical stance; they also make a political statement. Women's groups have worked not simply to interrogate the ideology of patriarchal relations at the level of theory, but also to disrupt its *practical* functioning. As a result, the pursuit of knowledge, which invariably exists in an ideological and hegemonic haven monopolized by an élitist few, becomes the province of *all* women on *their* terms.

2
Mapping Out the Ground:
The Contours of Planning
and Preparation

PAIN AND INSANE
MY LIFE IS FULL OF RAIN
DRIPPING IN TEARS
NO ONE HEARS
DO THEY CARE
NO JUST STARE
I'M MAD AND BAD
SILLY AND SAD
LET ME GO
WHO IS MY FOE
IS IT SHE
OR IS IT ME
LACKING IN LIFE
FULL OF STRIFE
DISTANT BUT NEAR
JUST ONE LOST TEAR

(Glenys Dacey –
women's group member)

Recounted in descriptive terms, the 'success' stories of the groups we established give an impression that the enterprise was an easy one. Nothing could be further from the truth. Using groupwork to break down the overwhelming sense of isolation, as contained in the above poem, can be exhausting, frustrating, fun, intense, powerful, overwhelmingly complex . . . the list is endless, and the potential gains infinite, but the costs can be equally high. For this reason, now is the most appropriate time to explore the theoretical and practical issues which are particularly buoyant during the planning phases of women's groups. We will consider a set of associated ideas and practices which emerged in relation to planning, thereby illustrating the range of paradoxes with which workers are faced when seeking to break new ground and offer a radical response to social problems.

What needs to happen before groups come into existence by way of the creative energy, clear thinking and communication skills required by workers, and the degree of commitment and ability to take risks

which women members need to evolve? We shall begin this chapter with a consideration of those crucial phases, namely:
(a) planning and preparation;
(b) structuring the group programme.

It will be seen that these phases involve considerable planning – planning which helps workers to clarify their thinking, to ask themselves critical questions. Out of this process of self-awareness can come honesty and openness with group members.

Planning and preparation

Creating the conditions for groupwork
The demand for a groupwork service can come to the worker's attention by a number of routes, each one generating different points of consideration. In our case, the impetus for groupwork was of our own making. Our decision to respond to women's isolation and despair through the establishment of women-only groups grew out of our belief in the centrality of social-structural explanations for social problems, and our own personal experience of gaining so much strength and encouragement from our sisters in consciousness-raising groups. This deliberate attempt to bring together two styles of working – feminism and groupwork – which had developed in different spheres of our lives, is a stance that is shared by Davies (1982), who writes about her involvement in a women's group on a post-war council housing estate in Glasgow, where she was a community worker.

Why was it felt necessary to reach out to women in the first instance, and then to assume that groupwork was the most appropriate way of dealing with the forms of social injustice with which social workers are confronted every day? When constantly faced with women in distress, we begin to feel immobilized by endless demands on the one hand and profoundly inadequate resources on the other. Because of the drain on both human and material resources of worker and client we believe that there *has* to be a more effective response to human disengagement than the traditional casework model. Shifting our focus from individualized and pathologizing problem-solving within families, to group, neighbourhood and community can reveal untapped resources. The support derived can begin to break down the hopelessness which so many women in poverty experience. Groups can occupy a unique position in a given locality, existing between the forces of the state and community.

Five common areas emerge as central to the wish to establish the groups:

1   an acute awareness of a gap in provision where women in such situations were concerned;

2 very similar statements about isolation, loneliness and confusion made time and again by women clients;
3 hearing repeated statements by colleagues about women that we disagreed with – that they were manipulative, inadequate, childish, hysterical, unresponsive and unreliable;
4 our own personal value systems and our belief that the constraints of the legal structures within which we work provide no space for women's self-exploration;
5 our wish to have an impact on attitudes towards and policies about working with women within our employing agency.

Throughout the initial planning stages of the group, we experienced a growing awareness of our own strengths and weaknesses, convictions and fears. Retrospectively, a pattern emerges of a conviction of the need for a group based on good intentions, coupled with a growing recognition of our own apprehensions. A group is always an unknown quantity, with fears arising particularly in relation to encouraging women to change in a hostile environment, and the risks of tackling violent men.

A decision to 'risk' groupwork faces workers with a range of dilemmas. Groupwork does not save time; it requires a high level of planning, research and evaluation if it is to be effective and worthwhile. Groupwork demands a great deal of workers emotionally, psychologically and practically, and invariably has to be fitted into an already overstretched work schedule. Groupwork is very much a poor relation in welfare agencies and there is therefore pressure for any group that is established to become the bottomless pit into which clients who are perceived to be difficult, entrenched or 'unmotivated' are thrown. No wonder many groups crumble. Neither is groupwork a panacea for all social ills: it can never be the sole answer to power imbalances and social injustice.

There is no dispute that potentially heavy costs are involved in groupwork, but we work and live in a society filled with contradictions, and whilst the existence of such risks is irrefutable, there is a high level of gains to be made. Indeed, as workers it is easy to construct dilemmas which in the end *prevent* any moves forward, thereby becoming a barrier to change. The first step in the justification of groupwork is to *convince yourself* that it is a viable means of intervention, and to realize that groupwork must reconcile apparent opposites in order to perceive the complementarity in contradiction.

Organizational and environmental context

Responding to organizational barriers   A major consideration when undertaking groupwork is the role of the employing agency in the provision of time, finances and resources. A group is more likely to succeed if colleagues and management accept and support its aims, and the potential contribution it can make to the institution. Added to which, no theory can survive outside a context which facilitates its implementation and expression. Thus one of the first considerations for the feminist worker is how to respond and act as a member of a minority group within her employing agency when she is in the process of negotiating permission for the group. In relation to feminist groupwork, clashes of ideology can immediately ensue between the predominant masculinist practices of hierarchical institutions and the co-operative, non-hierarchical methodologies employed by feminists (Hearn et al., 1989). How then can the worker understand the organizational processes operating around her, and what strategies can be devised to convince the organization of the potential gains of working with women in groups?

The worker first of all needs to understand the nature of the enterprise with which she is dealing, namely the workings of a patriarchal institution. Women have firsthand knowledge of the ways in which patriarchy operates against them. However, the organization can simultaneously contain within it a whole range of practices, be they benign, paternalistic, conflictual, ambiguous or aggressive, all of which deny women workers knowledge about the forms in which decision-making occurs. Women workers therefore need to devise methods of gaining access to these decision-making processes in order to challenge management definitions of women in groups.

Organizational and operational *constraints* are implicit in any attempts to introduce groupwork into the agency. Women workers face considerable obstacles in attempting to counteract the barrage of negative images that abound, where women are perceived to be either mad, bad or dependent, vulnerable carers. Social control mechanisms operate through this labelling process. The organization does not directly try to alter behaviour; rather it expects change to follow upon identifying, describing and defining an individual's attributes, social circumstances and public identity. Women therefore become public categories: 'She's not a medical, but a social problem'; 'It's not a family problem, it's a housing problem.' If a worker can describe what is 'wrong' with a woman client and then tell her what it is, the client should be grateful, sit passively through the verdict, but she will invariably continue with her preferred life-style, only to earn the label 'lacking in motivation', instead of 'demoralized by social work'.

How does the worker portray her intentions to an organization like Social Services in a way that leaves her feminist integrity intact? How can communication be effective in what is essentially an attempt at organizational change? There is a need for awareness of the interplay between the worker's own personal and professional philosophy and needs, the norms of the team and agency, and conditions which define the goals and tasks of organizational activity.

There are essentially two strands to the strategies which can be developed, as workers become irritants for change. The first concerns education and communication, and the second, negotiation and bargaining skills through the use of assertion.

1 *Education and communication* Agency response is mediated through the reactions of colleagues, who can actively approve or disapprove of the groupwork venture. Educating colleagues about the aims and purposes of the group, and the potential gains envisaged, as well as dispelling fears and myths about the potentially damaging effects of groups, are therefore crucial elements of preparatory work. Unless we deal with workers' reservations about groups they may inadvertently pass these on to clients, be dilatory in passing on referrals, or simply refuse to co-operate. Workers need to be convinced that there is something in it for them.

2 *Negotiation and bargaining* The incremental nature of policy-making in organizations means that there is room for manoeuvre. The art of persuasion and social influence comes into being. The worker will need to involve herself in negotiating and bargaining by:

(a) becoming aware of interaction patterns, who talks to whom, who initiates interaction and its frequency, in order to gain an assessment of power distribution;
(b) becoming aware of covert agendas in meetings and responding to those constructively. It is important that the worker constructs persuasive arguments which stem from a recognition of the attitudes and assumptions of those in the meeting;
(c) seeking out coalitions, alliances and interest groups, for a source of solidarity in the face of persistent masculinist arguments;
(d) developing the confidence to take risks, in order to respond to organizational pressure. This strength can emerge out of the maintenance of flexibility.

There is no doubt that the work undertaken in the preparatory stages for formal recognition of the group by the agency paves the way for the handling of difficulties in the future.

Responding to community barriers Turning to the environmental context, once a decision is made on the particular geographical area to be tapped, there is a whole range of considerations to be made in connection with the concepts of 'community' and 'locality'. If we begin with 'community', it soon becomes apparent that we are handling a chameleon. It is assumed that a single definition of community exists, transforming it into an ideological tool. Hillery (1955) discovered ninety-four different definitions of community, and that was over thirty years ago, so no doubt there are more to be found! Yet, despite this, the myth still abounds that particular kinds of social activity or relations are synonymous with a strong sense of community. Even limiting the meaning of the word to either social relations in a defined geographical area, or a sense of belonging to a group with shared values or beliefs, it becomes difficult to apply the concept to modern social structures. Yet, politically, the term has been applied to working-class and black people who are trapped in areas of deprivation, and who supposedly have a consensus about basic goals and values. On a pragmatic level, even when a group of residents have an *esprit de corps*, or have formed a 'community of mutual interests', they can be split up through the process of addressing themselves to a particular issue.

For women, however, the concept of community has a particular sting in the tail, as they occupy a marginalized position in relation to the sphere of production. In addition, they carry out individualized caring tasks and family responsibilities in such a way that they become *isolated* from any sense of 'mutual interest' or social relations within their locality (see Chapter 1).

Responding to a given locality The situation becomes even more complex when we concentrate on the term 'locality'. From the social work agency perspective, there has always been an assumption that 'locality' falls neatly within corporate management's decisions regarding the geographical boundaries of Social Services Area Teams (Cockburn, 1978). Morley and Warpole (1982, p. 3) assert that locality is not a power base, and it can be a screen to separate people from wider allegiances, thus producing a false togetherness. In the areas where we worked, women were indeed 'separate' (see Chapter 1), and there was little to be gained from wider allegiances.

Women's work largely revolved around child-care and housework in all its forms or low-paid factory shifts, cleaning or home-working, getting paid exploitative rates. The areas were poorly serviced, with an abundance of 'working men's clubs' but few child-care facilities. One woman in the rural women's group stated that 'You get used to not having services so you don't turn to them.' The picture that emerges is of a social structure based firmly within patriarchal demands, with a strict sexual division of labour, existing on scarce local resources. The sense of inadequacy amongst the women was completely under-standable, where financial stringencies made life a constant struggle.

Such a context of injustice and disadvantage would appear to make the development of a women's group pale into insignificance – a small fish in a large ocean, and a stormy one at that. It is in just such circumstances, though, that Egar and Sarkissian (1985) have outlined the development of self-help initiatives by local women in the Australian suburb of Adelaide, where community services and facilities were lacking and inaccessible. As with our work, the schemes developed were aimed at combating the social isolation which emerged as the greatest single problem for women in suburbia.

Membership

The small-group structure of consciousness-raising groups has been particularly suitable for the exploration of personal identity issues (Brodsky, 1973), growing out of the sense of 'restless constraint' (Friedan, 1963) felt by women whose lives are circumscribed within narrow confines. It follows that for a sense of trust, intimacy and self-revelation to be a hallmark of small women's groups, the only restriction to be made is on the size of the group – approximately eight to twelve people. In groups where there is fluidity of intention and purpose, slipping between support, information-giving and therapy towards change and influence on external concerns, it would be inappropriate to place further boundaries around membership, other than that women should attend of their own volition. The only other consideration is that women should be encouraged to generate their own choices and gain as much control as possible out of the proceedings of the group.

What effect do these principles have on the ways in which members are recruited to the group? There are multiple ways of generating membership, and whilst these may have a differential impact on the structure of the groups, from a feminist perspective it is inappropriate to lay down strict guidelines about the 'correct' way to proceed.

Despite our similarities in basic thinking very different groups resulted, with a wide range of experiences amongst group participants. During these initial planning stages, different thought processes were in operation across the rural and urban settings, which affected perceptions of the significance of certain factors surrounding selection. We need to look at what filtering mechanisms apply in the ways in which women are selected. Are these mechanisms overt or subconscious, or a combination of both? Are there women who end up being excluded inadvertently because we have not sought participants from appropriate sources? Is there a fine line between a self-motivated approach and unwitting coercion on our part?

If we make a comparison of the rural and urban groups, the workers in the former group undertook a wide trawl of the locality to publicize the group to as many women as possible in a particular area. Knowing the difficulties of reaching out to isolated, working-class women, we felt it was important to utilize as many different means as possible to generate interest and to present the group as non-stigmatizing. To that end we issued publicity and referral forms to social work colleagues and professionals from other helping agencies, as well as putting up posters in many local resources. When women themselves became involved the trawl was even wider, including door-to-door leafleting. As the group became more established, the most powerful advertising of all began, namely recommendation by word of mouth.

The net result of these diverse forms of recruitment was a considerable range of women who attended the group over the years in terms of life experiences, education, sexual identity, and physical criteria such as age and disability. In the first six months of the group's life, the women who attended ranged in age from nineteen to forty-seven; they had been drawn from third-party referrals, with a few women responding to publicity leaflets and word of mouth recommendation. A consequence of advertising, however, was that it began the process of getting the group known. The varied methods of recruitment bore their fruit, with the age range of the group increasing and women becoming actively involved in recruitment.

Within the urban groups there was, almost inadvertently to begin with, a concentration on working with women labelled as 'mentally ill'. Women with disabilities were not represented in these groups. Participants came predominantly from council housing estates or from inner-city housing association properties and two women came from owner-occupied homes. Whilst the oppression of multiple factors such as finance, health and violence remained the same in the urban and rural settings, the demographic concentration of these problems varied enormously. Women living in council accommodation, dependent on the Department of Social Security for their rent being paid, along with the myriad oppressions they face in other areas of their lives, can be seen as having the least autonomy in every respect.

There are two important qualifications to the representativeness of the urban and rural groups. First, all women were white Caucasian, and, secondly they defined themselves as working-class (see Chapter 1). Of particular importance in terms of breadth of differences that did exist was that as group members began to feel secure with each other, challenges relating to ageism, heterosexism and discrimination against people with disabilities began to emerge, and their own racism was addressed. The fact that the women attending the groups were all white is a reflection of demographic factors, underpinned by implicit or explicit local government policies which have brought about ghettoization on at least two levels. First, there is the rural–urban split, and secondly, within the city itself, black families are rarely housed on particular estates because of racism, hostility and threats to personal safety.

It is vital to recognize that, whatever action is taken in the planning stages, the worker is engaged in a value-laden exercise. For instance, in both groups recruitment took place on several levels at once, as can be seen from Figure 3. Women are likely to have internalized the opinion that it is appropriate for them to approach an agency for help because of their low self-esteem. A third party may have referred the woman direct, with or without her consent. If there is dependence on colleagues' interpretations of who will benefit from the group, the selection process presents yet another hurdle for a woman to be considered 'appropriate'.

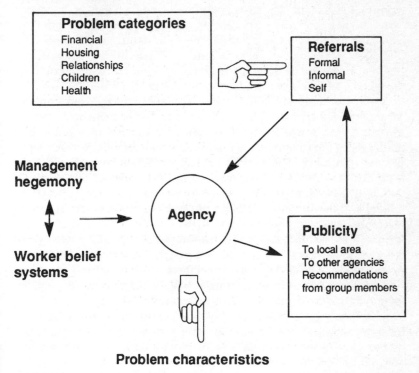

Figure 3   *The groupwork referral process*

As workers, we were in a position of power from the outset as regards deciding who should be invited to the group, and selecting the terminology that would guarantee referral for inclusion. How we move away from this position is a vexed issue. The only criterion for admission to the groups was being female, but for managerial purposes, it was necessary to phrase conditions more precisely. Figure 3 represents the dynamism of this process of selection. The interaction between management's cultural hegemony and workers' belief systems feeds into agency policy and practices, shaping responses to referrals and any publicity which is distributed. The net result from the agency's perspective is that certain problem categories are generated which become shorthand ways of reducing the pain of women's oppression to manageable proportions. These categories also reinforce prejudicial statements about women. Figure 4 lists the range of descriptions and stereotypes which were used by referrers, thereby creating a system of problem definitions.

Women only find services coming their way if they can be defined in relation to someone else, usually children, and then they must be seen to fail in their capacities as parents to qualify for advice. In Figure 4, it can be seen that a woman's public identity and status were ascribed on the basis of income, age and nature of parenthood. Invariably, reference was made to a continuum of violence which not only included a woman's personal experience of being abused, but also the risk of her abusing her children. Not one referral recognized women's strengths and fortitude. The catalogue of value judgements by others reveals a sexism which leaves women no room for negotiation and undermines the fundamental principles which feminist workers have set out to achieve. These value judgements are imposed because the scrutiny of women's behaviour is set against a masculinist standard and is always found wanting. Issues of class and gender expectations impinge, as the mechanisms whereby services are offered relate to a set of norms that simply does not apply in the lives of the women themselves. The process of categorization as depicted in Figures 3 and 4 may seem arbitrary, but it reveals a pattern of received ideas about womanhood which many group members had internalized.

Another factor to bear in mind is whether certain women end up being excluded because their backgrounds are not considered appropriate. For instance, were women inadvertently excluded from the groups because they were not oppressed 'enough'? Were they seen to be suffering an 'appropriate' level of deprivation, neither too much nor too little, by those referring them?

What conclusions about membership can we draw from our discussion so far? Even though the selection process used in the rural group was more open than in the urban group, the sense of purpose was the same. Participation in the group and the value of its existence for the women were similar for the two groups. We believe that groups for women can be set up in a variety of ways and participants can be drawn from a narrower or broader trawl. Despite the fact that this will lead to differences in membership and methods of working, there will

Problem characteristics

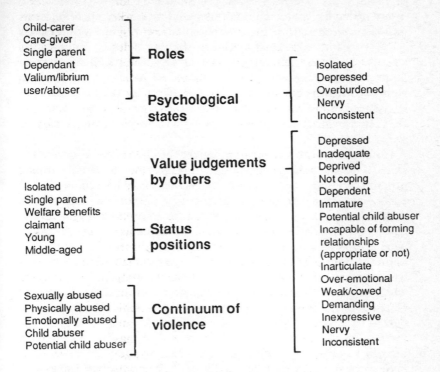

Figure 4 *Problem characteristics: stereotypical responses to women's group members*

always be similarities relating to women's unresolved experiences of oppression and the long-term impact of these. Our hypothesis is that this similarity will hold true for other women's groups.

To select or not to select A feminist perspective makes it inappropriate to use *selection* procedures in the establishment of a membership for the group, as potential members would immediately become aware of the workers' prior knowledge and judgements about them. Not only that, there are echoes of the social control element in selection to which we referred earlier (p. 32), and this does little for women's self-determination. Rather, it is important to have contact with potential members *before* the group starts in order to clarify expectations and responsibilities, and to provide the women concerned with enough information to enable them to decide *for themselves* whether the group would be useful to them or not.

Face-to-face contact with the worker(s) offers women the possibility of an initial assessment of the worker's trustworthiness. How should information be presented to women in order to facilitate their participation and afford them due consultation? Women want to know – and indeed have the right to know – what will happen in the group, who the other members will be, and, crucially, whether there will be an atmosphere of acceptance. The care that needs to be taken in helping a woman to identify her own needs and strengths, and relate these to the envisaged group aims, will make the difference between a woman who feels reticent about being involved, and one who is comitted to making the group work.

How much more reassuring, though, for discussion of hopes and fears to be undertaken with another group member. Once a rolling programme is under way women members can be encouraged to participate actively in initial interviews with prospective members. In the rural group, after approximately eighteen months, a scheme had developed whereby established group members were initially paired with new members in order to welcome and encourage them during the apprehensions of the first group sessions. This idea, originating from women's group members, began with those who felt more confident, who were later in a position to transfer their skills to others. In Chapter 4, we will be discussing the process of skill-sharing in greater depth.

Open and closed membership   Should a group operate an 'open door' policy to encourage women to choose their moment of joining, or should the doors be closed after a few sessions? Is holding a closed group contrary to feminist beliefs because of the risk of exclusivity? The creation of safety and trust has to be a priority in women's groups and therefore necessitates continuity of membership for a few weeks at least. The introduction of newcomers on a regular basis can inhibit self-disclosure and can be alienating for new members themselves, anxious to be accepted in an already established group. In our experience it works well to close the group during a sequence of sessions and then open the doors again for the beginning of the next programme. This compromise ensures that new members are integrated gradually.

We have spent some time raising pertinent issues about membership to illustrate that women's participation at the very beginning is a necessity. Otherwise the group remains under the ownership of the workers and never *belongs* to the women themselves.

Making it all possible: Creating the group
Belief in women's right to validation echoes through to the practical

arrangements for the group. Making a group happen relies just as heavily on material resources as it does on the subtleties of communication skills. Such practical arrangements carry with them symbolic significance, as the care with which they are undertaken will influence women's perceptions of warmth and safety, and of the respect they hope to receive.

Any decision about funding brings in its wake a plethora of difficulties. Funding from the worker's agency signifies formal recognition of the group, but may also bring with it organizational constraints and confine workers within patriarchal definitions. Both the rural and urban groups initially gained funding through Section 1 of the Children and Young Persons Act 1963, from money used to prevent the reception of children into care. The argument used to acquire this money was that women can only attend to the welfare of their children when they also have the opportunity to consider their own needs. The irony of this is obvious. On the one hand, we continually stressed that these were groups for women run by women, whilst at the same time we accepted with open hands a source of funding which reinforced women in their role as mothers. Ideology was pushed to one side for pragmatism, because at the time this was the only source of funding available. As the rural group became more established, workers gained funding from a community mental health project (trading in the 'women as mothers' trajectory for definitions of 'women as mentally unsound') and, latterly, from a county council self-help budget, which enabled the group to be totally self-directing. Such incremental developments, growing out of the dearth of resources available to women, symbolize the hold which patriarchy has over economic affairs.

Similar thought needs to take place in relation to the venue and timing of group sessions. If women feel vulnerable and physically uncomfortable in the group environment, then inhibitions will surface and mar attempts to explore problems and strengths. Searching out an appropriate venue deserves priority as a comfortable, warm room promotes physical and psychological safety. A room with a carpet, soft chairs, cushions and refreshments holds symbolic significance as it tells women that they are important, deserving of respect and privacy. The room should be so positioned in a building that ease of access is ensured for women with disabilities and those with pushchairs. The venue also needs to be accessible by public transport. Meeting these requirements may seem a tall order but premises with inherent problems will have a detrimental effect on the functioning of the group. The ease with which privacy and confidentiality can be destroyed highlights the importance of an environment free from interruptions, where women can shout, scream, and cry.

The timing of sessions again gives clear messages about women's self-worth. Knowing that women's days are always crammed with demands, it is crucial to agree on a time and frequency of meetings which will allow them space to attend the group sessions. For example, does the group meet during school holidays? If so, what arrangements are made for school-age children? Is it possible to provide a sitting service for the duration of group sessions for those women who care for dependent adults? How much travelling time are women expected to put to one side?

The list of questions is endless, and each answer contains a value position. The centrality of values is illustrated by the child-care issue. As this is a central feature of many women's lives, it is vital to ensure that child-care facilities are provided, and in our experience women see such arrangements as a key factor in deciding where to hold meetings. However, this faces workers with a dilemma: the provision of a crèche entails more low-paid or unpaid caring work for more women. A telling example of this was when one crèche volunteer in the rural group admitted that she would gain more from being a member of the group than from supervising the children.

Whatever the considerations, the goal must be to free women to concentrate upon themselves rather than others. In addition, acting decisively with practical arrangements, far from being peripheral, helps to create a secure framework within which women's groups can work more effectively. If such structures are developed, then workers can look to the clarification of the aims and objectives of the group, which can be shared with women and amended accordingly. To that end, we saw our task as providing a forum in which it was possible for women, whose identities are shaped in isolating and oppressive ways, to recognize themselves as members of a social group with the potential to alter their collective situation. We therefore devised both therapeutic and educative aims, consisting of the following:

1   to break down the walls of isolation by enabling women to share their experiences, and by facilitating friendships between women through relaxation, discussion and activity;
2   to build self-confidence and self-esteem by offering women structures they could take hold of, to develop their own potential;
3   to increase self-awareness and help women to understand and appreciate their bodies; to provide practical strategies and solutions to alleviate stress and its physical manifestations;
4   through an educative process to enable members to pursue problems and issues which affect their lives and to make links between these private difficulties and the structural oppression they experience;

5   to support women through any transition period from one stage in
    a relationship to the next;
6   to encourage women to reach and stay with whatever decisions felt
    best and were the most realistic for them in the circumstances;
7   to enable the collective expression of and solutions to personal
    experience and problems, through the recognition of individual
    and group power and control.

We were acutely conscious in drawing up these aims that women's
changing awareness would have a profound effect on how they saw
and behaved within family and public relationships, and that this
could lead to disruption, change and even breakdown of previously
existing structures (Chapter 6 looks at this in greater detail).

Most, if not all, of these aims are to be found in consciousness-
raising groups (Brodsky, 1973; Eastman, 1973), where the groups so
position members that they are likely to arrive at a political understanding of themselves – a recognition of the potential they have, as
members of that group, to alter themselves and their circumstances.
These aims are also similar to those developed by other statutory
workers involved in community-based women's groups (Donnelly,
1986).

Creating a structure in which feminist aims can materialize means
that a professional worker initially takes responsibility for recruitment
of participants, for administrative duties, and for the shape and
content of sessions. Subsequently, the group develops in a spirit of
greater self-sustaining independence as participants' confidence grows
in proportion to their awareness of the power and impact of
collectivity.

Co-working
Co-working the facilitator role is the embodiment of certain strands of
feminist philosophy. It is anti-establishment, it is a mutual recognition
of each other's skills, a journey of discovery of hitherto untapped
facets of self which are nurtured by mutual support. It also provides
women participants with a living example of what working together
co-operatively can entail. From both the workers' and the participants'
perspectives, co-working proves beneficial whilst at the same time
raising key issues for exploration.

As facilitators, the advantage of co-working is that we are not left
with total responsibility for what happens in the group, but can share
the role of observing how women are feeling. Co-workers' sense of
responsibility takes different forms, some real and quantifiable, others
imagined. The first of these relates to the sharing of organizational
tasks and practical arrangements, and the second to the wish to ensure

continuity of purpose. There is another form of responsibility, however, which proves unpredictable but never diminishing, namely the level of intensity which occurs in group sessions, where co-workers feel reluctant to send a woman home in a state of distress. There is a delicate balance to be achieved between the encouragement of emotional expression in the group and the co-workers' responsibility to provide a safety net.

Mutual support and criticism form the backbone of co-working, preventing each worker from being dogmatically entrenched in one position, or from undervaluing the support she herself is able to provide. Participants can learn that co-operation and mutual respect are possible, and that differences in approach do not mean distrust or disagreement. Significantly, the presence of a co-worker enhances and increases each worker's courage in trying out new, more risky exercises because she knows she has someone else to help her deal with the reactions to such an approach. Whatever the outcome of taking risks, no single worker should be left feeling at fault. She can discuss all these issues with her co-worker and, where necessary, begin to sort out those areas where she needs to make adjustments in her practice. There is no doubt that more sensitive and accurate assessments can be made of appropriate methodologies for use in group sessions when two workers are involved. Working alongside another person also facilitates a more realistic perspective on group events, as there are at least two angles from which proceedings can be seen.

The intricacies of the facilitator role open up a whole range of skills for co-workers, all of which aim to maximize the inclusion of all group members. Two workers are better placed for noticing who, for example, is wanting or trying to speak but finding it difficult, or who is looking withdrawn or upset. With mutual support it is possible for workers to encourage and reassure, be sensitive to levels of emotion, and draw out each member's potential. Throughout the group process workers can highlight and validate skills of facilitation which members can test out for themselves within the safety of the group and then risk using in their daily lives. These skills include the ability to support in a non-judgemental way, keeping silent and listening, knowing when to disclose details about personal experience, knowing when to offer appropriate information. On a more confrontational level, there are skills to be developed in handling conflict in a sensitive and constructive manner. The emphasis in co-working on modelling support, giving space and permission to speak, showing disagreement without antagonism, and responding intuitively to a woman's inner being helps to make feminist groupwork a reality.

Structuring the group programme

It is careful planning that opens up opportunities for spontaneity and imaginativeness in groups, because it allows each member to assess for themselves whether the group matches their expectations; if not, then challenges can be made. Structure facilitates our own thought processes, provides a framework for participants to relate to immediately and to present to management when issues of accountability come to the fore. Structure is crucial because participants in the group will inevitably come with individual expectations of involvement and control by themselves and workers. They will also require clarification of decisions to be reached as well as tasks and actions to be undertaken. They may approach the group with hope, anxiety, relief, scepticism, feelings of 'I've seen and heard it all before. Nothing's going to make any difference, but I'll give it a go anyway.' As workers, we need structure because we need to feel sure about what we are doing, not to be over-confident and dogmatic, but at least to present to participants an image of some degree of certainty and sense of personal worth, in the hope that this will be transmitted to all concerned.

What are the particular hallmarks of our women's group programmes? First, within them they contained a whole host of theoretical positions (see Chapter 3). Whilst believing in women's ability to support each other, we initially felt uncertain about which approach to take. Thinking on our feet was the order of the day, using improvisation and synthesis of a variety of theories and insights, whilst always allowing practice to determine what was true. The process of moving to a given ideological position occurred by testing out a theoretical principle and allowing experience to challenge and, when necessary, shatter it. A painful process, but crucial if we want to avoid adopting a particularly rigid stance.

Secondly, women shared control of the planning, co-ordination and facilitation of group sessions. This process can be symbolized by workers' acceptance of instructions from women members in order to encourage equity of task distribution. For instance, some of the early programmes of the rural group's sessions were organized around themes of women and stress, or women and health. When the time came to organize the content of the next ten-week programme, members lamented that they would rather have a variety of topics, so that each one could feed into and inform the next, without becoming repetitive or tedious. This was a powerful lesson. If the structure of the programme ends up reflecting the characteristics of the organizer, it offers women little scope for self-expression.

This feeds into our third point. In answer to the question 'How do we want to go about achieving our aims?', group activities need to run parallel to, and be an expression of, the group's original objectives. However, there always needs to be a distinction between the planned programme and what actually happens, to allow for creative spontaneity amidst purposeful activity. Out of fear, workers may either over- or under-organize, becoming so laid-back that the group runs away without them, or holding on to the reins so tightly that all movement becomes restricted. Structure must never intrude into individual needs. Within the organization of group meetings, there should be room allowed for as much flexibility as is required.

Fourthly, we believe that women's groups should experiment with as many different pursuits, activities and exercises as possible, in order to connect with the totality of women's lives and selves. As Davies (1982, p. 109) indicates, the immediate satisfaction of women having their hair done was a much more positive experience than a discussion about domestic violence or the social origins of depression. Our own trials and errors, and statements that women have made, have taught us that trips out and visits, the opportunity for fun, laughter and enjoyment, are just as central as psychotherapeutic exercises and socio-political discussions. It is our belief that group cohesion, conflict, commitment, identity change and the increasing value of time for Self, develop on a long-term basis out of a plethora of shared and differing experiences. We shall return to this argument in the next chapter.

So it was that in the rural group, over any ten-week programme, discussion sessions on sexual violence, women and the media, men and masculinity, unemployment, and so on, were interspersed with sessions devoted to self-assertion, relaxation, therapeutic exercises, or planning of fund-raising activities. Flipping between the overtly political and the overtly personal and therapeutic adds links to the chain of understanding about the Self in its political context.

Structure needs to be subtle without becoming obtrusive and an end in itself. It is manifested in the ways in which connections are made between different experiences and events, the ways conclusions are drawn and arrived at, the connections between public events and policies and private hardship and experience. In short, structure refers to the ways in which a picture is drawn of the whole rather than relying solely on the apparently fragmented, inconsequential series of events that life often seems to be.

This chapter has aimed to demonstrate the multifaceted approach used in the establishment and organization of the groups. We have shown that feminist groupwork is more than having good intentions which fizzle out because of lack of concerted action. Liberal-minded practitioners may have hearts of gold but so do hard-boiled eggs. We have shown that to make the group happen, workers must consider a plethora of factors revolving around organizational and environmental issues, membership and practical concerns, which expose our vulnerabilities and limitations. Strategies for dealing with other people's scepticism and hostility rely upon clarity in our thinking and flexibility of purpose. When it comes to planning the group programme, we have emphasized how important it is to be flexible and spontaneous within a given structure, and that co-working provides a constructive role model for mutual support and criticism. Above everything else, we have begun the process of locating working-class women's groups within a context of women's action and achievement.

3
Women Making Choices: Groupwork Revisited

Effective therapy in groups should encourage women to value and develop inner strengths, regardless of societal norms. The institutional and social barriers that have impeded women are so wide-ranging that their erosion must occur on numerous fronts. Any feminist approach must harness the growing unrest among women with the aim of recognizing the dynamics of oppression whilst avoiding pathologizing them as vulnerable, weak and dependent. There is a fine line to be drawn between the extensive reference to women as problem-bearers, which we saw in Chapter 1, as opposed to women as problem-solvers. The aim of groupwork must be to inspire women, not to demoralize them (Reinharz, 1983).

Using the planning phases and programme outline as a backcloth, this chapter will explore the ways in which activities undertaken in women's groups can encourage women's self-expression, personal development and change through the process of group interaction. To achieve this, we will analyse methods of work which can be used to get in touch with aspects of women's Selves which have hitherto been hidden, or misrepresented. Groupwork has to affect the cognitive, behavioural, emotional and spiritual aspects of women's selves if growth is to be encouraged. Techniques based on skill development (through assertion and problem-solving), in cognitive changes (especially new ways of viewing past experiences and new attitudes towards present and future), and in behavioural changes (through role play and goal-setting) (Loeffler and Fiedler, 1979) can therefore open up a world of spontaneity and imagination. This self-awareness is sustained through the direct expression of emotions and is located within a socio-political context, as indicated in our original aims (see Chapter 2). To achieve this we will explore the concepts of community education and action learning. It would be simplistic to suggest that this process can be developed through the use of a single method or approach.

Group activities within individual sessions

Amidst a variety of group activities it is possible to discern a range of dimensions which can help us to identify key concepts in the psychology of women. These dimensions are as follows:

1   *expectations* in undertaking particular group activities;
2   utilization of a *wide range* of activities in order to encourage the development of all group members' qualities and skills;
3   a *continuum of activities* from individually focused ones to those requiring maximum group interaction;
4   *transfer of knowledge* outside the group, where women are encouraged to build upon skills newly found in group sessions through re-enactment of such skills within their daily lives.

These dimensions indicate that change for women should involve an increasing range of goals and aspirations, to counteract the years of discouragement received through cultural mores.

Expectations in undertaking group activities
The use of any group activity carries with it both subtle and overt expectations and assumptions regarding members' willingness to participate. Experimentation with diverse activities can generate fear and anxiety, as well as excitement and hope. Participation involves discussion, self-disclosure, making connections with a range of experiences at different times of life. It can also involve fantasy, relaxation, physical exercise and laughter. It is not right to make assumptions about any individual woman's ability or willingness to participate in any of these processes, either at the outset of the group or in the course of its existence. Women's hopes and fears need to be addressed at every stage.

The moment that a group decision is reached to test out a new activity can face an individual woman, struggling to meet with group approval, with a frightening dilemma. Does she push herself over the brink and risk participating, thereby exposing her own felt inadequacies and lack of skills, or does she express her fears, refuse to participate, and risk group rejection? A woman's thought processes at this critical moment constitute the first steps in the assessment of her skills and qualities, as well as her weaknesses. The delight of using such a diverse range of activities is that women can learn the value of pooling individual resources, thereby casting different shades of light on to the same activity.

An example will clarify this further. An exercise involving drawing the Self in symbolic form was met with cries of 'But I'm hopeless at drawing' from several women. The expectation they had of the exercise was that other women would pass judgement on their artistic abilities. When it was explained further that drawing was to be used as a means to an end and was not to be scored or ranked as a pass/fail, women who had felt reticent agreed to be involved. They began to draw in a tense and rigid fashion, but, once absorbed in the exercise, one woman began to experiment with colour, whilst another, hanging on to a tiny drawing of herself surrounded by blank areas on the paper, described succinctly what it was that had precipitated her drawing. This example demonstrates that women's expectations regarding certain activities stem from deep-rooted constructs about their subordinate place in the world. If their skills are continually suppressed, they will hold back from exercises involving screaming, shouting, the expression of anger, because there are few existing messages which counteract their sublimation of Self.

These expectations, whether voiced or not, are likely to have a range of effects. First, no contribution in a group session should be coerced. Despite the fact that women's abilities may not have been exploited for years it cannot be assumed that they will want to take advantage of the opportunities offered. Challenges enough will exist within the group's very structure without women feeling pressured to 'perform' in a prescribed way. It is important that the encouragement the worker sees herself as offering in good faith is received as such by the women concerned, and not as coercion.

If a woman refuses to participate in a particular activity, the group should give her space to make such a choice and not ridicule her in the process. Indeed, a woman's refusal is a mark of assertion and can offer the group a source of discussion and growth. T initially refused to participate in relaxation exercises which involved lying on the floor. She later disclosed her embarrassment about being overweight and the difficulty she had in getting on to the floor. However, when she witnessed other women laughing about their own cumbersome methods of lying down, with bones creaking and much rolling over as they attempted to maintain their balance, her fears began to subside. Initially, she felt comfortable with deep breathing exercises from a sitting position, but once women offered her reassurance and physical support, she attempted to lie down. This development opened up discussion regarding body image and patriarchal attitudes towards women's body-weight.

Secondly, a woman may not consider it appropriate to discuss and name her feelings, particularly those involving self-blame, where detrimental events in her life are perceived to be consequences of her own behaviour. It may seem to her that talking about them is not right. It is likely that a series of painful events will have led to her feeling defensive about looking at what is happening. This will inevitably affect whatever she is able to say.

Control, self-control and coercion are therefore central features of all group activities. Women have no tradition of self-assertion, and thus an introduction to any exercise will appear non-negotiable. This stems from the internalization of ideas that others have to be pleased for the woman herself to be liked. Particularly where maximum group interaction is concerned, it becomes difficult to maintain that women are not being made to do things against their will. For example, there is a game in which each participant in turn throws a ball at another, whilst calling out a positive statement about her. The person who has the ball is in a powerful position, as she is the one who speaks, who has control, but can also exclude other members. Non-participation in this could be misinterpreted by others as superciliousness, shyness, embarrassment, pride, 'It's beneath my dignity'. In reality, it may be attributable to the paralysing fear:

> I can't possibly play this game, no one will have anything good to say about me. These people don't really know me, they haven't seen me in all situations.

The construction of these thoughts demonstrates the coercion a woman may experience at any point in a group exercise. These feelings emerge in direct proportion to the fear and anxiety a woman suffers when faced with a certain request. In contrast, elements of control are perceived as an external force, free from the aspects of fear contained within coercion. However, self-control is a learnt response developed through consideration for others, where a woman gains the ability to wait and judge the right moment to speak or act. These three facets can coexist, with any woman shifting her perceptions about the degree of control she has within any given session. It is possible for a woman to feel confident in one exercise, yet vulnerable in another.

As workers, how do we counteract the inhibiting effects of these expectations? Above everything else, the demonstration of our belief in participants' worth and their inalienable right to self-expression creates an atmosphere of choice and self-determination. From the perspective of the woman participating, this may free her from previously felt inhibitions, but this process can only occur at her own pace. We recognize too that the ideal of 'free participation' is impossible to achieve and is circumscribed by group pressure. The nearest we can hope to get to this is the development of a woman's judgement of when it is right for her to engage in a certain activity.

For instance, direct discussion of 'What I feel like at the end of the day, in that moment between having got the kids off to bed and waiting for X to come in from the pub' is too difficult to handle, because it touches the heart of fear, pain and self-disclosure so acutely. However, representing these emotions in a symbolic fashion, through drawing, through shouting out suggestions for a brainstorm, through a role play in which each emotion gets its own characterization, may be more manageable. This may be because it is fun, and each woman can hold on to, reveal as much or as little of her feelings as she wishes. In a more formalized discussion, this 'withholding' of feelings and information may be more obvious because of silences, facial expression and apparently inconsequential statements.

There is also a sense in which using a range of group activities shatters expectations about working-class women's 'limited' capabilities. In particular, the view that working-class women do not possess verbal skills is rooted in negative assumptions and stereotypes, formulated by the middle classes. The argument inherent in such class oppression runs along the lines that working-class women are inarticulate, ignorant and incapable of developing sophisticated ideas. Expectations about their limitations are so internalized by women themselves that statements such as:

> It's all just common sense really.
> I can't talk about that, it's beyond me.
> I don't understand all this politics stuff, it's not for the likes of me.

reinforce the constraints under which many working-class women are placed. Whilst the group provides an arena in which such negative expectations can be slowly eroded, the view women hold of themselves is prompted by years of being perceived as objects of other people's action (Freire, 1970).

Disagreeing with such expectations accrued over the years requires a level of confidence which the group can help provide. Each woman's growing realization of what she is able to derive from and contribute to the group builds an environment in which participants can encourage a woman who is feeling marginalized to examine and confront the roots of her inhibition. In this way dealing with expectations becomes a group responsibility.

Using a wide range of activities: The unfolding of insight and innovation

Any group concerned to formulate and deal with pertinent women's issues must attempt to incorporate as much variety as possible. This boils down to the principle that group activities must reflect in microcosm the range of knowledge, beliefs, values and ideas which need to be called upon to deal with any problematic domain. The need to *increase variety and diversity* of learning methods in groups, as a way of getting to grips with our oppression and formulate challenges to it, is a task recognized by all the women with whom we have worked. Learning in women's groups requires a pluralistic approach.

Activities also need to involve a broad range of possible responses, skills and abilities on the part of the women. Through a variety of mechanisms, women can discover skills in representation, humour, imaginativeness, the ability to laugh and make others laugh, all of which lead to a release of tension. We need to encourage them to recognize their own potential, and that any limits on this are artificially constructed. We do not underestimate the enormity of the task, but stress the need to face up to and, by whatever means possible, deconstruct these limits.

To illustrate this, we will now look at some of the range of activities it is possible to use and the consequences and effects of these.

Physical movement   Basic 'physical education' warm-up exercises can be used, shaking out hands and feet, stretching limbs and moving the head round slowly on the neck. Finally, the whole body can be shaken from the hips. Enhanced circulation and a flow of energy will result from this, enlivening the atmosphere generally, but also encouraging the participants to feel more confident about joining in group activities. Other positive effects are a loosening up of cramped limbs, stretching the trunk and therefore facilitating deeper, healthier breathing; a growing awareness of sensations in different parts of the body and the pleasure to be derived from responding to this. A recognition of the connections between mind and body emerges. Some inhibitions will be lost and self-consciousness in front of others will diminish as fun ensues.

Physical movement is not an end in itself. Its invigorating effects inspire women to take risks in what they will disclose in the group. A short period of physical exercise provides scope for looking at the general lack of enjoyment and relaxation in women's lives. Women express jealousy about the fact that men are allowed their social freedoms. Men cannot be expected to hang around the house all day, uncomplaining and participating in domestic tasks. We recognize that the scale of activity is no form of compensation, but having fun together and breaking down isolation yet more should never be underestimated.

Role play   It is common for people to find role play a difficult activity. They feel they are not going to 'get the part right', that they will give a bad performance and look stupid. Many people expend a fair amount of energy rationalizing their unwillingness to participate in such an approach. Often, this very energy could quite simply be used to participate immediately in the role play in question. The more quickly and deeply the person becomes involved, the less likely they are to feel inhibited.

Once group members take the risk of engaging in role play they can develop confidence and lateral thinking. Role play also provides a rehearsal space for actual encounters. Feelings of egalitarianism are enhanced in that everyone has the chance to tell others what to do and there is plenty of room for debate. Role play provides endless scope as a group activity, not only in terms of learning different strategies for dealing with painful situations, but also for discovering hidden talents and emotions. As with physical movement, role play can be fun, leading to the release of tension.

Within the context of role play, a person can choose to represent another's emotions and to plumb that feeling to its depths. Social niceties, conventions and constraints no longer apply if she herself assumes responsibility for all that is happening within 'her' character. A woman may prefer not to participate in a role play but be happy to 'direct' one, dictating to others how the action should proceed. She can instruct them in the subject-matter but what is actually said depends on the performer's spontaneous reaction or decision. This may lead to new, deeper insights for the 'director', both about her own circumstances and feelings, and about ways of reacting to what is being represented in the role play. This enables the whole group to participate in discussion about her most appropriate course of action.

Relaxation   Space for ourselves is difficult to come by. Guilt is piled on that this is wrong and self-indulgent. For women in general it runs counter to the ethos of being there to serve others, always thinking ahead. The psychological and political messages internalized by women are that domestic labour and childbearing and rearing do not constitute work because they have no market value. Women not in paid work have 'all the time in the world' to engage in this 'non-labour'; they therefore have no right to complain about its never-ending nature, about the emotional and physical toll it exacts. If what they are engaged in does not count as toil, then how can there be an expectation that there should be any relief from it? If something does not exist, then how can it have an opposite? But ask any woman and she will tell you what this 'non-labour' is like.

Relaxation acknowledges women's right to time out. It throws into relief the relentlessness of the daily round by showing that there can be an alternative. The mind and the body deserve their own time and space and the permission the group gives for this can be extended elsewhere. Engaging in relaxation techniques is more personally demanding and goes deeper than participating in physical exercise. It throws a woman back more on to herself and her inner world. By letting the internal mechanisms of the body take over, it becomes much easier to get in touch with blocked fears, joys and needs. Relaxation identifies areas of the body that are cramped and tense. It can help us to understand how we carry ourselves, which physical positions we unconsciously adopt when faced with particular problems.

As women also become more in tune with their emotions, their awareness increases of the ways in which conventional methods of treatment mask the causes of anxiety. The dulling of symptoms through psychotropic drugs may lead women to feel temporary relief and to think that things have changed, although in fact they may have even less control over what is happening to them. Relaxation does the exact opposite by giving women the scope to take control.

Relaxation may have a calming influence on a short-term basis, but does it have any long-term effects? There is endless scope for practising its techniques, as women test and adapt the control they have learnt across a host of situations. Relaxation serves its purpose not only in a reactive sense as a woman realizes that she is in an anxiety-provoking encounter. She can also use it pre-emptively before a difficult situation has arisen.

Self-assertion exercises   Through role play and relaxation exercises, the group offers women a variety of approaches for discovering aspects of themselves hitherto untapped. Role play, by its very nature, is dependent upon the group functioning as an entity where women can explore the significance of scenes and emotions in a concrete way. Relaxation, whilst enhanced as a group activity, nevertheless offers women their own personal space bubble which can be transported wherever it is needed. Once women become aware of the range of qualities they possess as a consequence of such exercises, it is appropriate to engage in work on self-assertion. It is only at this stage that it will make sense; in isolation it is purely mechanistic, operating within strictly behavioural principles. From the woman's point of view, the reductionism of behavioural change can lead to cognitive dissonance, as actions become disconnected from her beliefs about the Self.

Our main aim in using self-assertion (Butler, 1981; Dickson, 1982) is to give women permission to think exclusively of themselves and prioritize their own needs, to think and speak a series of 'I' statements freely and without criticism or recrimination. Such an experience may never have befallen them before. The moment a woman does this, she gets in touch with a whole range of aspects of herself which may have remained dormant and hidden for years. For example, she may learn about the strength and power to be derived from making, or indeed shouting out, demands. Although this goal is accessible to *all* women in *some* ways, getting there is a lengthy, uphill struggle. When invited to say what they want out of life, women frequently make statements like: 'I want the children to be happy; I want enough money to buy the children all they need; I want him to have enough money to go out every week.' It proves very difficult for a woman to believe she has the right to say: 'I want a paid job with some security; I want decent child-care facilities; I want time, peace and happiness for myself; I want to be treated like an adult.'

Women will declare wants spontaneously, which are obviously ready to burst through the surface, but will immediately retract them on the grounds that such desires are self-indulgent. The common feelings of guilt and fear quickly follow. These reactions stem from inhibitions, arising from messages received through socially constructed roles, coupled with the derision of their physical and mental capacities. Dealing with behaviours in the here and now does little to address and change the effects of all-pervasive and well-ingrained oppression. It is crucial that women are constantly reminded of their *right* to assertive forms of expression and also of the sources that inhibit them from owning this right. *Repetition* of these rights is one important way to break down cyclical thought patterns such as:

> Sometimes I can say 'I want', but then I stop because I feel guilty. Sometimes I think that life would be better if I *could* say 'I want'. Then I realize I can't do it because it's too demanding. It's my fault then, isn't it, if I can't do it? I'll just have to dream about what I could ask for.

The impact of the group as enabler, supporter and confronter comes into its own at this point. Repetition of these rights by an individual can be reasonably persuasive, but, when repeated by the group as a whole, they take on a power of their own. If a woman feels unable to accept these positive statements about herself, her only defence is anger and frustration. If, on the other hand, she tentatively begins to accept the truth of what is being said, the next step is to use the effects of this belief in situations outside the group. Thus she begins to have a choice between feeling disappointed and angry with herself and succeeding in what she wants.

Using self-assertion demonstrates the supportive nature of group activity and collective working, and shows women how they can give and gain in the same exercises. This encourages women's feelings of self-worth as they recognize what they have to offer others. As they learn to accept advice and support from their peers, they begin to see more clearly the sources and depth of their own need. The capacity to be assertive in our own right is notoriously difficult. To recognize such behaviour as a valid activity is to say, 'I am a worthwhile person, deserving of greater respect and recognition', and the achievement of this is a major step.

Fantasy and creativity   The quality and richness of interaction between women in groups can be harnessed further through the use of techniques which raise the profile of intuition, aesthetics, creativity and fantasy. Such methods rely on images and symbolism, which act as a signpost for future directions. Hence, a woman's shift in perception occurs through a process of association, rather than through connections based on rational modes of thinking which can raise barriers and defences.

The group is encouraged to employ such imagery by building up a representation of some aspect of individual or group experience, thereby increasing self- and group-awareness. To the intellect, such symbols may seem unrealistic; hence women need to be encouraged not to condemn themselves for irrationality if they shrink from the images and memories which come into focus. The value of this symbolism arises out of a woman's ability to imbue the image with qualities and emotions dredged from personal experience. It provides an additional mechanism for tuning into thought processes which affect behaviour and attitudes. A few examples of such techniques will convey the impact and exhilaration of symbolism.

First, in 'guided fantasy' group members are encouraged to relax and, with the facilitator as guide, imagine a symbolic situation which can be explored, such as a magical journey, a walk in the countryside or by the sea (Ernst and Goodison, 1981, p. 174). Inner depths of the Self, a woman's sexuality, her relationships, her body image, can be revealed as she discovers the significance of certain symbols. An added dimension can be for women to generate their own symbols and to visualize images for different parts of the Self, whether it be the head, heart, stomach, or their sexuality. Guided fantasy encourages women to develop a holistic approach to their daily experiences, giving validation and shape to previously half-guessed at or submerged ideas and feelings.

There are other ways of breaking down patterns of interaction which have accumulated over time. Exercises such as the 'Hidden Personality' or the 'Magic Shop' (Ernst and Goodison, 1981, pp. 39 and 211) can be used to tease out aspects of individual experience, as well as patterns of group communication. Such exercises give women permission to reveal beliefs or aspects of the Self about which they feel embarrassed or which they have failed to acknowledge.

In the 'Hidden Personality' exercise each woman introduces an aspect of her character to the group which usually remains unexpressed. The character is given a name and takes on a life of its own. This can lead women to validate these characteristics and then act on them. In the 'Magic Shop' exercise women trade in aspects of themselves for qualities or values contained in sweet jars, for instance, love, caring, patience. Women often find it extremely difficult to recognize parts of themselves they wish to abandon, whilst at the same time wanting to 'buy' a new quality. From this, it is possible for women to explore their new quality, see whether it is a good 'fit' and identify what it is that prevents them from giving up the familiar and well-worn aspect of Self.

Our discussion of the benefits of fantasy work highlights that creativity may be within us all, but it has to be nurtured. Added to which, the very act of expression is slow and cumulative (Lury, 1987). A look at creative writing in the groups provides an illustration of this. Several women in the groups began to write poetry, fictional stories, and personal accounts through diaries and notes, all of which were located in their own experiences. The style of writing reflected the fragmented nature of many working-class women's lives, and the ways in which women grapple with the multidimensional nature of their identities. There are so many conflicting demands that personal identities become shaped in a diffuse and diverse way. Much of this writing shared a direct and honest style which needed no excuses, no apologies or further explanation. The honesty of women's poetry in particular released emotional responses in other women who understood the cultural and structural context in which the writing had emerged. Women may have written in a personally significant manner, but they also appropriated and made sense of salient features of social relations that were shared by other women.

The exploration of fantasy and creativity identifies without doubt that the usual channels of communication are not enough to deal with the oppression in women's lives. Group activity needs to draw on our imagination, touching a source of powerful insight and spirituality. We can learn how our reality is embedded in the symbolic forms through which we realize our everyday world, and out of this we can identify areas for change in our lives. Creativity for women is therefore about immersion in forms of self-expression which stretch our potential and enrich our links with others; it is certainly not about distance and detachment from the Self. Ultimately, creativity is about direct access to our own and each other's emotions.

Regression and art work   The inadequacies of habitual forms of interaction can be thrown into sharp relief through the use of paraverbal techniques developed through music, dancing, drawing, play and painting. In many groups, verbal communication is developed at the expense of other forms of self-expression. It is our belief, however, that the development of other senses – taste, touch, smell, observation – can only enhance a woman's engagement with herself. Operating as wide a remit as possible therefore accommodates the needs of women with a range of physical disabilities who may, for example, be partially sighted, but have already gained an acute ability to listen or to discern through touch.

Natural mediums, such as water, mud, clay and sand, provide space for self-exploration, can trigger connections between influences in present relationships and past patterns, or provide echoes of past and current attitudes to body image. One woman was very reticent about using clay with her hands, as she heard echoes of her mother's voice in her childhood, telling her 'Don't get yourself dirty.' She began to squeeze, pull, punch, stroke the clay, feeling its texture and smelling its earthiness. In so doing, emotions of anger, betrayal, rejection, fear began to surface, although the source of these was too painful to acknowledge. The relaxation to be derived from the use of natural mediums is the exact antithesis of many of the synthetic products with which women come into contact. In addition, the significance of water should never be underestimated. One woman washed her hands and arms continuously during a session involving play materials. She wanted to peel off her white skin because she felt dirty and blemished. As a child she had been sexually assaulted by her father and in her mid-twenties she was raped by a stranger.

A major step in women's group development comes when women acknowledge the validity of play as a means of communication and source of pleasure. Many group members had little time for fun and pleasure amidst the exhaustion of life's responsibilities and traumas. Raising the profile of play also challenges the embarrassment women feel about the creativity and fantasy of childhood because of the self-exposure entailed. The separation of play from work brackets children's activity from 'serious' life and trivializes their experience. By integrating play activities into group sessions, the multiple layers of meaning of play can be revealed and used as a purposeful vehicle for growth, providing a fresh approach to adult life.

All of this is viewed with much trepidation because it involves risk-taking and self-exploration into a past women may have spent years burying. Strangely enough, it is the close ties which surround the fates of women and children that can be used to overcome any discomfort and self-consciousness. For instance, it soon became apparent when running the crèche at one group that members were curious about the play equipment provided and wanted to join in activities with their children – not for themselves, but to 'help out' with the child-care. It then became relatively easy to transfer some of these play materials into the group room. Women began to disclose that they had never painted or run their hands through clay before, that in fact they did not know *how* to play and expected us to provide them with a magic formula.

The message we gave was that the ability to play comes from within each of us. The difference is that the group provides the encouragement and opportunity to focus on our inner worlds within the context of learning from each other. It becomes legitimate to feel the pleasure, feel the pain, and to discharge emotions, not half-heartedly, but in a way that enables women to connect with and ground themselves in their bodies. Playing, above anything else, enlarges women's range of emotions and provides a close-up mirror that alters their self-reflection.

This is reinforced further through painting (Liebmann, 1989), where group members are asked to paint their world on paper, using curves, shapes and colour, channelling women's energy into overcoming vague and uncomfortable sensations. There is a sense in which the process of painting becomes an enriching experience in its own right and can spill over into the creation of a group picture.

The role of sensory activity and play acknowledges the depths to which women must go to connect with the social oppression they experience. Women can become enlivened once they begin to fit their responses together, like pieces of a jigsaw puzzle, and perceive the edges of the jigsaw pieces as finite and sharp, rather than as blurred and confused.

Discussion/verbal techniques　We have waited until this moment to analyse the role of discussion in groups because we wished to raise the profile of skills which do not rely solely on verbal or conceptual ability. There are considerable dangers inherent in an over-reliance on discussion as a means of learning. Women's ability to articulate will be dependent on a host of factors, such as the level of education reached in school, the opportunities for maintaining this subsequently in reading, writing and discussion. A woman may have had specific educational abilities which have been ignored or even undermined, which have left her feeling inferior to others even before she hears them speak or tries to make contributions herself. We will explore this process of self-deprecation further through our analysis of the concept of community education.

There is another consideration beyond women's own perceptions of their verbal skills, and that is their use of language itself. The combination of gender and class issues here is explosive and directly challenges the relationship between thought, language and action. Ruptures in communication often occur because of the constant struggle to balance language and reason, which end up constraining and confusing a group's conceptualization of an event. The key question about words is whether we use them too little or too much to express what we need and want. For some working-class women an ability to be direct, to demystify and avoid intellectual banter, means that language can cut through to the core and pin-point certain revelations. But how often do we hide behind those sounds called words? The supportive environment of a women's group can help us to throw away unnecessary words, words which confuse and mask meaning.

Bearing these doubts in mind, discussion about a given topic does not have to be confined to the group circle arrangement, with individual members passing comments to each other, invariably leading to an interpretative free-for-all.

> Well, I don't think she's saying that.
> The trouble with what you're saying is . . .
> We all feel the same.
> Everyone goes through it.

There is a likelihood of inaccuracy in all of this. What gives the first woman the right to speak on behalf of someone else? How constructive is the second speaker's judgement? How can the third and fourth speakers know what we are all feeling? Developing accurate speech can be encouraged by asking women only to speak for themselves, to use 'I' statements rather than generalities or impersonal constructs. Women find it difficult to *own* their speech, as 'I' statements appear self-congratulatory and self-centred, ultimately leading to the disparage-ment of the concept of 'Self'. Laughter about the dangers of boasting or appearing big-headed rationalize women's defensiveness. It is therefore highly appropriate to use sentence completion exercises to break down this reluctance and to open up the powers of self-description. This route to self-discovery speaks for itself:

> I am kind and friendly. I am loving to my family. Most of all I am hard-working, looking after two children and a sick husband who is bedridden.
> I am a mother of four boys and married to one who thinks he still is.
> I am trying to diet.
> I go out to work, but he expects everything doing in the house as well. Women have brought all this equality business on themselves and we've lost out. I can't do anything about it.

From clear statements such as these, the group can begin to identify contradictions in societal expectations, thus demonstrating the extent to which we have internalized and continue to act upon dominant ideologies.

Debates and syndicates also offer a different forum for the use of verbal techniques and skills, hence avoiding repetition and superficial responses. Members can divide into subgroups and take up differing positions around a certain topic or point of view, for example, the abortion campaign; conflict in the group; lack of nursery facilities in the locality. Each subgroup is asked to demonstrate consistency in its behavioural and verbal forms of expression. Such a technique gives women permission to try out a certain belief system and subsequently discuss how comfortable they felt with it, thus allowing for shifts in attitude. It is also an exhilarating method of testing out assertion skills.

Discussion, then, when used in an imaginative way, can become participatory and exploratory, and is effective in encouraging attitude change. Discussion, if coupled with the imaginative techniques referred to earlier, can precipitate a heightened awareness of how to tackle obstacles, set goals and develop solutions, growing out of an increase in self-expression and recognition of cognitive processes. This is not to suggest that discussion can be neatly packaged, with the rough edges, the half-spoken truths, smoothed away into simplistic answers. Rather, a discussion is constructive if it sparks off group members' enthusiasm, not to create order and discover clarity, but to understand the chaos better.

Trips out   It is often said that group activity involving trips and social occasions is compensatory, offering members opportunities which hitherto have been denied them because of material and economic deprivation. Whilst this is true, there are other equally important reasons for building social occasions into the group's life. First, trips out can be fun, can involve adventure, excitement and risk-taking. Each women's group session is a social occasion for members, and for many it may be the only opportunity to escape from the confines of the house:

> It gives me a break from the kids.
>
> It gets me out of the house.
>
> I meet other women just like myself and we laugh about our problems.
>
> School holidays are a stressful time for all of us, and our visit to the working farm and other social outings took away the frustration for a while.

Secondly, such outings can give women a rare chance to try out physical skills and improve their co-ordination. Women can become permanently stooped through walking with pushchairs and carrying heavy shopping. Thirdly, a successful outing can strengthen mutuality and reciprocity, promote trust and co-operation. In Chapter 4, we examine the importance of these elements of group identity development, but we must never play down the role of social occasions.

There is yet another dimension to trips out, that of opening women's consciousness to their environment. A re-evaluation of their community takes place, their streets, their factories, the landscape around them, leading to a recognition of its capitalist and patriarchal roots. Women begin to value the historical boundaries of their locality and the networks which have been sustained, despite economic hardship. For women in the rural group, mobility was strait-jacketed by cultural and economic ties. However, visits to local textile and pottery factories, farms, historical sights and homes of local literary figures began to shatter the taken-for-granted outlook and acceptance of women's lot. What had previously been seen to be 'just an ordinary place, it's where I've grown up, there's nothing more to it' came to be seen as a place of local historical significance, albeit a history created by male working-class figures and aristocratic landowners. The role of women in this history had never been acknowledged. With the dawning of this realization, the Self can be placed not only in a social, but also in a temporal context. A woman's ability to concentrate on her environment improves as she learns to assess its assets and deficits. This gives her a more acute sense of how demands can be made on powerful institutions in the locality.

Through trips out, information from the environment can take on a new signifance and can transform the erosion of the past into part of our present cultural heritage. In addition, the ability to perceive the social injustices surrounding each group member is heightened. Women usually experience themselves 'living in' an external world that is independent of them. We tend to subscribe to the idea that 'seeing is believing' rather than 'believing is seeing' (Morgan and Ramirez, 1983) and our actions are circumscribed by the past. Trips out can encourage women to re-examine familiar situations to see what *possible* directions for development emerge.

Continuum of group activities: Using individual and
social transformation
Group interaction, by its very nature, presupposes a collective approach to work, whatever the activity. Across the infinite range of group activities, however, it is possible to discern differences between those that depend solely on the responses of the individual, and those requiring maximum group participation. Nevertheless, the transition from one of these approaches to another does not occur on a linear basis and cannot be said to be a true continuum. There is a constant ebb and flow between the overtly individual and the group focus, and in this section we will explore a few examples of such fluctuations.

Starting with the 'Personal Pen Picture' exercise, this can bridge the gap between an apparently individual task and shared discussion, analysis and evaluation. In this exercise, women are asked to describe their character not using hard, factual information, such as 'I'm twenty-seven, I've got three kids, I live at . . .' The purpose of this exercise is to encourage women to identify and feel proud of aspects of themselves, to imagine meeting someone new for the first time, and to feel able to present this new Self to others without fighting through any existing preconceptions. Even though the exercise is based in individual response, it acts as a catalyst for group discussion around the difficulties we face in 'displaying' ourselves in a positive light. It is still possible for each woman to decide just how much or how little she will join in a particular discussion, and just how much of herself she will make known to others. Learning self-control is possible here too.

Likewise, paper and pencil exercises, initially undertaken as individual activities, can alter the mood of the whole group and channel energy into a task with easily understood procedures. Such exercises do not require literacy skills because if any woman has difficulty in writing she can be helped by another group member who can record her thoughts on her behalf. Thus, sentence completion games, 'I get angry when . . .'; 'I feel tired when . . .'; 'If only I could . . .'; 'I'm happiest during . . .'; 'I'm really good at . . .', get the individual to focus on the Self. The sentence 'If I got angry I would . . .' gives permission to express fears about individual levels of anger and the extreme forms these may appear to take. This allows for a discussion of how exaggerated many fears are in relation to anger, and for plans to be made to express anger constructively (see Chapter 5). These exercises also foster decisions about the use of personal will and choice, rare activities for women pulled in all directions to the point of fragmentation.

'The Poster Game' is an equally important way of seeking out self-validation and group approval. In this exercise (Ernst and Goodison, 1981, p. 55) each member draws her name very large in the middle of a sheet of paper using bright colours, and then writes positive comments about herself around this name. Everyone then writes on each person's poster the things they like about her. This exercise, beginning as it does with concentration on the Self, opens up into a group activity, generating thoughts about other group members. The process of moving from the inner to the outer succinctly highlights the pull between recognition of Self and interdependency. In addition, the fact that the poster can be kept, taken home and looked at time and time again provides a constant injection of the potency of other people's compliments. The route to self-worth is opened.

As far as maximum group interaction is concerned, a technique such as sculpting can involve each member in a spatial representation of the interpersonal dynamics of the group. Sculpting involves asking group members to form themselves into a living sculpture or a photograph, whereby certain postures, facial expressions, gestures and proximity to others represent the main characteristics and feelings of an event. A group member who is experiencing difficulty in self-expression can be asked to direct the piece, moving people to the positions she feels reflect the themes of an incident. Such a director may only be tangentially linked to the way an issue is initially defined, but may in the end have one of the most important ideas to contribute.

Women are then asked to comment on the position they hold and its relation to other members. Their awareness of the potential for change may be raised. The sculpt is then reconstructed in new positions, demonstrating the consequences of group members' actions. The way in which such an exercise can open up honesty and revelations about others' perceptions of behaviour encourages collaboration. Women can also reappraise the physical space they occupy. The power of this exercise stems from its ability to catch hold of and freeze the affective and attitudinal content of a specific encounter. There is a strong message that any moment of a group's life can yield enough data for us to learn something about our perceptions, our habitual patterns of dealing with others, and our conflicts.

Group construction exercises (Brandes and Phillips, 1977, s. 21), where members form themselves into a train, a tree, a lawnmower, and mime the actions accordingly, provide lessons in seeking out the support of others whilst concentrating on your own particular activity. In this exercise, what happens when there are changes in circumstances, or the constructed machine has to deal with something unexpected? If the machine's parts are not working together, then it will break down because it is not clear which part will know how to deal with the new problems posed. If few parts have an overall view of the machine, action taken by one part causes problems for others. One section of the machine ends up working against the interests of another. It is important to learn how the part can take its specific shape at any one time from the nature of the whole. Each element also needs the capacity to question what it is doing, to determine whether what is being done is appropriate and adjust its actions accordingly. This exercise can begin to encourage women to act in a manner *informed by* an awareness of the interrelations that define their situation, rather than by the conventional dictates of fixed societal roles. The group thus becomes self-organizing and self-generating.

An exercise examining confrontation can develop similar skills. Members form themselves into two lines, in which they hold each other, arms round back, and line A keeps shouting YES at line B, who keeps responding NO (Houston, 1987). After a while, the roles are reversed, amidst exhilaration, laughter and frustration or anger, as memories are evoked about previous handling of confrontation. The physical energy required in the exercise can spark off maximum interaction concerning women's responses to shouting or being shouted at, competition and its meaning, and the values placed on NO and YES.

METHODIST COLLEGE LIBRARY
Fayetteville, N.C.

The need for activity which requires participation from all members is particularly important. Only then can women begin to recognize and value the power of inductive learning, of gaining ground in relation to each other, of pooling skills and qualities with the aim of perceiving a problem or issue in its entirety. The separation and segregation of women's activities means that often this is a difficult lesson to learn, as years of oppressive socialization need to be counteracted. Every member has something of value to contribute to an understanding of the group, and this resource should be tapped in as many ways as possible to enhance the learning capacity of the whole.

Transfer of knowledge: Linking the internal world of the group to the external world
Such an array of approaches and exercises has value in itself as it offers women a range of different views of themselves, as well as company and brief respite from home and child-care concerns. Nevertheless, it would be disingenuous to deny the hope on the workers' part that new-found self-awareness and confidence could be transferred to other aspects of women participants' lives, and, indeed, to our own. The learning process was constant for all concerned. In this section we will review opportunities for the transfer of knowledge outside the group which took place on different planes and by a variety of mechanisms.

Women's changing attitudes towards themselves and others inevitably led to differences in self-expression and behaviour which surprised even themselves, let alone those whom they were addressing. They may have found themselves better able to deal with the demands of children, because of the respite and relaxation afforded by the group. They may have gone home from a particular session – for example, on tenants' rights – with a set of statements being repeated over and over again in their heads, and as a result have been inspired to make appropriate demands immediately of the relevant authority.

We will be exploring the nature of group change in Chapter 4, and its impact on personal and public relationships in Chapter 6. For our purposes here, we will concentrate on group change which can occur because it is deliberately planned. Women can hang on to moments of personal growth in a more systematic manner when 'homework' tasks are set on a weekly and monthly basis, so that they can prove to themselves and other group members that learning is taking place as a result of discussions and exercises. For example, the attempted resolution of specific issues can be role-played when it is known that the risks involved in re-enacting this in 'real' life, outside the group, are not life-threatening. Take the example of a group member whose ex-mother-in-law still held a key to her house, turning up uninvited and unannounced, ready to assume control of the children and the household at any time. Through role play, she was encouraged to assert herself in the face of such an imposition, to make it clear that she was mistress in her own house, that she welcomed assistance when she sought it herself, but at no other time.

Women were encouraged to take practical steps to enhance the circumstances in which they lived, whether this entailed discussion with children, partners, Department of Social Security workers, or Housing Department officers (see Chapter 6). In a systematic way, the information was conveyed to women that they had rights as parents, as tenants, as patients, as consumers of legal services, but that under-pinning all this were their rights as individuals. This can lead women to feel more confident to make demands over issues that are of a more personal nature than tenants' rights, for instance. Women were encouraged wherever possible to take time for themselves during the week, whether this meant spending one twenty-minute session engaged in relaxation, walking in the park or leaving their children with friends. The pleasure and invigoration afforded by such activities enhance women's positive self-image as they begin to believe that they are worthy of what may hitherto have struck them as impossible indulgences. Once there has been the chance to experience these activities a few times, women will want to carry on doing so.

Exercises serve several purposes. First, whilst recognizing the need for silence and 'quiet times', there can be periods in group sessions where it seems that discussion and movement are becoming proble-matic, that people are getting stuck (see Chapter 4). An exercise, carefully chosen for its apposite nature and for the thoughts, feelings and statements it is likely to generate can help get the group moving. It is no use introducing an exercise as a random piece of work, without giving any forethought to its place in the structure and process of the group.

Secondly, structured exercises at regular stages in the group's experience can be used as a way of crystallizing and demonstrating to women the changes taking place within themselves and their lives. Listed below are exercises which can tap into individual and group change:

1 Hidden Personality;
2 Personal Pen Pictures, not including basic factual information;
3 the Magic Shop;
4 stating feelings and owning them;
5 working on recognizing and expressing anger;
6 recognizing the right to be assertive, devising an assertiveness 'ladder' and climbing it;
7 a discussion of the origins of the discrepancies between each

woman's wants for herself and the expectations she feels are
imposed on her by society, family and friends;

8   the Card Game (see below), looking at how many levels this can
be played on and the different reactions women have to statements
made about them by others;

9   painting, using colours to describe personality and Self;

10   looking at a range of media images of women and at ways of
creating an autonomous picture to counteract these.

Some of these exercises need to take place over more than one session.
Building the assertiveness 'ladder' is a prime example because women
often want to add more rungs to their 'ladder' once they have practised
the strategies described and discussed in previous sessions and once
there are more areas of their lives in which they want to experiment
with assertion techniques. The notion of this ladder can be introduced
at a relatively early stage in the group's proceedings, with reference
being made to it, for example, every three weeks in a fifteen-week series
of sessions. This gives women ample opportunity to discuss their
feelings of pride and encouragement at having practised a certain stage
on the ladder and at being able to maintain a certain level. It must be
emphasized that such a structured approach must not be used to
measure 'success' or 'failure' (see Chapter 4) and that discussion and
comparison of individual ladders should be used to offer advice and
encouragement, never criticism. The ladder can be represented
pictorially and women can keep it as a measure of their achievement
and change throughout the group's meetings.

All the exercises listed can be repeated over time and demonstrate to
women in a graphic way any movement in their self-awareness. In the
Card Game, for instance, approximately thirty cards are prepared with
complimentary statements written on them ('The person with the
brightest eyes'; 'The person with lots of interesting things to say'; 'The
person with the smallest feet'). The cards are placed in a single pile face
down and each member in turn picks up a card, reads it silently, and
passes it to another group member if she thinks the statement on the
card applies to her. If the woman picking up the card does not wish to
pass it on, she places it face down on the floor/table, in a new pile. This
continues until the whole pile of cards has been picked up and seen by
at least one person. This means that participants can get an idea of
what is on the cards and see that the statements are positive and
non-threatening.

The procedure is repeated, only this time each card must be passed
to another woman, so that finally no cards are left. Each member in
turn then explains why she passed a particular card to a given woman.
For example, what qualities does she think the woman has? What

thoughts did she have which inspired her to give the card to a particular woman? Once positive statements are made about each group member, the recipients describe their thoughts, feelings and reactions to getting the cards. If the card is a surprise, does it offer an opportunity for a different self-perception? When this exercise is repeated at intervals during the group's life, it can lead to an analysis of how we function in relation to others, of how we act in ways we think others expect of us, rather than as we would wish to ourselves. We can learn how readily we misinterpret others' behaviour, that often we are not observant about physical appearance, and that if this is the case, then it is equally likely that we will misinterpret psychological states. It can lead to a reappraisal of self-image.

Finally, the keeping of a group diary as a record of change and development provides immediate proof of different stages of thinking, to which women can refer as time goes on. Thus, women can take it upon themselves to expand and test out their confidence and self-assurance through structured as well as informal mechanisms. 'Homework', in this sense, can either be consciously set up or be a consequence of women's changing perceptions.

The fluidity of theory and method

Our purpose in sketching in the various dimensions of groupwork methodology is to emphasize the experiential nature of the enterprise. However, identifying *how* methods can be used to satisfy the aims of group learning is just as important as the methods themselves. If workers do not know *why* a particular exercise or discussion is being used, then members' investment in a session will understandably subside. Clarity about the purpose of an exercise or topic for discussion, and sharing this with group members, are key elements in harnessing women's interest. In addition, groupwork should not be used in a mechanistic way. If there is fluidity and cross-referencing between exercises, then this allows time for review and elaboration in order to draw out threads of analysis which can be woven into the next part of a session. Techniques are meaningless unless grounded in a vision which increases the capacity for learning.

The general theoretical principles which we outline offer a definition of possibilities for feminist groupwork and are not meant to be taken as a set of optimal procedures. The ideology of women's groups allows for the use of psychological theories when they are grounded in socio-political explanations, and when the relationship between *form* and *content* is continually reviewed.

Our first consideration relates to the *ideology of women's groups*. By their very existence such groups give the opportunity for creating space in which to make demands for personal needs and wants. It is invariably the case that women in circumstances of poverty feel that they have no significant role to play in what is happening in their lives, and that events take place around them. We sought to encourage women to hang on to the validity of their own explanations and feelings, and to question expert views and opinions through learning to trust their own judgements.

This stance is reinforced by the use of *behavioural approaches* which encourage an analysis of the sequential nature of what happens 'inside' a particular pattern or set of events. Through the use of role play it is possible to encourage women to recognize the patterns of behaviour and responses that they fall into, for example, in dealing with children or other dependent relatives. By breaking a behavioural sequence into small manageable units, a woman can learn to take greater control of each part of an event as it happens and, ultimately, to feel more in control of herself. For this to have a lasting effect and be generalized to other situations, however, there needs to be more than the largely mechanistic process of behavioural work.

Cognitive restructuring can be criticized by feminists as encouraging women to examine their behaviour and reactions, then analyse and redefine them along traditional masculinist lines. It may be seen as a coercive process, with women coming to accept the representation of Self offered to them by societal norms. However, it is a process that can be turned to feminist ends. Given that identity is both personally held, in that it is a process of progressive differentiation and, in addition, is socially constructed, cognitive restructuring can play a key role in helping group members to gain control over their environment. Used particularly with women experiencing depression, cognitive therapy seeks to assess a person's 'cognitive triad' of negative views about themselves, the world, and the future (Beck and Greenberg, 1974). In addition to having selective perceptions, people with depression are said to draw arbitrary, pessimistic inferences; to make over-generalizations based on one negative incident; to magnify particular unpleasant events, and to focus on one unhappy detail (Beck et al., 1979). The cognitive approach teaches people to monitor their 'automatic thoughts' and to recognize the type of cognitive distortions that they habitually use (M. Scott, 1989). A feminist gloss on each thought or behavioural pattern can have a liberating effect by encouraging women to:

1 recognize patterns of self-protection, self-blame and self-effacement from the past, and to articulate the reasons behind the need for such behaviour;

2 express distress and anger at the extent to which direct, honest

self-expression has been denied them. The strategies they have employed to persist in these thought patterns or behaviours can be unravelled;
3 recognize such behaviours and cognitions as survival mechanisms, rather than pathological disturbances.

Learning to identify and articulate these interpretations of behaviour and cognitions can help construct a world-view in which a woman can become an agent as regards her own actions, having accepted the influence of the past on the present. An exploration of deeper levels of consciousness through fantasy and relaxation can further increase a woman's sense of control.

This process of rediscovery and redefinition is kindled through *socio-political explanations* for action. At no point is it appropriate for us to offer such explanations to women without them first drawing out their *own* analysis through discussion and questioning. Women know where power lies and what a struggle they have to grasp any in their own right. We have no wish to send women away feeling disgruntled and dissatisfied, powerless to effect any change. This was particularly the case as we knew that women in the groups were frequently in the position of going home to a life of material and emotional deprivation. Statements made in the group, though, can provide a basis for enquiry, for putting forward ways of viewing the world that can be discussed:

> Women's lib has just made things worse. It hasn't made my life easier.
>
> I enjoy being a mother. I don't want to go out to work. Stop taking that from us.
>
> It's alright for you feminists fighting for abortion rights. I had an abortion in hospital and I didn't even know I was having one. There's *no* choice for the likes of us. It's either that or sterilization.

Contained within these statements is a call for feminism to accept the paradoxes of limited choices if the Women's Movement is to be relevant to as many women as possible. For example, a working-class woman should be able to express her anger at the lack of tangible changes in her life that she feels the Women's Movement has brought her. For the second speaker, concentration by white feminists on employment and career moves for middle-class women has led her to fear that motherhood has become even more devalued than previously. The third woman voices her challenges to the priorities of the Women's Movement, which by default has denied the institutional violence experienced by women in poverty. In such circumstances, gynae-cologists have stereotyped women not only in terms of their reproductive role, but also in terms of their low-income status.

The expression of thoughts and beliefs such as these should be encouraged in the group, as the potential for a positive outcome should outweigh the risks women have to take, the risks of moving on or deciding to stay where they are. The process of risk-taking in women's groups pin-points the need to make connections between various theoretical and methodological elements. The approaches we have outlined can then be transformed by imbuing them with feminist beliefs and principles, thereby providing group members with a pool of challenges to dip into. In our next section, we will outline the philosophy of action learning which underpins the range of theoretical and methodological strands explored so far. By fusing therapy with community education principles, women can make the links between oppression, their survival mechanisms and the socio-political context.

The concept of community education

From institutional education to action learning
A hallmark of women's groups is learning to frame, enquire about and reframe ideologies and forms of knowledge. Yet one of the many legacies which some working-class women bring to groups is their negative experiences of formal education through the under-resourced state school system. Some working-class women have internalized a deprecating self-assessment and sense of inadequacy *vis-à-vis* those with formal educational achievements. Indeed, there is ample documentation of the ways in which institutional education contributes to the process of gender differentiation, the exclusion of girls (Spender, 1982a; Spender and Sarah, 1980) and the perpetuation of racism, classism and heterosexism (City of Leicester Teachers' Association (NUT), 1987; Jones and Mahoney, 1989).

The memories evoked by schooldays involve the underestimation of any skills and, instead, place emphasis on the need to prepare for motherhood. By way of contrast, women's groups have to rely on a radical and inspiring definition of education which draws out women's potential and offers them the means to a better future (Thompson, 1983). Such a stance has strong links with the process of conscientization described by Paolo Freire (1970). Through his work in Brazil and Chile, Freire sought to increase peasants' literacy skills, whilst at one and the same time opening up their perceptions of social, political and economic contradictions. For Freire, consciousness-raising for the oppressed involves *reflection*, searching out an understanding of dehumanizing social structures, but also *action* aimed at altering societal conditions (Longres and McLeod, 1980). To avoid the danger of this process becoming a tool for further oppression, in which an ideological perspective is forced on unsuspecting people, workers can engage in *dialogue* (Freire, 1970, p. 61). Through this, all participants in the discussion learn from each other; there is no value to be gained from the banking concept of education where an expert fills the empty head of someone without knowledge.

The essence of women's group learning must reside therefore in the idea that we all learn through action. Action learning aims to enhance women's capabilities to enquire and investigate, thus empowering them to become critically conscious of their values, assumptions and rights *within* social contexts (Morgan and Ramirez, 1983). Learning to learn again involves freeing women from fixed frameworks for interpreting situations. It involves breaking free from the vicious circle of assumption and consequence by democratizing learning. Given the opportunity, all women are able to *own* their learning, to be reflective and act upon the environment. Social change starts and ends with each of us. Such reflexivity enabled women in the rural group to attend local community education events and International Women's Days with the ability to concentrate on themselves, to talk and share experiences.

The encouragement of personal awareness through women's issues material

The principles of action learning are revealed especially through our use of women's issues material, which was interwoven into all group discussions and at times presented as specific topics for debate. These related to sexuality and sexual violence, women's health issues, domestic labour and paid employment, men and masculinity. It is impossible to operate from a feminist standpoint when working in groups with women without such areas of discussion assuming considerable if not paramount importance. In this respect, feminist groupwork will be seen to differ radically from traditional approaches.

In feminist groupwork, members aim never to make a particular subject seem taboo. It cannot be guaranteed that total freedom of expression is possible, nor that workers will pick up all available cues and messages. Neither can any predictions be made of the ways in which different women will react to the raising of certain matters – rape, sexual assault, or child abuse, for example. It may be that they will be completely unable to participate in the discussion at a particular point because of the pain this generates. Allowances need to be made for dealing with the reactions some women know they are likely to have.

Feminist groupwork seeks to raise levels of awareness of, first, the structures inherent in maintaining women in subordinate positions, and, secondly, ways of challenging, confronting and, where possible, changing these structures. It does not exist to encourage women to accept the positions they find themselves in, but to question them all the time. The argument often put forward against such an approach is that it will only make women unhappy because they become aware that things could be different, when they are not in a position to change anything. The forces that need to be contended with are far too strong. Such an argument is an insult to women on several counts:

1 It does not recognize the misery that many women face in their day-to-day lives, the degradation caused by bad housing, poverty, burdens of caring, violence, isolation.

2 It does not recognize women's tenacity and strength of character and determination to improve at least their children's, if not their own, circumstances.

3 It assumes that women will sit around and wait for change to occur somewhere else further up the male-dominated social hierarchy, and be grateful for the minor improvements this might bring about in their lives. The history of revolution tells us enough to know that such an approach is never beneficial to women in the long run.

What group discussion *can* offer is the space to discover the contradictions of the patriarchal capitalist order, as reflected in prescribed social roles for women. Working-class women can begin to identify the received ideas which permeate major institutions, and the ways these ideologies have become ostacles to their own development. This can be achieved through an exploration of women's insights into how things really are through their own life experiences, the learning experiences in the group and elements of their 'common sense' (R. Davis, 1988). Once holes begin to appear in women's descriptions of dominant ideologies, then the possibility of change in their perceptions can occur (Kirk, 1983). Such an appreciation and analysis serves to demonstrate to women the processes and function of their oppression; the reality of it they will have been aware of for a long time already. The awareness gained reveals the ubiquitous, pervasive nature of different forms of discrimination, leaving women with the realization that they do not carry individual responsibility or blame for their own misery. Nor can this be explained by their 'inadequacy', 'hysteria', 'manipulation', 'illitcracy' or whatever term is chosen.

It is a truism that an understanding and knowlege of oppression often functions as a 'ripple effect', as an individual woman begins to acknowledge that the serenity and peace of mind she is told she should be experiencing are extremely elusive. Masculinist attitudes towards working-class women's involvement in the labour market will help to clarify the links to be made between personal troubles and public issues. Within our women's groups, some men wanted to be able to control their partners' lives to the extent that a few women engaged in very short shifts of paid work. For example, an hour and a half's cleaning was undertaken when their partners were out at work, in the desperate hope that they would not be found out. Money earned in this way was used to supplement the household budget, not to line the woman's pocket. Amongst male partners, there were some who deemed it inappropriate or even immoral for 'their' woman to work outside the home, considering it right that the woman's place was exclusively in the domestic sphere. One man wanted details of any visitors a group member had during the day, or visits she herself had made. J would come home from work, run his finger along a shelf and, if it was dusty, assume that L, his partner, had been out all day as she obviously had not been in cleaning. Being out could mean being with another man, and that would warrant physical violence.

Women's group members thus effectively become prisoners in their own homes, their entire lives, their every action, shaped by the reaction they might expect from their partner returning home. This is unpredictable, but experience shows that it is wise to err on the side of caution. This means that when 'treats' are offered – a night out, a new outfit, 'permission' granted to see a particular friend or family member – then these have to be grabbed when the chance is given. There can be no planning, no personal control over the shape of life and activities undertaken. Everything is a risk, everything is overshadowed. Such a pattern inevitably takes its toll, with women's coping mechanisms becoming more and more strained.

It is not surprising, therefore, when analysis and explanations of such a life-style are offered that women engage enthusiastically in discussion about oppression and liberation. Taking steps to liberate oneself from the round of risk, uncertainty and abuse may be extremely frightening, and it is not something that can be undertaken lightly. The ripple effect grows, with awareness spreading of how this oppression works, contaminates, distorts and suppresses experience. The connections between actual physical or sexual violence and the less immediately obvious forms of violence such as inadequate policies on education, housing, health and public transport come to be made.

Personal awareness of the links between an individual's position and the plight of other women around her leads to a breaking down of the isolation and loneliness she has been experiencing (see Chapter 1). A feeling of impotence develops, which is soon converted to anger and rage, the need to speak out and retaliate thus precipitating debate on possible individual and collective action. The greatest achievement is that women recognize their own strength and power and take pride in this.

Throughout the group experience, there are key elements of action learning which will always remain the same, no matter what methodology or theoretical stance is chosen. The aim is to establish a basis for personal and collective transformation in which a woman is encouraged:

1   to recognize the shared basis of responses which have denied women the right to take action for themselves;
2   to trust and own her cognitions, counteracting messages received from elsewhere;
3   to recognize that group decision-making is not a mark of indecisiveness on her part;
4   to recognize that group decision-making means collective response, validation and, in some instances, collective activity.

Fundamental to our arguments in this chapter has been the belief that groupwork methods should be hallmarked by flexibility in order to break down the limitations imposed on women's choices. A holistic approach to activities embraces the diversity of women's expectations when undertaking a particular exercise. It also encourages recognition of every aspect of Self and a developing group identity. When all of this is framed by and imbued with feminist principles concerning action learning and the politics of therapy, it is possible to use groupwork methodology as the springboard for conscientization. Being proactive, using our own resources and energy levels to the full in groups, provides a strong basis from which to counteract and challenge the misogynistic behaviour with which we are all surrounded.

4

Group Transformation: The Dynamic Process of Change

I don't really talk to other women. Don't get me wrong, I'm a chatty person, y'know. I'll pass the time of day with women on the estate, but we only talk about the kids. Anyway, my bloke would think I was off my rocker if I turned to women all the time. No, I've never really given much thought to women friends. (Anne – women's group member)

Virginia Woolf described the relationships between women as 'that vast chamber where nobody has been' (quoted in Rich, 1979). Indeed, such is patriarchal power that it has shaped our preferences with regard to social relations, and has limited our sense of possibilities. This chapter focuses on attempts by women to move from this isolation from each other to the identification of a group consciousness, that sense of belonging which leads to concerted action. It is our contention that the collective creation of knowledge is precipitated not only by the feminist methodologies referred to in Chapter 3, but also through group process. Together, these relieve the pain of exorcizing social myths and personal images which are deeply embedded in the Self. It is group process which provides women with the experience and the tools to comprehend the political and personal dimensions of existence. We shall make it clear that changes in perceptions of identity and social reality are affirmed through the positive language of social exchange and the symbolic language of group ritual.

This chapter is structured in four sections to help us understand more fully the significance of group process and group identity. First, we will examine how structural patterns within the group challenge ideological constraints. Secondly, there will be an analysis of group interaction and continuity over a period of time, as these influence the definition of group identity, cohesion and the negotiation of group values and beliefs. Thirdly, we will examine the connections between group process and identity, and the development of women's friendships. Finally, we will look at how groups change and what value is placed on this by group members. Running throughout this, we will speculate about the ways in which group process breaks through the impasse of patriarchal definitions of contemporary life.

Structural relationships

We have already referred in Chapter 1 to the dishonesty of calling for unanimity between participants by hiding our different socio-economic positions. What we now wish to explore is how structural relationships in groups can be made explicit in order to throw light on conflicts and tensions regarding individuality and interdependence. Structural relationships are also at the root of the politics of feminist process in groups. If we accept that patriarchal social order affects the psychological functioning of individuals, then our concern has to be the extent to which this may impinge upon the relations between workers and women members.

The relationships between women workers and group members

We are all products of our socialization as women; this is perhaps, paradoxically, supremely so for women workers, who have chosen a field which requires them to emphasize their emotional sensitivity to others and their care-giving abilities. Yet, beyond this, there are issues of power relations within women's groups, which, if ignored, can breed mendacity and obfuscation. Barker (1986), in her honest discussion of her work with two women's health courses, accentuates the mistakes which can be made in relation to the *process* of feminist organizing. She indicates that there are dangers of workers falling into a 'false equality trap' (1986, p. 82) where differences between women are minimized. This conjures up a mythology of equality which glosses over structural positions in the group, and differences in experiences of oppression and in possession of knowledge and skills. Barker's practice, therefore, was to avoid domination by merging into the group, but such informal and structureless discussion can breed frustration and, as has been said by Rowbotham (1979), a coercive form of consensus. The covert exercise of power can manifest itself at any point, leaving a nasty taste in the mouths of women members, who feel divided and patronized. Far from developing group cohesion and sisterhood, Barker's mistakes created dynamics which were the opposite of those intended, widening the gap between workers and women members.

As Longres and McLeod (1980) have stressed, women workers have knowledge and information derived from their formal education and professional experience which *can* make an important contribution to the group. Information is power (Freeman, 1984) and if workers can be clear about their boundaries and the power invested in them by virtue of their role, they can impart information which is relevant to the group's endeavours. In our experience, this leads to direct questioning from women and sets the tone for honest communication. For example, we may all share experiences of loss and bereavement, of sexual violence, of breakdown in personal relationships, but workers need to stress the access they have to information and resources which potentially give them more freedom of choice to deal with such crises. In contrast, many working-class women are expected to manage their family resources unaided, are stigmatized for failing, and yet are those with the fewest resources. In addition, they know about societal rules and expectations regarding eligibility for services – show deference, dependence, deservingness and just the right degree of 'inadequacy', not too little or too much. Women workers, who enjoy greater social and economic advantages, should therefore encourage members to recognize the immense efforts they have made in difficult circumstances over a considerable period of time. Sisterhood does not mean obscuring the fact that women have different and unequal material circumstances, and acquire knowledge and skills through a range of routes. What feminist process should attempt to achieve is recognition of such structural positions.

The legacy of leadership
Deciding who occupies which structural positions in the group can expose the problem of leadership. Stripped of obsession with hierarchy and sensitive to the immediate needs of members, women's groups can harbour queries about the relevance of leadership to the group. Skill-sharing is an accepted goal of feminist organizing (Barker, 1986), but there are problems and dilemmas in finding methods of communicating these skills without slipping into condescension.

Lack of example, lack of role models, lack of encouragement, lack of interest in what is proposed, lack of opportunity to do, lack of appreciation for what is done – all exert considerable pressure upon women to avoid testing out new ground. Women therefore have little self-confidence to declare 'I can and I will.' They still sometimes expect designated leadership roles. This is the result of years of women discouraging each other from being 'successful' by outwardly conforming to male-determined standards of female behaviour (Rendel, 1978). Women in the groups quickly indicated the ways in which they punished themselves for expressing any instrumental skills. 'Let him believe it's his own idea' and, 'Let him know you've got weaknesses, because if you're tough, then you'll get the whole lot dropped on you' was the advice given by one group member to another during a role play of an argument between a man and a woman.

These obstacles do not stop there because women have difficulty in assessing how good or bad their work is. Within the groups, achievements were often qualified by 'But you'd have done it better', or 'I've had a go at this. See what you think, although I've not made a very good job of it.' The absence of an appreciative response to achievement creates difficulties for women in groups, who either have to put themselves down or set their judgement against that of society. Throughout this process, the group will at times turn to the workers for advice or support, and we have to decide how to act, how to speak and not replicate the patronizing responses women have received repeatedly from many others. Such phrases as 'It's up to you', 'You could think about such and such', and 'There might be other ways of doing it' all need careful consideration before utterance. It is still too easy to fall into the role of 'expert' because we think we can see certain plans of action that are likely to be more beneficial than the one being contemplated. It is vital to let participants find out for themselves even if the process is painful. Whilst acknowledging people's different learning needs, we must not put ourselves in a position of preaching or teaching. Offering information is one thing, about whom to approach in the council, or where to get cheap photocopying done, but telling people how to do things is another matter, and likely to lead to resentment. Workers' awareness of the complexity of structural positions in the group must be supported by the need for flexibility in skill-sharing.

Differences between women: Divisive or diverse?

Explicit recognition of structural issues is a necessary precondition for raising members' awareness of inequalities which may be operating within the group. This is particularly so when differences between women based on age, disability, sexuality, race and ethnicity are played out in the group. It has already been said (see Chapter 1) that the diversity of membership in the rural group led to a rich tapestry of learning, as contradictions relating to oppression were explored. However, this process of discovery was marked with intense disturbance at times as conflict between women occurred. This was based on lack of honest communication regarding stereotyping and prejudice. J, for example, had ended a lesbian relationship and was now caring for her elderly father at his home. After several months of hearing other women in the group talk about their heterosexual partners and their child-rearing practices, she suddenly shouted out that she was sick of women making heterosexist assumptions about the 'normality' of sexual relations with men, that she felt excluded, and that it was further assumed that choosing to have a child-free life made her incomplete. For months she had felt marginalized and oppressed by other women because of the inferences with which she was surrounded. There were few positive images of lesbian women which she could catch hold of. Initially heterosexual women in the group were astonished by her statements, so unaware were they of their actions and behaviour.

In a similar vein, S, an older woman in the group, had been saying for weeks that she was prepared to run a few sessions of yoga and relaxation as she had considerable experience in these areas. Group interaction was such that her statements fell on stony ground, and were not followed up by other women. At one point a woman, T, said that she did not feel such sessions were appropriate for the group. S then backed off, feeling dismissed and ridiculed. Towards the end of the session, another woman indicated that she had felt uncomfortable about the way the group had treated S, and she thought this might be to do with group members' prejudice about older people assuming responsibility. T replied that she was not sure it was right for the group to open its doors to women over sixty anyway, and shouldn't the group set an upper age limit? The devastating effect of this comment led to a wealth of angry responses towards T, who was scapegoated, thereby diverting attention from other members' own ageist assumptions. As Macdonald and Rich (1984) have stressed, the fear of the stigma of age and the total ignorance of its reality in the lives of women has separated women of different ages from each other. Thus, the younger women had denied the older woman's strength, courage and sorrow. She was seen as having no future, treated as having no past and a highly marginal present. The bewilderment that can spread amongst group members as their ignorance begins to sway is testimony to the power of prejudice and stereotyping. There can never be enough occasions for us to learn that individual differences are important and valuable.

Once these interactions are made explicit they provide a basis for learning about the differences between women and how these can be harnessed for positive ends. The process of stereotyping can be broken down by constantly redefining and negotiating the exclusive possession of roles in the group which may become solidified over time. If a woman becomes stuck in the role of scapegoat, or clown, or saboteur, for example, then other women's responses will become rigidly defined and repetitive, leaving her little room for manoeuvre. Such roles also provide an escape route for other women who can hide behind the actions of the woman in the role, whilst at the same time disclaiming responsibility for her. Like all unspoken rules, it may be that one group member can express discontent and anger easily, thus conveniently leaving everyone else in the position of 'likeable women'. If other members want to express their anger in a subversive way, this can always be turned into righteous wrath at the 'angry' member.

All behaviours serve their purpose, but interactions such as these can be disconcerting and dangerous, leaving women with raw and unacknowledged feelings. At these times, the group needs to stop in its tracks and work hard to deconstruct the behavioural patterns which gloss over deeply held attitudes and assumptions. We all need to test out the fluidity of roles, tease out their component parts, and gain awareness of the values placed on certain behaviours. During such incidents, we learn to confront ourselves, offer up our doubts, and allow the possibility of a shifting subjectivity. Words spoken in a moment should not be seen to represent a woman's total belief system. If this happens, then women will become reticent about expressing their views for fear of negative judgements.

The empowerment of group members

Amidst the playing out of structural positions in the group, one of the most striking messages which women's groups convey is the need for women to take power for themselves. The realization that each interaction point is an exercise of power negotiation can energize women to tread the rocky path towards self-control. What develops is an internal legitimation of the constructive use of authority and influence. These notions may arouse discomfort and suspicion amongst feminists, clinging to the political ideal of unity amongst women grounded in equality of participation. Paradoxically in our view, women's group members very quickly assess each other's authority – who has knowledge and skills; who is an appropriate role model; who holds influence in the group as regards decision-making. It is easy for these thought processes to remain ambiguous and for control to be seen only in a negative light. However, control intersects at too many points with the caring aspects of women's behaviour for such fragmentation to be sustained.

Seating arrangements   Equality of participation can be encouraged through recognition of direct and symbolic forms of structural group processes. There is movement from looking at *what* is happening to *how* it is happening. To minimize the perpetuation of members' powerlessness, attention can be given to seating arrangements during discussions, as these can inadvertently reinforce exclusion and marginalization. For example, if a subgroup is beginning to form it is more than likely that these women will sit together. If a woman sitting near this group is feeling vulnerable and is reticent about speaking, then she will be paralysed even further by the force of the subgroup. In such circumstances, it is appropriate for women workers or other members to draw attention to this inadvertent marginalization and the ways in which this may be inhibiting participation. Group members can become aware of the *form* of interaction that is thrown up by such seating arrangements, *which* options are available for changing such inequalities, and *how* these can be achieved.

Interactional sequences   There are other ways in which group process can be made explicit in order to facilitate member control over the group, over their own lives, and over the ways they are perceived by others. An interactional sequence between two group members, for instance, will invariably draw in a third party, which can be constructive, but at times when the group dynamics are under strain this triad can create negative feedback.

At one particular point in the group, three women were making negative comments about another group member who had been silent and withdrawn for a few sessions, but they were not communicating directly with her. On examination of this closed triad, two of the women were exchanging angry statements about the other party, whom they felt had not been prepared to discuss personal facets of her life. The third woman was using placatory comments such as 'It wouldn't be fair to tell her how we're reacting to her. She couldn't handle it.' These regulated the exchanges of the other two and hence preserved rather than changed what was going on.

When alliances such as these become a power-base leading to the oppression of others, it is possible to bring this interactional sequence into focus by splitting the triad. If the placatory member and one of the angry members are left together, the third woman can be asked what it is that is preventing her from speaking directly to the silent member. It is then possible to ask her to imagine the perceptions the excluded woman may hold of the triad, and how her 'guesses' are related to the non-verbal cues she is displaying. Triad members can be asked how they have handled similar situations in the past, outside the group context. The silent group member can be encouraged to share what had happened to precipitate her withdrawal. Directing similar questioning to *all* group members conveys the need for difficulties to be shared, breaking down structural positions in the process.

Our understanding of patterns of interaction is enhanced further by group members' changing perceptions of workers and the effect this has on group process. As women begin to see workers in a clearer perspective then we take on less of a significant role in discussion. This fluctuates depending on the subject-matter being looked at, the state of mind of participants at that particular moment, and the workers' own need/wish to interject or intervene. The interplay between these three elements means that key moments of tension occur when workers see participants as having knowledge in a specific area which is worth sharing, but the participants themselves may be feeling particularly vulnerable or confused and welcome the thought of workers taking control of the debate. Once workers have recognized that the balance of power has shifted, they need to keep their interventions to a sensitive minimum. If this happens in a relatively smooth way women will cease to direct questions, observations and interpretations solely to the workers. Our aim should be to make ourselves redundant. The point at which women begin to make direct reference to each other signifies members' growth away from dependency; they are not prepared to sit and listen to 'professionals', but have things of value to say for themselves and to each other.

When an awareness of structural group processes begins to emerge, women can review their social representations of themselves in the group and learn how these directly affect the topic for discussion or group exercise. We have also shown that when group integrity is under threat through the formation of fixed and habitual patterns of interaction, these can be regulated by active refocusing. The increasing frequency of social exchanges *between* members, rather than via workers, also signifies the breakdown of women's customary mode of listening to others whilst questioning and denying their own thoughts and beliefs.

Development of group identity

Once women's responses to particular group dynamics are awakened and intensified, then they can discover and appraise their own behaviour and functioning as group members. Group identity, fed by feminism, offers a status and security beyond the group's boundaries, and assumes a greater and clearer role in women participants' lives. There are several ways in which the broad outline of group identity takes shape. First, the knowledge of the certainty of the group's existence, its weekly regularity, serves in itself to provide a sense of collective activity and experience that is not achieved elsewhere. Secondly, in contrast to a woman's emotionally bereft life, the group can awaken her ability to respond to others' wants and needs, thereby developing a more perceptive understanding. Then can come the confidence in her personal ability and *right* to make commiserative statements to others, to offer advice and counsel based on received wisdom and personal experience, and ultimately to offer practical assistance. Giving and taking become the mainstay of the group.

Thirdly, the power of the group can be realized through each woman's *self*-discovery. Women often feel prevented from expressing strong emotions out of a fear of destroying and overwhelming the group. Once it is learnt that the group gives permission for each woman to describe, share, cry over, be angry about personal experiences, and that the whole remains strong and protective, then the depths of her responses can be tapped. Fourthly, the unflagging, yet questioning, support of the group may be a wholly new experience for some working-class women and will be met with incredulity. Listening to a woman wholeheartedly and accepting her exactly as she is at that moment is the antithesis of women's experiences outside the group, where attention is taken up with diverging demands. The luxury of concentrating on one thing at a time is denied. Indeed, Ellis and Nichols (1979), in their comparative study of feminist and conventional group assertiveness training with women, found that the very fact of being in a women-only group had such a powerful effect in itself that the particular content of a group session was a bonus. Statements made by women highlight that group identity is activated as life takes on a greater polarization, with positive events standing out against negative experiences.

The relational dimensions of group identity
The common theme in the above four factors is that group identity development for women emerges out of *relational* dimensions, where group process and interpersonal skills create a co-operative and sensitive environment. Reflection is a key principle in all this, as the group generates structured opportunities for action–reflection–action, which leads to an analysis of socio-economic and political factors within women's lives. This emphasis on reflective sharing is supported by other studies of community women's group development (Eastman, 1973; Egar and Sarkissian, 1985). Attention to the origin, maintenance and growth of group identity reveals it to be an open-ended, rather than immutable, entity. It is forever in motion.

There are certain concepts inherent in the dynamism of group identity that can be unfolded and displayed as signifying patterns of growth. The concepts of *group identification, trust, reciprocity* and *mutuality* become the corner-stones of the group as they gain in value and emotional significance. These concepts are revealed through the principles of *open self-disclosure* and *positive feedback*. Out of these the group develops a certain distinctiveness, a social identity which draws on a belief system that all women are to be valued. The ensuing intimacy precipitates total investment in the group:

> I feel important in the group. It's a support and sanctuary I can invest in.
>
> I find a lot of sharing and understanding in the group and it helps to know you're not alone with your thoughts. It sometimes feels as though we're all sisters, we all help each other.
>
> I'm not one for gadding about so I haven't got anyone else to talk to. We're all sort of close with each other. If one of us cries, there's plenty of hugs 'cos we all know what it's like.
>
> The group is a bumper against which we can take out our frustrations and speak freely, knowing all our conversations are confidential.

The protective functions of the group are readily apparent within these statements by women. The nurturing, comforting atmosphere provide not only a shield against the social injustices of daily living, but also a source of strength and reserve energy in the face of opposition (Hyde, 1986).

Group identification   How does the strength to be derived from identifying with the group develop? This hinges upon psychological integration with the group, as members tussle with the expectations they hold about matters *for* the group and that which is to be excluded. Group identification is certainly not the same thing to all women (Brown and Williams, 1984). As indicated earlier, women's statements highlight the significance of the group as a sanctuary and source of sisterhood, but the group was described by the same women at different times as 'Rocking the boat', as 'Too much of a challenge. I can't cope with it at the moment.' However, the growing ability to differentiate between attitudinal shifts in Self and in other group members reinforces the collective ability to sustain the group's social identity.

Trust   For many working-class women the ability to trust and be trusted will often prove an uphill struggle. Trust may have been shattered through breakdown in personal relationships, or through self-disclosure to an untrustworthy person. One of the aims of women's groups is to encourage women to *expect* co-operative behaviour from group members and to *risk* placing their faith in others. Invariably, processes associated with trust are activated by the way a woman *expects* others to respond to *her* behaviour: 'I thought you'd all laugh at me if I told you'; 'I just feel so guilty about it that I know you're going to accuse me.' Once the risk-taking involved in trust-building has been tested and the rewards are reaped then seeds of group cohesion can be shown.

Reciprocity   Intimate acquaintance with the social milieu of women's groups reveals a third concept, reciprocity. Reciprocity specifies that we should repay help with help (Meeker, 1983). For women who have experienced distorted relationships, the ability to differentiate between harm and help may have become skewed. After years of domestic violence and oppressive heterosexual relationships, any offer of help for several women in the group was met with a harmful response. Once this was discussed openly in the group, members who had themselves reaped the benefits of positive reciprocity set into motion the mechanism of goodwill in social relations between women.

Open self-disclosure   It is the principle of open self-disclosure by workers and members that can provide the testing ground for empowerment. From the worker's point of view, considerable fear is generated by women's self-disclosure because of doubts about the degree of intensity and intimacy she can face hearing and dealing with. If workers can create reciprocity of information between themselves and women to counter any misconceptions about women workers as 'problem-free' people (Barker, 1986), then women can assess workers' limitations and, in addition, look to themselves for guidance and advice. Although there is a fine line to be drawn between workers disclosing personal concerns and burdening women with their own experiences, in feminist practice there is no better way of precipitating mutual learning.

Self-disclosure can present women with mountainous pressures in view of their reluctance to place their trust in others. In the daily lives of group members, their experiences of closeness and support are often short-lived, offering only a partial response. As a result, the unremitting support of a women's group can be difficult to accept and deal with. Previous life experiences have left many women bereft of intimacy and of the type of friendship that may disagree, dispute, but never undermine and unquestioningly shares their burdens, sorrows and joys. Women's group members had fantasies about such relationships, fond memories of times when they existed, all overlaid with a degree of scepticism that such hopes were unrealistic 'and not for me'. The negative reinforcement of such thought processes was plentiful in personal relationships outside the group. Because of the jealousy of a male partner, one woman had to sneak out of the house, under the guise of doing extra shopping, to visit her sister for half an hour. The search for such simple pleasures was invariably viewed as a misdemeanour by the male partner.

Set against such a background, it is hardly surprising that it may take weeks, even months, for women to feel safe enough to overcome the anxiety associated with self-disclosure, fearing both real and imaginary consequences. It is difficult to break well-entrenched patterns of behaviour, especially if these involve self-protection. In the early stages of a group's life, it is to be expected that women will avoid speaking out because of the fear that no one will listen to them. Alternatively, women retaliate, fighting against negative experiences that have pushed them into self-blame by acting in confrontational ways within the group.

Once women feel able to reveal degrading and debilitating experiences, on finding themselves in an environment where this is not only possible but expected, there is an initial sense of relief. Later on, this may lead to fear, shame and anxiety about rejection. Fear is often felt on the basis that disclosure of degrading experiences is tantamount to statements of:

> This is the sort of person I am. If these things have happened to me then I must be wicked, must have deserved them. You'll think the same of me too. I

need to be able to say these things; it feels fairly safe to do so here, but I'm stuck. Either I continue to hold on to all of this and feel really bad about it all, or I reveal it to you and run the risk of you saying you want nothing more to do with me, that I'm a slut, no-good, I asked for it.

The process of discovering that this is not so, that other women can identify with what is happening and begin to offer comments on the speaker's and their own experiences, is extremely moving and revealing.

Positive feedback The capacity for action learning to which we referred in Chapter 3 can be encouraged through an essential element of feminist groupwork, positive feedback. Feminist groupwork does not set out with the assumption that change will occur, but if in the course of discussion women make it clear that change is what they seek, then encouragement will be given to facilitate that. Sustained attempts should be made to pin-point and nurture women's capacity to recognize and validate the strengths and positive qualities in each other, and as an extension of this, but far more difficult to achieve, to begin to make similar statements about themselves.

Positive feedback offers scope for evaluation of change in the way women appear to behave in group meetings. For example, a woman who at the beginning of sessions had been silent and reluctant to express any opinion, fearful about describing her own experiences or venturing any sort of explanation for them, acted in a far more assertive and self-confident manner within a period of a few weeks. Her physical appearance altered along with how she expressed her emotions; she walked into the room looking as though she knew she had a right to be there. This led to conflict with other group members once they felt that their own space was being impinged upon, but this was discussed and renegotiated. The extent of this growing assertiveness was a process from which other women could learn, but it was made possible through the interchanges of positive feedback.

In acting as role models, we as workers can demonstrate our changing awareness of the ways in which women's behaviour and attitudes are perceived and valued, and the influence of mainstream psychological thinking in this respect. We can offer descriptions and explanations of how we have come to value our skills as carers, as mothers, daughters, nieces, of how we have come to see the intricacy of our daily lives as requiring a level of sophistication of response and organization that goes unrecognized in the world of male-dominated 'real work'. This is not to try to dupe women into thinking that there is a particular dignity and nobility in housework and other tasks. Rather, we seek to encourage women to value themselves and their actions, whatever they are doing. If this encouragement is provided consistently on a mutual, reciprocal basis, then there is a good chance that it can withstand the influence of women's socialization.

Mutuality It is the element of mutuality that allows the women's group to be perceived as distinctive in positively valued ways. Group relations may fluctuate within and across group sessions, and this distinctiveness is not in itself static. However, the overarching significance of the group is upheld through the development of shared beliefs and tacit agreements between group members about which facets of the group they find beneficial. Within the women's groups, the values which emerged as worthy of praise and approval were:

- a belief that all contributions should be considered and if not used, then appreciated;
- a belief that mutual support is an effective buffer against stress and oppression;
- a belief that confrontation should be communal;
- the validation of efforts by members to change their behaviour, attitudes or life-style;
- a belief in sisterhood and collective action.

The development of a shared consciousness is crucial to the group process and structure. Over time, group identity becomes profoundly historical and symbolic, as the excitement accumulates of recalling when something was achieved, or when women had an impact on their locality, however small.

The finding that positive feedback, self-disclosure and group cohesion may be *necessary* conditions for women's group identity is crucial, but are they *sufficient* conditions? For instance, does the enhancement of group cohesion necessarily lead to greater learning within the group, or can it degenerate into cosiness? In women's groups the emphasis placed on encouraging participation through the creation of openness, trust and respect can result in a number of difficulties which revolve around 'the personal is the political'. The stress on the use of personal example in arguments can make it hard to disagree with someone's view without appearing to dismiss them (Lury, 1987). There is also a sensitive balance to be achieved between the degree of criticism that is fair as far as the individual is concerned, and the issues which are important to the workings of the group. Should critiques always be weighted in favour of the group? The question of what 'recognizing' or 'respecting' the 'validity' of other women's experiences might mean is problematic. The strength of group identity can therefore come into being only through alternations between individual accounts and critical but supportive group questioning.

The challenge of diversity in group interaction

By looking at the finer points of group interaction we can demonstrate the subtle mix between shared language and understanding, and the challenge of diversity. Group interaction generates sets of common assumptions about the way things are, how these interrelate, and the degree of importance they hold for group members. However, group interaction also needs to grapple with differences in assumptions, beliefs and life experiences which will give women the *choice* needed to make their own decisions, rather than complying with a set of agreed parameters. How is meaning confirmed or disputed in group interaction? In our view it is generated through the dual configurations of *interdependence* and *independence*. The construction of a reality unique to the group has to be fed by a range of beliefs in order to confirm or call into question the spectrum of social realities presented by women members.

How, and to what extent, are patterns of interaction able to construct a group identity fed by constructive challenge, as well as consensus? To address this question we will assess the role of *speaking turns, interruptions, silences* and *confused communication patterns*.

Speaking turns   We have indicated already that members may undervalue each other's contributions, thus causing resentment. Often this dismissal may arise out of another woman's eagerness to 'get it off her chest', particularly if her story has never been told before. This process echoes the patriarchal structures of society, where competition and control are valued above co-operation. Our inclination is to disparage other women rather than to recognize these tendencies as signs of internalized misogyny.

Co-operation can be encouraged through the use of speaking turns, where group members focus on one woman's current problem and rally to give her support and empathic feedback. Some women commented that their thoughts were totally constricted, bursting forth once they were given their own space in the group, with speech becoming incoherent. Such freedom can be so new to women that they search for as many opportunities as possible to speak in the group. Assumptions may follow, with a woman declaring how much she is like other members without first listening to their contributions. With the search for approval that ensues, it is possible to look at the role of speaking turns and learn that there is space for everyone, but that sometimes one's own concerns can wait. Feedback can be encouraged by asking group members if they have any comments or feelings about a particular woman's contribution.

Building upon such patterns can establish the process of dialogue referred to in Chapter 3, where the aim is to draw in as many women's viewpoints as possible. This is particularly important when women are feeling overshadowed by other members. L's contributions in the group in the initial stages were always cautious and apologetic, and she addressed issues for herself by questioning others. Her confidence was nurtured by asking her to give feedback on other members' contributions which could then be used as her own speaking turn. The more women get a hearing, the more they are listened to and encouraged to speak, the greater the change in women's attitudes towards themselves. Each woman becomes aware of what it has cost her to reach the stage where she can speak out and in time can empathize with others who are experiencing similar struggles.

Interruptions   Our previous arguments raise the controversial subject of interruptions. Who has the right to interrupt, and are some interruptions to be valued above others? Is the timing of interruptions important? What was seen to be significant for group members was the frequency of the interruptions, rather than the quality of what was said. Members would become particularly frustrated if interruptions diverted attention away from the task. However, there was a positive role for interruptions if a group member was holding the floor and another wished to talk about the impact of the speaker's statements on herself.

It could also be asked who has the influence in the group to decide what is relevant. This is particularly the case as women have differing motivations for attending group sessions, and how can a group meet each of the many expressed needs anyway? It is easy to see how a split can develop between those women who are willing to open themselves up with honesty and sincerity, and others who want to maintain distance. Such developments can be connoted positively by balancing time for burgeoning self-revelation with analysis and abstraction of political dimensions. Women become engaged at varying points in the proceedings, with the effect that statements are interspersed with interruptions, laughter, several women speaking at once. A pattern emerges where a woman may become the temporary focus by revealing charged material and this sharing may act as a catalyst for other women. Others may provide a cognitive frame of understanding, or offer supportive, mediating comments. Each contribution has a role to play and can be understood as the group experiments with different means of achieving a common purpose.

A toast to silences and absent friends   Group identity is manifested through the distinct energetic qualities of group interaction, emotionally and physically charged. We have already conveyed the warmth of co-operation, but the cold of silence and indifference, of absenteeism, can precipitate strong reactions from group members. The precarious balance between exploring/revealing and withholding can be disrupted through discussion and speculation about women who are absent or have left the group. As a way of dealing with this, individual fantasies can be aired that relate to fear of exposure and absent members' assumed lack of commitment to the group.

The weight of silence in the group may be oppressive, embarrassing, uncomfortable. Usually it is assumed that silent member(s) negate the purpose and direction of the group by engaging in flight activity, or sabotage the group by exercising a subversive form of power and influence. Yet women have had more practice in keeping quiet, backing off or retreating than in standing ground and demanding to be heard (Robbins, 1983). Silence may signify the need for separation or personal survival. The learning to be derived from handling silences increases members' abilities to take heed of non-verbal responses (Houston, 1987). It is important for silent members to hear about the effect their behaviour has on others, as many women end up feeling that such members are passengers in the group. Women who have been silent for any length of time comment that the longer this continues the harder it is to say anything at all. Women fear that their voices will be inaudible and that their delivery will be mistimed. In such circumstances, group disapproval will only intensify a woman's negative thoughts. The group needs to check out the significance of any silences and not immediately conclude that it is negative.

One incident conveys this. For many weeks D had been silent in the group, sitting with her arms folded during discussion, staring at the floor. Other group members were uncomfortable with D's behaviour, and tried to draw her into the conversation, but when this was unsuccessful they gave her sideways glances. Frustration was expressed covertly outside the sessions. There was a debate in the next session about domestic labour in which women were sharing dilemmas about cleaning their sons' bedrooms. D suddenly said, 'I'm on strike.' Her assertive statement was met with shock and disbelief from other group members. D then indicated that during her stay in, and since her discharge from, psychiatric hospital her husband had been responsible for all domestic and child-rearing activities, so she now felt redundant. She saw little point in reclaiming any role in the domestic sphere because she felt superfluous to the household, and she had carried on her withdrawal of labour in the women's group. What had encouraged her to break the silence and speak out? Her initial statement was precipitated by the expressed wariness of other women who were pulled between letting go of aspects of domesticity and still feeling the heavy responsibility of men's and children's dependency. She, on the other hand, *had* let go. This was an important learning point for the group in terms of not only the *content* of her statements, but also the discovery of the significance of silences and of empathic responses.

Communication patterns in confusion   In all of this it can be seen that effective communication is a prerequisite for the evolution of group identity, as the exchange of information needs to draw upon co-operation. There are times, however, when incidents occur which will lead to a fracture of communication and the cyclical effect of confusion sets in. Working-class women in comparable situations to group members have been silenced for years and it is no surprise that at times speaking turns may be unconnected, as women experiment with the rhythm of communication (see Chapter 3). Problems may occur when messages are misunderstood by the listener. There are also occasions when verbal messages and non-verbal cues may be inconsistent. Equally, a listener may avoid responding to a woman's statement immediately and misplace their reaction on to someone or something else: 'You hurt me because of A, but I'll get angry about B.' The lines of communication can become crossed so easily that it is no small achievement if we communicate effectively at all. There is a net across our senses that blurs images and their processing through our consciousness. This is more profoundly so for isolated women whose perceptions may have been frozen for years: 'I just can't get through to you'; 'Why aren't you more open about that?' The desperation of confused communication can be softened by women learning to *own* their values, their meanings, their responses. They can learn to take responsibility for statements they make, and for sending out clear, simple and specific messages.

Paradox and contradiction in group identity development
Earlier in this section we asked whether safety and acceptance were enough to precipitate group identity development and change in women's groups. We have highlighted through patterns of interaction and social exchanges that the answer to this must be a resounding NO. It is our view that the experience of paradox and contradiction is also central to group identity formation. The warmth and cohesion of women's groups provide the support that is required for the group to meet the second prerequisite for changing group identity, namely *the interconnections between apparent opposites.*

There is a real concern amongst feminists that differences between women based on race, ethnicity, religion, sexuality, class, age and disability should be bridged (Caplan, 1983; Hyde, 1986; Pheterson, 1986). Also, women must be vigilant in avoiding the trap of prioritizing the fight against sexism over racism, or vice versa. As Reid (1984) stresses, what purpose is served by trying to determine who suffers the most? She quotes black leaders such as Jesse Jackson (1980) who have exhorted their constituents to work towards the eradication of both racism and sexism, as true liberation can only occur when *all* human potential is respected. For Hyde (1986), in her exploration of the work of women activists in the labour, peace and feminist movements, building bridges involves confronting prejudices, rather than ignoring them to create an illusion of solidarity. The women activists all stressed the importance of raising these differences as a means of furthering group development.

The probable effects of such confrontation are outlined by Pheterson (1986), who was involved in the Netherlands' 'Feminist Alliance Project' which aimed to further a theoretical and political understanding of divisions between women. Over a two-year period the Project formed parallel groups of five months' duration to address the racism, anti-semitism and heterosexism that divide women. Each group's structure consisted of seven women from an oppressed category (black, lesbian or Jewish) and five from a dominant category (white, heterosexual or non-Jewish). The patterns of internalized oppression and domination that occurred were assumed to be shaped by external systems of domination.

What emerged in the groups was that oppression breeds psychological processes that distort reality and weaken personal strength. Feeling angry, isolated and defiant were identified as participants' reactions to oppression. Feeling guilty, dull and confused were identified as reactions to dominance. These feelings spiralled into blaming, needing and excluding other women, or seeking out protection, reassurance and approval from women in the dominant groups. The effective counterforce to these dynamics was the building of alliances between women, who have differences but whose interests are in essential ways akin.

Pheterson's experience is in many ways similar to our own, as we learnt that it was crucial to gain from the richness of diversity whilst building upon the interconnections of apparent opposites. An example will stand as an illustration of this point. When P disclosed that she was a lesbian, a gulf developed between her and V, who had pride in her mothering abilities and heterosexuality, and these factors prevented either party from learning about each other's diverse life experiences. V became angry when she felt that P was belittling motherhood, and she slipped quickly into stereotypes and misconceptions about all lesbian women being child-free. P retreated into a position of passivity, feeling fundamentally different from other women in the group. What began to emerge, tentatively and painfully, were other women's statements about the ambiguity of their sexuality and the pressures that had pushed them into heterosexual relationships. One woman disclosed that she had had a crush on her best female friend at school, and that she thought this was a phase all women go through. Homophobia and identity confusion surrounding sexuality began to emerge, albeit a difficult process.

At certain points in the interaction, women would retreat to the relative safety of discussion of motherhood. During one moment, when women's barriers were lowered slightly, one woman jokingly said: 'There's no difference really, in what you're doing, P, from bringing up babies. Whilst you're changing your Dad's incontinence pads, some of us are changing nappies.' A connection out of apparent opposites was brought into sharp focus. In caring for her elderly father, P's tending tasks were similar to the mothering skills undertaken by V. The degree of physical care which P was expected to provide was no less socially determined than the child-rearing patterns of women who are parents. We are still expected to clear up the mess. Out of a fragment of common ground, V and P, with the group's support, were able to build up a respect for each other's differences.

The fluctuation between diversity and similarity creates a rhythm which permeates every facet of a group's existence. Two women who are locked into differences during one session may in the next be sharing a common concern in a different subject area. Two women who may have much in common in terms of the choices and pressures that have shaped their lives based on age, sexuality, class, and so on, may demonstrate diverse responses on a micro level. They may have developed different strategies for psychological survival. Masculinist notions of individualism, as internalized by women, encourage a fear of and alienation from a true knowledge of feminine identity. Paradoxically, understanding the restrictions on women's potential opens up our humanity. Out of these different perceptions, group members are able to speculate about why it is that women with very similar life histories can internalize different world-views.

As individual vulnerabilities and anxieties begin to feed into group cohesion, paradox emerges in response to the untenability of sex-role stereotypes. Stereotypes and prejudice hinder adjustment to the challenging situations faced by the group. Women's groups can increase flexibility so that group identity responds with a far wider range of behaviours amongst members than patriarchy would have us believe is possible.

The role of group pressure and influence   How these subtleties and complexities can be accommodated within group identity is a vexed issue. Breakwell's (1986, p. 132) view is that consciousness-raising groups provide a powerful means of changing attitudes and beliefs because the individual is subject to conformity pressures. She goes on to state that far from offering women choice, the group provides a pre-packaged solution in accordance with a new philosophical and social awareness. It is important to take note of the powers of persuasion and group pressure because there *are* dangers inherent in situations where women are left feeling that there is a 'group norm' to which they have to aspire. When attitude and behaviour change are not based in free will, women may believe that they have failed in some way and are not doing themselves and/or the group justice if they do not follow such a norm. All this reinforces the negative self-image that they may already have.

In many other respects, though, Breakwell has missed the point in our view. The deliberations and struggles which women experience together invariably lead to the stage where different views can have a hearing and be respected. Attitude change will occur only if it is based on an assessment of women's self-control. There may be instances of compliance as a woman feels persuaded to go along with another's wishes or views. However, change in behaviour will be sustained only if it emerges out of her *choice* to adapt and change, and if women perceive paradoxes between received ideas, their personal experience and the different perceptions of other group members. Huws (1982) is nearer to the mark when she declares that women's groups build a new perspective on the world out of collectivity. The transition in knowledge base and social reality, this rite of passage, is sustained through group pressure which, far from being controlling, is drawn from a realization of the *power within*. So many answers to questions lie in our inner worlds, if only we could give ourselves time to explore. Group influence can help us to identify this source of personal power. In this sense, the pressure of group identity runs parallel to the discovery of individuality.

The role of resistance Group pressure and influence can have the opposite effect to Breakwell's (1986) assertions, namely that at times there will be a marked *resistance* to change, where feminist organizing is called into question as painful areas are avoided. The realization that group identification can mean increased pain and risk-taking faces group members with a range of dilemmas. The struggle to maintain group identity as it is may be protracted and intense, leading to sabotage, exclusion, scapegoating and walking out of the group, in an attempt to balance any fear regarding group identity change. If we take sabotage as an example, when this occurs women may be giving very clear signals to put the brakes on discussion they are finding uncomfortable. Such developments can best be dealt with honestly by all women discussing their emotional responses to sabotage, the images and memories that are evoked by those feelings, and the ways of coping we are choosing or evading. The message needs to be conveyed that group resistance to change serves an important function, in that group stasis maintains an equilibrium which protects the group and its members. Women can talk about their avoidance and feelings of threat by recognizing that each member needs to find her own pace.

The conflicts of oppression and growth It should be clear by now that any safe environment can never be conflict-free. When the need for support and acceptance is of crucial importance, it is predictable that interpersonal conflicts will be merely alluded to but not allowed to surface. It is unrealistic to expect perfect harmony in a group's life, and women often express vague dissatisfactions with aspects of the group. Although women say that it is important to express feelings when they are happening rather than allowing them to escalate and become distorted over time, there is still an inherent fear of challenging another woman. Indeed, grappling with the need for interpersonal confrontation can be halted at any point by the fear of expressing anger and hostility (Eastman, 1973).

Where does this fear originate and what effects does it have on group identity? Miller (1983a) has stressed that women experience internal conflict which stems from living in subordinate positions and from the legacy of socialization which is systematically woven into our psyche. External conflict pulls us in every direction, so it is no small wonder that society condemns us to the inner conflicts of depression. Structures abound which attempt to suppress external conflict and maintain the status quo. In all of this, there is enough confirmation within the interpersonal and cultural milieu for us to maintain our own current psychological forces.

There are also times when women's group process *reflects* what happens in society by way of jealousy or competition between women. Women learn not to value each other, are threatened by each other, are deeply afraid of being seen to be dependent on each other, and resort to manipulation to get some leverage in personal relationships. All of this demonstrates the profound internalization of oppression. How can this well-established pattern be broken down within women's groups? Miller (1983b) makes a distinction between the *conflict of oppression* and the *conflict of growth*. Group members can reclaim conflict as a step towards wholeness by breaking down internal conflicts and perceiving external conflict in the group as a mark of growth.

An example at this point will illustrate the interconnecting properties of *conflict as growth*. During a group discussion on sexual violence, E queried why women did not fight back when raped by a stranger. She added that she sincerely believed that rape was not a woman's fault but she thought women ought to defend themselves more. At this point F, who had herself been raped at night by a stranger, walked out of the room in tears. Another group member followed and offered her much-needed support and comfort. F in her distressed state, repeatedly asked why E had to say such things, saying that her question had hit her like a body blow, pushing her back into self-blame. She added that 'E is always so self-confident, she's everything I'm not.' With F's self-esteem plummeting, this incident precipitated a rift in the group, with some women offering constructive support to F and others feeling so uncomfortable that they were immobilized. At this stage, no group member had challenged or offered E a different way of conceptualizing rape by a stranger. With E still reeling from the consequences of her actions, F entered the room again, physically supported by two women, who angrily shouted at E that she should not have said such things. The blame, the complaints against her came spilling out, but in a way which emphasized the gulf between E and F. By this point F was slumped in a chair crying, and the more E tried to retract her statement, the more she dug herself a bigger hole. With such intense heat and high emotion in the group, the comfort offered to F was of paramount importance, so that she did not feel completely betrayed.

In a conflict which generates so much fear and confusion, women automatically draw on forms of behaviour which intensify oppression. Resolution at this stage in the group meant soothing the vast amount of distress, but nothing had been done to deal with the cause of the original confrontation. The group had handled the conflict by reinforcing the separation of two women from each other, which did not change what was happening. In order to encourage a *conflict of growth*, the group decided upon a clarification stage, where each woman examined her responses to the conflict, the judgements she had made and the consequences of those judgements. It was important that each woman was as specific as possible – 'You did A and I did B.' This then gave F the right to reply to E's original question and to talk about the impact of this question on her. F expressed her feelings:

> I've heard men joking about how women ask for rape, but it's a million times worse hearing it from a woman. I never thought a woman could. I just feel betrayed and punished again. I don't feel at home in the group any more.

E was full of remorse by this stage, apologizing continually; the only way the group could move forward was to ask each other what they now wanted and how they wished to go about it. It was possible to undertake pairing exercises so that the main protagonists felt supported whilst they searched for value out of the conflict. If conflict is to be constructive the task for the group is to see how they can live with such an outcome.

Interpersonal confrontation does not come easily to women, but once space is allowed to discuss the elicited and aroused feelings then these can be worked on within the group sessions more effectively. As a result of conflict, E gave her commitment to re-examine her constructs concerning rape, and she was assisted in this by more analytical members of the group who had undertaken reading on sexual violence. Direct experience of conflict in women's groups has convinced us that a redefinition is required which breaks away from its conceptualization into such opposing conditions as conflict/co-operation and approach/avoidance. When conflict is seen as growth, these socially constructed polarities need to feed into each other. Conflict is likely to be based in perceptual differences, feelings of distrust and verbal or interpersonal difficulties. However, the ultimate irony is that for conflict to be expressed there needs to be effective communication within the group which provides an outlet for disagreements. In addition, the spatial and temporal characteristics of the group are such that any conflict which is generated invariably involves a review of past action plus a shift in balance of power. The implications for group identity are multiple. If conflict in women's groups involves moving from current behaviours and attitudes to new constructs and behaviours, then the potential for wholeness is a step nearer. Conflict can make the group stronger and can transform pain into possibilities.

In summary, a developing sense of group identity requires conflict as well as cohesion. From the outset, women participating in the groups recognized the common ground between them and the ways in which they could offer each other support. They each came to the group with their own pain and hopes, and this sense of individuality remained but with a shift in emphasis from that of isolated and oppressed, to aware, strong and able to take action. Alongside this personal change grew an awareness of the cohesiveness of the group, its sense of purpose, and the fact that it was not solely a collection of individuals, but had an identity of its own. This was clear in a number of ways. The group would challenge the behaviour and/or actions of one or both workers, making demands for greater or different input, more variety, deeper analysis or more time. There would be requests for disclosure of personal experience, a degree of openness and honesty that workers would have to acknowledge they expected from other participants. Such challenges were made possible by some group members meeting between sessions and making the decision to have such a confrontation, or they would arise spontaneously within discussion. With the development of group solidarity it is easier to challenge each other and not feel undermined, but also to challenge workers, within and outside the group.

Group identity and women's friendship development

The hope of wholeness which is derived from a growing group identity is advanced further by the development of women's friendships within and outside the group. Friendships contribute to personal growth, support or change (Davidson and Packard, 1981) and are positively associated with women's psychological well-being (Goodenow, 1985). Women's groups themselves provide ample evidence of the links between self-disclosure, a growing kinship system and the validation of women as friends. These connections are endorsed further by the tradition of a highly intimate and supportive female friendship which predates contemporary feminism (Faderman, 1985). The value and acceptability of female friendship through the centuries and the recognition of its supportive and protective function in a range of cultures is well documented (Eckenstein, 1963; Faderman, 1985; Mavor, 1971; Raymond, 1986). This historical documentation can contribute to women's feelings of self-worth, of belonging to a group with strength, sensitivity and compassion. Such testimony goes a long way towards counteracting images of women as helpless, passive, feckless, dependent creatures with no will of their own. If we can be reminded of how our great-grandmothers were expected to behave towards each other, then we can have confidence in the resonances in our own psyche of the need for female companionship.

Yet female friendship flies in the face of masculinist doctrines which have created the dislocation and invisibility of women from each other (see Chapter 1). The net effect is that women can become rootless in their own group identity and this contributes more than anything to the non-political perception that many women have of the world. Barriers to friendship can appear so insurmountable as to prevent lasting intimacy between women. When this is coupled with the realization that the hetero-relational world-view erases and ignores the historical and cultural diversity of women's associations with each other, then it is easy to see how patriarchy exerts considerable pressure on women to exist only for men.

It is the ways in which women have been trained to *wait* which prove to be the real impediments to the formation of female friendships. Hetero-relations demand that women function as men's audience, as this is the only bond that receives social, political and economic sanction for women. In the waiting game, from the audience's point of view, if the male 'star' is not present how can anything worthwhile happen? The amount of waiting in which women are involved is considerable. Despite frenetic activity in any day, it is time filled against 'his' return or arrival.

Many women have swallowed the pill that their most meaningful relationships are with men. Yet it is men of whatever persuasion who turn to us for validation and support, for the freedom to express their emotionality in a way that will not leave them feeling ashamed or emasculated because they have escaped showing it in front of other men. Frequently, we provide this emotional pillow for our partners, lovers, sons. We are socialized to believe that this is one of our main roles in life; it makes us feel wanted, we enjoy giving and we desperately hope it means men might offer us something similar in return. Hope that things might change is a strong force.

The net effect of these barriers is that women's talk in the groups was for some time constantly focused on men. This kind of relating fosters superficiality where discussion is frequently drawing on how to support your man more, how to attend to his wishes at the expense of your Self. Indeed, the consistent focus on dealing with the relationships in which many women are immersed reinforces the fact that meaning is forever to be derived from relations with something external to the Self. It serves as a deflection from women's needs. The concomitant effect is that the time and energy devoted to talking about men reinforces anti-woman behaviour and statements. This occurred where women in the groups disliked other women or, at best, were indifferent to the significance of female friendships. They talked of women's bitchiness, their fickleness and unreliability, their gossiping, and sometimes declared that 'women are their own worst enemies'. Whatever our understanding of the origins of these internalized attitudes, it does not assuage the awful reality of anti-woman conduct when it happens within the group context. This is particularly the case when such anti-woman discussion is supplemented by the historical *silence* about women always loving women. This double message serves to stonewall the evolution of female friendship.

The implication of all this is that women's group members feared that if they did evolve friendships with other women, this would be seen as a threat to their heterosexual relationships. Indeed, women together for whatever reason are often seen as a threat by men (see Chapter 6). This fear is based in the incredulity that women should have anything to discuss of any significance without men around. Women need men to direct the conversation because they always have matters of more importance to talk about. Men also fear women's personal and political movement towards each other because of the threat to the established order when women realize the extent of their oppression and that they have simply had enough.

Whatever the dimension or manifestation of women's friendships, men will often want to know what women together have been talking about. This is partly out of disbelief that women are sensible enough to sort things out for themselves, and partly because of a wish to know, and keep power and control over all that they do. Not giving men this information is a crucial element of female survival. Women together in quantity become inaccessible to men. How much more unapproachable are women who are joined together by choice and affective bonds.

The very fact that women in groups share, think, act, feel and talk together begins to shatter the myth of men as women's greatest adventure. Women begin to question their expectations about a lively future with men. The ideal of a restrained and tamed woman is disputed once women notice or miss the lost possibilities of a vibrant female friendship. Yet women's group members often expressed fear of taking the initiative in female friendship. Some women had felt responsible in the past for maintaining friendships when they had been let down and had given more than they had received: 'I'm always the one that has to give her a ring. I'm fed up with it'; 'She only wants me when she needs something.' Women also commented that in times of adversity, 'You certainly find out who your real friends are', and 'A friend in need is a friend indeed.' There are betrayals of women by other women. Women can hold such unrealistic expectations of friends that when these are not fulfilled they feel disillusioned and abandoned. It is important to help women distinguish between the betrayals and the unrealistic expectations. Coming to terms with the sense of loss and grief can help women to untangle the origins of the lack of respect women have for each other, and to avoid perceiving such betrayal as similar in character to the victimization women experience at the hands of men.

Sorting out the hopes for a caring, respectful and responsive friendship on a profoundly existential level occurs once women begin to take power for themselves, and to re-evaluate and reconstruct their thoughts on female friendship. How does this process of reappraisal occur within women's groups? There is a connection here between the redefinition of female friendship as valuable in its own right, rather than as second-best to relations with men, and self-disclosure within the context of group identity. As the group grows in strength and participants gain in self-awareness (see Chapter 5), so the levels of interaction between women become more numerous and more complex. More and more layers of experience and emotion are peeled back and revealed, more and more connections between life-styles and events, between hopes, wishes and fears, become evident, and empathy and solidarity grow as a result. Close relations develop both within and outside the group through the very act of sharing intimate and painful information, and the barriers to friendship are broken down. This is not just a case of victims clinging together in adversity in the way male relationships and camaraderie develop in times of war and conflict. It is women wanting to join together to hold each other up, literally and metaphorically, name the awful things that have happened to them, and move on from there.

The development of friendships within the group is a clear signal that group process and shifts in group identity are under way. Once the barriers to female companionship are broken down, friendship becomes hallmarked by affective exchange, not just talking about feelings and emotions. Indeed, friendships are based largely on intimacy (Rose, 1985), and it is group cohesion and mutuality which provide the fertile ground for this to blossom.

Going full circle: Group transformation

Our progression through the territories of structural relationships, through the landscape of group identity and friendship development, has brought us full circle. What does all this tell us about the nature of group change? Change is a dynamic process which occurs constantly and on several levels at once. Yet within our dualistic system of language and representation, the word 'change' is situated typically on the side of 'progress', with the hidden rider of 'failure' if the group does not match up to certain objective criteria. Group change is measured against such a yardstick and it is assumed that the group moves towards its goals in a linear fashion. The notion of progress therefore implies that there is a norm towards which everyone must strive. However, the circularity inherent in women's group development makes the use of a word such as 'progress' highly problematic. It is arguable that progress is not a feature of women's groups, that there is no given point to which each woman or the group as a collective entity is moving. Women's group activity and process is organic in nature, with scripts and patterns unfolding as social exchanges take place.

Amidst the dynamism and creative context of group identity development there is a need from the start for regular and consistent evaluation of the process of change, both for the group and for its individual members. Workers need to safeguard against such total involvement with the group that they might cease to be able to judge it with any degree of objectivity. Does this use of the term objectivity impose any sort of moral dilemma for a feminist account of working with women? 'Objectivity' equals male subjectivity (Spender, 1980) and it offers no moral, intellectual or philosophical basis by which to evaluate female experience. Why do we need to use such a term in this instance then, and does doing so undermine the validity of what we claim to be setting out to achieve, namely the enhancement of women's self-esteem and the prospect of greater liberation?

The need for evaluation with a built-in measure of 'objectivity' derives from the structures within which we work. We had responsibilities not only to group members, but also to our colleagues and managers. When practice is seen to be innovatory, an assessment needs to be made of the use of worker time and the effectiveness of the group as a way of improving women's lives. We cannot entirely escape such bureaucratic procedures, and our pragmatism told us that if we wanted to retain the resources essential to the survival of the groups, then evaluation threaded with objectivity would serve our purpose. Women workers also need to stand back and evaluate the extent and nature of interactions in the group by checking this out with group members.

When change is measured on a subjective scale, evaluation revolves around each person's statements about what feels right for her, which can be demonstrated through the structured exercises to which we referred in Chapter 3. As each woman feels more competent to present an analysis of the situations in which she finds herself, these can be used to reappraise the position of others. This allows for alternative explanations to 'Well, that's how life is – you'll just have to put up with it.' Inevitably, such personal evaluation presented as an explanation to other group members will give rise to conflict, but without this, change is hardly likely to occur.

Couched in these terms, group development is not inexorable, but is a product of a particular balance of factors acting both within and outside the group. Group change hinges on the reciprocal effects of individual psychology and behavioural change, and patterns of social interaction. This reciprocity is framed by the dynamics of structural relationships which are themselves influenced by socio-economic and political forces external to the group. In more specific terms, the hallmarks of cohesion in women's groups, namely positive feedback, open self-disclosure and mutuality, precipitate differing manifestations of a changing group identity. There is a concomitant shift in the power structure affecting the relationship between workers and participants, symbolized by growing interactions between women themselves directly rather than via workers. Our baseline for change was for each woman to begin to recognize and accept her own qualities and to evolve trust in beliefs that were right for her, including a set of individual criteria against which she could judge herself. Such recognition and acceptance inevitably leave their mark on the group, changing its nature, demarcating any subgroup it may contain more sharply, and also providing the basis for solidarity.

What has gone before is not a description of the inevitable path a women's group must follow, but rather a selection of pointers which will assist in the anticipation of probable group directions. We are certainly not advocating a strict adherence to a particular model because the process of each group transformation is ultimately unique. The mapping out of group identity development can only ever be part of the territory. In the next chapter, we will add to the features of our particular map by taking a look at the elements of group process and development which are necessary for the creation of personal identity change.

5
Women's Groups as Windows into the Self

CAN YOU SEE
NO ME SEE ME
I'M ME NOT SHE
OR COULD IT BE
THAT SHE IS ME
IF I AM SHE
THEN WHO IS ME
AM I ME
NO I AM SHE
WHO IS SHE

(Glenys Dacey –
women's group member)

How do women in groups experience 'me' and 'I' within the physical and social circumstances of the group? How do societal expectations affect women's selves and their resultant behaviour? How do women's groups offer members the opportunity to act as they would wish, rather than in ways they think others expect of them? The temptation to delve into personal identity has been resisted until this point as a way of mirroring the difficulty women have in forming a self-description and self-definition. We need to develop a clear understanding of the Self in relation to group process, dynamics and structure, in other words, of how a changing group identity has an impact on the individual psyche. Current societal norms leave women little space for thought or for any appraisal of their position in life. Women's groups offer one means of resistance to the distortion and corruption of androcentric belief systems. Women's groups also exist as a vehicle for personal change, as women's identity shifts and develops along one major continuum, namely that it becomes something they learn to define for themselves.

Breakwell (1986, p. 15) queries whether the existence of both personal and social identity is merely a definitional and theoretical trick which creates an arbitrary boundary. Yet in groups, women *do* distinguish personal from group identity. Women assess their distinctiveness through social comparison. At the same time, there are moments when personal identity responds to the vicissitudes of the social context in a similar way to the dynamic and rhythmic processes of group identity development (see Chapter 4). For women, the Self is always in active interchange with other selves (Miller, 1984), and women's groups provide the scope for exploration of this interdependence and independence.

This chapter will draw out the developmental patterns which highlight personal identity as inextricably bound up with social interaction and social context. We shall explore the effect of socio-political meaning upon individual identity, hemmed in as it is by social values and beliefs. Above all, this chapter will recognize what Washington (1981) has called 'The Divided Self' within women – the compartmentalizing of our reality, our talents and our dreams. Whilst referring specifically to black women, Washington's characteristics of women's identity are equally applicable to our discussion here. She talks of the 'Suspended Woman' who is severely limited in her opinions, destroyed by pain, pressure and violence. The 'Assimilated Woman' adopts dominant cultural values, alienated from her roots and socio-economic context. In contrast, the 'Emergent Woman' has self-awareness and confronts issues of her reality. Whilst these three characterizations may appear simplistic and reductionist, they can help us to unpack the tensions and drama which ensue at any given moment in a group's life. This chapter is about the adaptability of women's identity, the growth of self-reliance, and the harnessing of survival for positive ends. It is about the significance of the coping abilities which women develop when experiencing core aspects of Self in transition. It is also about the ways in which personal dissatisfaction and strength feed into collective discontent and power.

The first part of this chapter will be devoted largely to an examination of women's self-definition and the role of paradox and contradiction arising out of environmental values and beliefs. This analysis will be organized around the key identity concepts of caring, a sense of well-being and sexuality, which emerged as fundamental to women's groups discussions. It is one thing to outline the dimensions which shape a woman's identity but it is another matter to speculate about how the choice of these dimensions is determined. In rectifying this, the next section will elaborate on the operational dimensions of identity in terms of self-esteem, differentiation and continuity, and the cognitive resources available to women as they gain in self-realization. The process of identity change will draw on the themes of fantasy and creativity which facilitate a clearer self-representation. Our particular emphasis will be on methods of self-protection and on the constructive use of anger as a way of mobilizing change.

Self-definition

Structural aspects of identity
There has been a great deal of theorizing about the study of Self in psychological theory, most of which has become preoccupied with the separation of oneself from the matrix of others (Erikson, 1950, 1970). The state of separation has come to signify the highest form of existence in white, male Western thought (Miller, 1984). Yet this drive towards separated individuation has been markedly ideological because the bulk of the hegemonic representations of Self are those of a powerful and articulate minority. Few men ever attain such self-sufficiency as every woman knows. Yet if these models fail to reflect men's lives, then they are certainly discredited as far as women's experience is concerned, and have therefore been scrutinized and attacked by a range of feminist researchers (Gilligan, 1982; Miller, 1976; Peck, 1986; Sherif, 1982). These prevailing models operate as a powerful force because they make prescriptions about what *should* happen. They affect men, but they have become erroneous, restrictive and destructive teachings for women. They are used to mock, taunt and disparage women's psychological development because emotional connection to others is undervalued. For their part, many women perceive the prospects held out by the model of Self in separation as threatening and alien.

Are there any formulations which can be used as a framework for women's experience of identity? We can turn to Breakwell's model (1986) for some guidance. As discussed earlier (p. 19), Breakwell asserts that identity is a dynamic product of the interaction between the individual's cognitive resources and the social context, and is structured across two planes: the content and the value dimensions. In the former, the constellation of properties concerning group membership, roles, social category labels, values and attitudes marks the person's individuality. Such properties have differing degrees of centrality and relative salience. In addition, each element in the content dimension has a specific positive or negative value. We shall return to values and attitudes shortly but first it is important to clarify key aspects of identity as revealed through groupwork. We will use self-structure as a primary concept to describe the manner in which a woman organizes and subjectively experiences her various identities (roles, activities and relationships) (Ogilvie, 1987). A distinction is made here between social roles and identities. An activity can be said to reflect both a role and an identity, but the latter label is used when a woman considers it to represent an important aspect of Self.

In terms of the meaning of being a woman, group members initially find it easier to articulate properties concerning group membership and roles, than they do to draw out core aspects of Self revolving around emotions, thoughts and goals. In the 'I am . . .' sentence completion exercise referred to in Chapter 3 for instance, over a third of the women initially could offer no self-description whatsoever. Other women offered descriptions of physical characteristics ('I'm small, I'm overweight, I've got greasy hair') or uttered with great difficulty an external range of internalized statements, presented largely as facts ('I'm twenty-seven, I've got three children, I'm only a mother'). Most had little idea of their own future goals or purposes. Yet why should this be the case? To a large extent, self-description is linked to the establishment of trust and self-disclosure to which we referred in Chapter 4. But there is another dimension which feeds into women's negativism, namely that it is social roles which provide a structure for women's self-description. It is easy to see why this aspect of identity dominates, given women's socialization and beliefs that their actions are worthless. These shape explanations of facts and lead to conclusions about self-description.

Given the support, companionship and safety of the group, aspects of identity do emerge as significant to women. Our hypothesis is that identity becomes the problematic axis of individuality, based in and reinforced by notions of group continuity. An understanding of how women come to define and redefine themselves in groups bears this out. Feminist groupwork expects an appreciation of a woman's creation of self-knowledge through her experience of others as an individual-in-society (Peck, 1986). Self-definition is dependent upon a woman's perceptions and assessment of herself within the context of the social roles she possesses and the impact of group relations on her. Self-defintion also holds that women construct their own reality (Unger, 1983), are capable of understanding their own behaviour, and are able to communicate this sense of Self to others (Peck, 1986).

Such discussions about the content of personal identity and self-definition prefigure a thorough transformation in our thinking unless we look to the ubiquitous concepts of Self which revealed themselves in group sessions. The central properties in women's self-structure revolved around the *Caring or Relational Self* and the *Agential Self*.

The Caring Self   There is no doubt that for women's group members, in common with women from every walk of life, relationships and caring occupy a position of significance in respect of women's self-knowledge. Once women are able to articulate their internal representation of Self, it is based on *connection* with others, not *separation*. We have mentioned before the ways in which women are socialized to be sensitive to the emotionality of others, especially men (see Chapter 4), and to pay special attention to those qualities that maintain and enhance relational ties. Women's development occurs within a complex and sophisticated relational network, evolving into women's *Relational Self* (Gilligan, 1982; Kaplan et al., 1983; Miller, 1984).

Emotional connection with others is desired by women and it becomes a primary motivation of women's actions. Working-class women in the groups aspired to a better life for the family unit, not for the Self alone: 'I love my family very much and regard them as very important and put them before anyone else, including me.' This belief runs parallel to the statements of black and immigrant women who have argued vehemently against the individualism promoted in the West and the approach of white feminists, who have not comprehended black women's commitment to their families (Meleis and Rogers, 1987). The goal for women is to be attuned to the feelings of others, understanding and being understood by the other and thus participating in other people's development. The incipient effects of this are reflected in women's assessment of themselves in the here and now, and how they would like to be. When asked to describe themselves as a Liked Person, two-thirds described their caring abilities, patience and tolerance as being an integral part of themselves. Other statements revolved around an ability to love others, to understand and help others. Disliked Person and Me at My Worst included constructs grouped in terms of the Relational Self and not caring enough. For example, two-thirds of the group felt negative about losing their temper and demonstrating aggression; other constructs revolved around having *no* patience, especially with children, feeling guilty about the Self, and giving in easily to others. How I Would Like to Be *always* included statements about the capacity to care and respond to others' emotionality. Whilst there is much to be said about group members' fear of expressing anger and the internalization of nurturing skills as core self-concepts, the priority which women give to themselves in relation cannot be ignored. We shall explore constructs in transition, particularly attitudes to anger, at a later date, but at this point we want to accentuate women's expressed need for satisfaction through their caring relationships (Kaplan et al., 1983).

In Gilligan's (1982) studies of morality, she postulates that a central dilemma for men is between life and property, whereas for women, the conflict revolves round the disruption of human relationships. She also demonstrates that men and women perceive danger in human relationships under different circumstances – men when there is closeness and women in separation. For women, the injunction is 'care' whereas for men the moral imperative is to respect the rights of others. Noddings (1984) defines *caring* as the apprehension of the other person's reality, feeling what she or he feels as nearly as possible, and acting on behalf of that person. The commitment to act and to be continually interested in the person cared for must be sustained over time and constantly renewed. Caring involves engrossment with the other person and being motivated towards the welfare, protection and enhancement of the cared-for person.

The Agential Self The second dimension of relevance for women's identity is our use of agential qualities – the ability to act to further our own needs and wishes (Kaplan et al., 1983). A developed capacity to assess our own qualities and to exert influence on the environment, to display courage, self-confidence, a willingness to make ourselves conspicuous and to take risks – all these aspects of identity mean that women can become self-defining, rather than being defined continually by others. Although women often submerge their aspirations, struggles for autonomy and assertion do occur. Women's capacity for agency is, however, responded to by others as threatening to relational ties. This is where social belief systems exert influence on women's self-development, in the sense that women pay a heavy price for their relational selves.

Women's groups can deal with this psychological damage by allowing for the expression of the Agential Self within an atmosphere of mutuality. Women can be encouraged to recognize instances when agential self-expression has been thwarted or misrepresented through hierarchical relationships. Some women had acted conspicuously in their private and public relationships, feeling that they had intimidated others, controlling and exerting power over them. Women assume that having influence in the environment means acting out of self-interest and stepping over everyone to get what you want. If we suppress our Agential Selves as a result of this, indirect forms of expression develop and our personal boundaries become diffuse. Caring without agency stifles us within our interactional networks.

By constructing a political and historical context, women's groups present the Agential Self as a necessary part of personal growth. This can be achieved by:

1 naming certain behaviours and group dynamics as examples of agential action, which is a powerful message in itself;
2 recognizing women's courage and facilitating spontaneous emotional expression;
3 presenting risk-taking as a resource for action and change in oppressive conditions, being tested out through the group's interactive processes;
4 allowing for the identification of women's impact on each other, so that group members can listen and respond unconditionally to a woman's attempts at agential self-expression;

5 encouraging responses to conspicuous acts which do not originate from feelings of attack, defensiveness or being diminished;
6 encouraging the reappraisal of agentic actions as necessary for survival in hierarchical relationships;
7 encouraging the *direct* articulation of experiences within the group.

To varying degrees, women were already actively involved in resisting mediocrity and compromises. Yet the Agential Self is so submerged that it is a struggle for women to own such actions. The conspiracy of silence which surrounds this aspect of identity keeps women in positions of isolation and exploitation. The costs and benefits involved mean that group members need to practise agential self-expression a great deal, which has the effect of focusing, clarifying and energizing relationships.

The relative value of caring and agency The translation from cultural paradigm to individual psyche is mediated through family, friends and group membership. The values attributed to aspects of personal identity are therefore subject to perpetual revision as they interact with and are fed by group membership and interpersonal networks. The actual *value* of an identity element is not absolute, it is relative. What are the affective dimensions of identity, especially relating to caring and agency? Elements of identity have different values attributed to them on the basis of social beliefs in interaction with previously established value codes (Breakwell, 1986). For instance, dominant ideologies hold that the Relational Self is odious and signifies weakness, therefore possession of that characteristic is demeaning, except when it becomes a political expedient. Group members, on the other hand, associated positive affect with caring relationships and placed a high degree of importance on the emotional aspects of their lives. In contrast, negative affect arose from the competition and discriminatory responses associated with agency (Williams, 1984). Already we are beginning to see the difference in emphasis and affective content of caring and agency for group members and for the dominant social order. It is to these issues that we now turn.

The present societal arrangements which expect a specialization in expressive and instrumental functions on the part of the female and male respectively play a key role in limiting women's self-definitions. As a result, the devaluing of relational ties, coupled with the perceived threat of self-motivated behaviour, means that to act out of one's own interest and motivation is experienced as selfishness and aggression. Women and girls are taught to swallow slights and indignities: 'Don't make scenes'; 'You're making yourself conspicuous'; 'You're making a fool of yourself.' Women are not supposed to use activity for their own self-initiated and self-defined goals or for their own development. As a result, women use *selective inhibition*: actions which further their own goals are strongly inhibited, but they are distinctively active when displaying support or enhancement of someone else (Kaplan, 1984).

Given such a scenario, caring becomes bound up with *responsbility*. Women's descriptions of the Self in relation to caring unanimously referred to statements around 'Having no one to do things for me. I always have to do things for others.' In addition, caring involved a complete package of domestic responsibilities in which working-class women, with limited financial and material resources, had to juggle a finite amount of money against an infinite range of demands. For group members, the devaluation of the Caring Self involved the following:

> Planning what to have for tea, making sure I've shopped for it and hoping I've got enough money.
>
> Being responsible for my home and children twenty-four hours a day.
>
> Dealing with children without the training or skills to do this.
>
> Partner not listening to me at all.
>
> Being so busy thinking about others, having no time to plan my own future, and having no personal space.

The frustration and disenchantment of responsibility is summarized in the following statement 'No sooner have I put the carrots in the pan than she's taking them out again' (referring to her eighteen-month-old daughter). The devaluing of relational qualities has a constricting effect on women's capacities to care, but it also limits our self-motivated actions vastly.

Just how demeaning caring becomes depends upon the sphere of influence in which a woman lives. The characteristics which make up the sum of a woman's relationships either foster or impede the clarity and certainty within which self-knowledge can develop (Peck, 1986). What is important as far as the affective dimension of personal identity is concerned is the *quality* of the interaction with a significant other. Many group members had been told often enough that connection with others was a sign of 'dependency', 'smothering', 'possessiveness', leading women to doubt and even fail to recognize the value of their own endeavours. Within the primary context for caring relationships, the family, women had experienced failure, frustration and fear in their attempts at affective connection: 'People hurt me all the time.'

In terms of heterosexual relationships, women continually expose themselves to the merry-go-round of men's demands and defer their own needs in the process. Ultimately, they take responsibility for relational failure. Even if the partner is not living on the premises, and regardless of his employment status, he is still likely to exert a considerable influence over the woman and her household. It may be that a woman never knows when he is likely to appear, that she is in a permanent state of anxiety and anticipation over not only his arrival, but also his mood. Confirmation of beliefs about relational failure are further endorsed when repeated attempts at connection are made in the hope that renewed efforts will succeed where past attempts have failed:

> I get myself into situations where I try a bit harder in the hope that he'll change. I keep thinking there must be something I can do 'cos if I don't, then I'll have failed.

The energy which is expended in repeating these patterns of relationship wraps women in an inexorable fatigue.

Loss of confirmation of core self-structure   The spiralling effects of such cognitions are exacerbated by dominant ideological mechanisms revolving around social stereotypes. Discrimination and stereotyping have a marked impact on intrapsychic processes, as lack of validation leads to a loss of confirmation of women's core self-structure:

> I'm completely taken for granted. As long as the food's on the table, and I don't cause much fuss, then they all let me be. I'm just a cosy old sofa with all the padding coming out.
>
> When I get in from work, they're all just lounging around on the settee, watching telly. None of them makes me a cuppa tea. I just start makin' dinner even before I've got me coat off.

Internalized oppression become embedded in the Self at the expense of positive aspects of identity and without regard to external reality. Group members had withdrawn from self-awareness in the face of feedback from the world, unrelenting in its negative and derogatory connotations. Given the persistence of multiple disadvantage and the effects of oppression, continuous exposure to the misogynistic fray would be tantamount to masochism. Shutting down becomes a coping strategy which eventually annihilates the Self: 'I come in my house at night and no one speaks to me. Not even Hello. I end up thinking I don't exist at all.'

For many women the notion of an 'identity' eluded them. They were left genuinely uncertain of who or what they were and where they could go next. Women had experienced identity as distorted, ignored or eliminated because of restrictions on them. During group sessions, pictorial representations of women's lives, their descriptions of what it felt like to be them, would often include images of mountains, mountains of conflicting interests; screaming, importunate demands being made on them; fear of being swamped and overwhelmed, of there being no way out. The cognitions with which a woman is left are obviously confused, whilst the frustration and disenchantment this can engender are denied.

Principles of paradox and contradiction in identity
This pattern of women severely inhibiting their own strivings and actions to preserve relationships (Eichenbaum and Orbach, 1987) emerges over and over again because aspects of identity feed on *paradox* and *contradiction*. Just as group identity is generated through conflict (see Chapter 4), so the pulls for and against the Caring and Agential Selves act as a constant source of tension and hope. Internalized oppression and internalized domination interact not only between different persons, but also intrapsychically within one person. Oppression and domination are experienced as a mutually reinforcing web of insecurity and rigidities (Pheterson, 1986). The fear of violence a woman experiences in her heterosexual relationships, for example, reinforces the fear of revenge she feels as an agent of oppression. The guilt felt for dominating others reinforces the guilt felt for her own victimization. The more guilty the white woman feels about her racism, the less adequate she is likely to feel about effecting change and the more dependent she will be on black women to do the work of changing racist attitudes. The more a heterosexual woman seeks out male approval, the more threatened she will be by lesbian autonomy. Every human difference becomes a confrontation with Self.

The spectrum of relationships is experienced as paradox and contradiction because caring is both women's hope and their downfall. At its best, women hope for and want varying degrees of involvement in relationships as the prime factor in a clearer self-definition. Such movement is empowering as women can see the effects of their own influence upon people around them and, in so doing, can begin to differentiate the Self by exerting control over the extent to which others' needs and expectations affect their own behaviour and concerns. The growth of a differentiated Self (*independence*) is commensurate with the growth of a positive and enriching relational network (*interdependence*). Increasing others' capabilities and resources enhances the power of others and simultaneously our own power (Miller, 1984). Caring does have its rewards, including pleasure in the ability to care and delight in seeing the growth of the one cared for. Many of the demands of caring are not felt as demands, but are the occasions that offer most of what makes life worth living (Woods, 1987).

At its worst, the extent to which women can act and feel empowered by their caring capacities is highly dependent on the extent of societal mixed messages at any one time. On the one hand, the accentuation of our weakness and dependency and our supposed need to be in a relationship where we are subordinate leads to an interpretation that fundamentally we are stupid. On the other hand, it is brought home to us daily that we carry the sole and total responsibility for the material and emotional well-being of our families:

> Most of my waking day is spent feeling guilty that whatever I do for others – me kids, me bloke, me Mam, just isn't good enough. I just don't seem to be able to manage the kids, and me Mam says I ought to try harder. And I just can't keep up with all the housework. I worry about it all the time.

The frequency with which women spoke about conflict in caring came as no surprise. Women hoped for strength in personal relationships, whilst at the same time they experienced a fundamental lack of understanding from male partners and a subsequent lack of control in these same relationships. Women were pushed up against the demands of child-care, time-keeping and housework with little relief. No wonder that caring involves considerable costs. Not only do we carry much in terms of how we bring up our children, for we are judged by their behaviour, but they are also judged by ours.

The emotional exploitation of women's role as mothers and carers increases as fewer and fewer services are provided on a statutory basis and as the impact of mass unemployment and an increase in lower-paid jobs is denied. Further, the effects of a decreasing medical and housing service for those unable to pay their way is not seen as having any significance. The policies that rapidly strip away any safety net of statutory services ensure that women are left with a manifold burden. Such incompatible demands thus breed tension and guilt, where the cared-for person becomes the target for women's unrest and any conflict of interest separates the carer and cared-for from each other. Added to which, economic dependence constrains many women from making the break from an oppressive partner to the poverty of Income Support (Carew-Jones and Watson, 1985). Despite, for example, the disaggregation possibilities in the payment of Income Support, the Department of Social Security still looks upon a woman as financially dependent on a man if there is the slightest hint that she is enjoying more than the most transient of relationships with him. The impact of legislative and police involvement in a woman's experience can underline further the assumptions made about her ability to cope and care alone (Pahl, 1985). As a woman travels from agency to agency, seeking the help they purport to offer, she frequently finds the blame and responsibility pushed on to her shoulders for the unfortunate events that have caused her to seek help in the first place. Borkowski, Murch and Walker's (1983) study based in Bristol demonstrated that women approached a minimum of seven agencies after experiencing domestic violence before they obtained a constructive response.

All of this points to the energy which women expend in the achievement of relational connection (Eichenbaum and Orbach, 1987) and in the acquisition of expressive and instrumental attributes which enhance this. The irony is that the expressive qualities of nurturance, affection, warmth, gentleness, loyalty, empathy and understanding are the very attributes of stereotyped femininity (Butler, 1981) which have been perceived constantly as infantile and passive. Such trivialization constantly reinforces the gap between goals, hopes and reality which is experienced as cognitive dissonance. We now want to concentrate on this dissonance by highlighting four elements of paradox in caring which emerged during group discussions. These are the balancing act involved in caring; women's mediating role; fear of abandonment; and the pulls towards closeness and differentiation.

First, the challenge of managing multiple social roles (both of oppression and of domination) calls for a balancing act in which group members weigh personal concerns against societal motivations (Swanson-Kauffman, 1987). The implications of this prove to be far-reaching in that caring involves a fair degree of control (Lewis and Meredith, 1988) which opens up choice as well as placing limits on it. These can be both a source of celebration and an aggravation.

Secondly, women act as mediators in caring relationships as they manage a whole host of conflicting demands, rights and obligations which are experienced as support, pleasure and pressure (Woods, 1987). Group members talked of having to keep their heads in a thousand places at once, as they juggled with their responsibilities. Women experience their mediating and negotiating roles as sometimes engendering activity and self-control, whilst on other occasions the different strategies used to keep agencies at bay encourage passivity and control by others. Such inconsistencies abound within the complexities of women's self-structure and develop into our third element, the fear of abandonment.

If caring is a core identity element for women, then its very existence must provide *continuity* across time and situation, giving women a framework in which to handle society's mixed messages. The continuity of caring in all its forms gives a degree of predictability in an unpredictable environment. Caring provides a whole host of self-defining properties. As a carer a woman knows what to think and what value she has. However, the overwhelming constraints of caring as it is constructed within patriarchy mean that women strive to remove the Self from total enmeshment in relationships whilst at the same time attempting not to hurt the people for whom they care. This is the fear of abandonment. Societal expectations for self-denial in women may severely limit their choices, but at least such restrictions are well tried and tested. Partners, children and relatives may expect a woman to put their needs foremost in her life, and although this bargain breeds terrible dissatisfaction, she hopes that it will equip her with a measure of security.

In contrast, women are afraid that if they display agential qualities their interpersonal network will suddenly disappear. Yet there is nothing inherently threatening to women's Caring Self about agential self-expression being encouraged (Kaplan, 1984). Nevertheless, being assertive and angry have come to be equated with the loss not just of another person (Eichenbaum and Orbach, 1987) but, more important, of one's capacity to care about others. Loss had already been a major feature in the lives of group participants and the fear of further abandonment loomed large. Loss of friends and family; loss of children through death, custody disputes, irregular access arrangements; loss of partners, through death, separation, or divorce; loss of accommodation; financial insecurity; lack of recognition by professionals; loss of continuity in one place; loss of stability for themselves and their children – all take their toll. How is a woman to cope with and make sense of all that? The contradictions inherent within continuity and fear of loss precipitate the pulls towards closeness and differentiation.

The diverse identity elements which cluster around caring jostle for position through the constant pulls towards closeness and differentiation within the group. There are many occasions when a woman will assert 'I'm just not like that' in response to a given situation or group discussion. The nature of identity is such that it works to produce distinctiveness for an individual woman because this is valued in white Western culture and therefore has power to guide identity elements and the process of their evaluation. Yet this desire for interpersonal differentiation is dependent upon and tested out through the specific network of relations in the group which pertains at any time.

The tension between connection in and separation from personal relationships often goes unrecognized by women. This oversight is not surprising given women's lack of awareness of their hopes for autonomy. Women effectively conceal these aspirations from themselves as a result of the internalization of sex-role stereotyping (Sayers, 1986). The effect of this is that group members may offer each other overwhelming nurturance or err on the side of distancing in group sessions, giving space which the individual is too vulnerable to use and which she experiences as rejection.

The relationship between these four elements fluctuates, with any given element achieving salience and cogency through the influence of the group. The pluralistic nature of caring as a core aspect of identity requires the individual woman to check out the tensions between the four elements through social comparison. Women can begin to appraise and evaluate their caring attitudes and behaviours through an assessment of the similarities and differences in others' opinions. One group member, for example, expressed intense reactions to her children which fluctuated between extreme concern for their welfare and action which signified control and power over their lives. In response to this, another group member declared that 'I'm not like that' by describing her mechanistic and routinized responses to her children, which in effect reduced child-rearing to rigid and clearly defined tasks. Reason had destroyed feelings for her, and for the first woman feelings had produced forms of control in caring which she herself experienced as 'beyond her control'. The articulation of such a struggle, born out of social comparison, points to the fact that group members strive for separation *and* interdependence within any one session, and they are both active and passive in this process. As Urwin (1984) has said, women can be acutely vulnerable, but are also capable of assertive action.

Yet paradox and contradiction within identity act as catalysts for the exploration of Self in women's groups because connection with others is a key component of action and growth. For instance, the sense of responsibility and commitment women have to caring and their desire for emotional expression can enhance connections with other women (see Chapter 4). Ironically enough, this fosters the gradual evolution of a differentiated Self, a Self with its own clear properties and wishes. However, this Self achieves articulation through participation in and attention to the relational process (Kaplan, 1984).

Women's groups can foster this self-development by reassessing the value of caring. An aspect of identity which is negatively perceived can become a source of satisfaction when viewed comparatively. The centrality of relational ties in women's lives means that a woman can find knowledge of herself through the impact of group relations on her. The teachings of women's groups lead, therefore, to the development of the Caring Self within an atmosphere of mutuality. Hence, women end up perceiving each other as allies rather than as rivals.

Similarly, women's adaptability to varied roles whilst at the same time transcending social barriers can be reframed as an illustration of significant coping abilities. If we carry such potent responsibilities, then surely somewhere we must be thought intelligent and capable, we must be self-reliant if we work out how to juggle the plethora of conflicting demands. It *is* possible to retrieve caring as a positive force by choosing to compare past and present identity content with others in the group. Women can then re-evaluate their beliefs and attitudes which stem from *social exclusion* and instead seek out support which points to *social confirmation*.

Within the context of the validation of caring, group process can have an impact on personal identity by confronting women's *unrestrained* caring. Women give and give, extending themselves constantly, performing emotional labour that obliterates their ability to think. The challenges and warmth of women's groups allows women to think about what it means to respect and consider another's needs rather than acting automatically. This movement towards thoughtful caring also exists dialectically with a woman's conversion of her Self into the original friend (Arendt, 1978). Once it is discovered that a woman can converse with her Self, and in so doing can enrich her conversations with others, then a belief in Self is awakened.

Steps towards a sense of well-being: Effects of devaluation of the core of identity
There is a sense in which the awakening of self-awareness runs parallel to women's self-esteem, which itself is connected intimately to self-knowledge and self-definition. So important is this to our discussion that we will now explore the effects of devaluation of core identity elements on women's self-esteem, particularly as this proved to be a common experience across all women's groups. How can we get to grips with women's understanding of self-esteem? What has emerged from the previous section is that women gauge their self-esteem through relationships with others, where emotionality is bound up with and feeds into such connections. Self-esteem is generated, therefore, through action within the context of relationships, the effectiveness of which is assessed by the individual concerned (Breakwell, 1986). Social competence is judged through feedback from the social world about the consequences of our actions, which in turn contributes to our self-knowledge.

It is our belief that institutional and social barriers impede women's growth because it is only when action achieves a desired outcome that it is deemed efficacious and has the power to create self-esteem. Being at the bottom of the social heap had for the most part prevented the validation of women's group members' activity, apart from occasional glimpses of gratitude from friends. Let us take caring as a prime example, as it illustrates the mixed motivation of guilt, love, hate and duty, as well as the kaleidoscope of changing emotions in changing situations which have a dramatic effect on self-esteem. The conclusion that emerges from our previous section is that the performance of emotional labour, coupled with its constant societal devaluation, have a deleterious effect on women's health and sense of well-being. The shaping of identity through unrelenting caring provides little sustenance because of the scarce opportunity for the development of any personal capabilities.

We need to recognize fully the links between material and emotional deprivation and mental distress. Women carry the burden of financial poverty. The totality of women's responsibilities is mediated by the establishment and enforcement of standards of material subsistence, through social security services, which severely restrict the capacity of the poorest to develop their personal powers. Management of so many women in poverty can only be maintained through their self-denial, self-restriction, and sacrificing of their health, opportunities and freedoms. Women end up feeling ill at ease with the world as the practices used to propagate the ideology of the dominant societal groups mix in with their own identity structures. Women in poverty learn about their disadvantaged social positions from a multitude of sources, all of which are impregnated by the prevailing ideologies' influence on gender relations. The extent and impact of the feminization of poverty (Glendinning and Millar, 1987) pushes through to the core of women's identity and self-esteem.

Our identity is shaped for us constantly, to the extent that the more people tell us certain things about ourselves, the more inclined we are to believe them. Our ways of living are so individualized that any group member's embryonic attempts to offer herself explanations for feelings and behaviour would be dismissed by 'experts'. We are led to believe that any disagreement with the rest of society means the fault is in our own psyche. We might be deemed arrogant, selfish and demanding for presuming to think differently. The way in which women's lives have been reshaped and reinterpreted by others focuses particularly on mental distress and reproduction.

Mental distress and the uterine woman   It comes as no surprise that the majority of women's group members joined with a history of 'mental illness' (see Chapter 1). This 'history' had been written by someone else, with many chapters and embellishments added along the way. The frequency with which women's expression of emotionality had been redefined as a problem, as endogenous depression, as self-inflicted, and treated by chemical intervention or worse, gives us an explanation for the erosion of any opportunity for self-definition. If you are told frequently enough that you are mad, it becomes very difficult to sustain any level of self-esteem. The vestiges of self-approval and self-love you may have had left over from childhood, or from a few isolated adult experiences and relationships, are gradually fragmented.

The processes of social influence and injustice which have exacerbated and prolonged women's vulnerability to mental distress may be inconsistent and reflect the differing interests of dominant social groups. One way of coping with these contradictory prescriptions is through repression and self-deprecation. Women renounce any

positive attributes in order to comply with conflicting social pro-
hibitions. However, holding on to these expectations exposes a woman
to considerable levels of stress. Women often complained of perpetual
tiredness, of loss of memory, of dull headaches and tightening of the
stomach. There was also much irritability and frenetic activity which
proved counter-productive but used up what little energy a woman
had. It is symbolic that women's reference to headaches is an accurate
reflection of the pain they experience in trying continually to make
sense of the incomprehensible. In such circumstances, women cannot
allow themselves to get in touch with affective responses – the pain and
fear appear too overwhelming. The majority of group members
indicated that they suppressed 'bad feelings' and avoided naming
them. Self-denial and stress affect women's perceptions of themselves
in relation to their surroundings. This is due to:

- limitations in choices;
- feelings of being out of control of events and social relations;
- initiative being seen as potentially destructive;
- difficulty in identifying positive ways of handling stress;
- not knowing how to *use* their feelings.

For women in violent relationships, the threat of retribution creates
an additional climate of fear and suspicion: 'It's normal to be afraid,
normal not to be heard, not to speak out when you're told all the time
that you're doing wrong.' When you are at the bottom of the social
strata, there is little margin for error as you are scrutinized continuously
by the state:

Professional people treat me like an idiot.
Those professionals just aren't honest with me. They use soft words and
bland phrases, but they cut through me like a knife.

Climbing up from the bottom is thwarted by women's entrapment in
impoverished life-styles which push only their unhappiness to the
surface: 'I feel backed into a corner. There's no escape. I wake up and
I'm afraid again, just the same as the day before.' Smoking, abuse of
alcohol and prescribed drugs, overdoses, other forms of self-harm, not
eating, obesity, sleeping problems, menstrual or gynaecological
problems, obsessional behaviour, agoraphobia, depression, anxiety,
paranoia, self-neglect, neglect of personal hygiene – this list of
desperation was compiled by group members who quickly realized
how the use of substances or behaviours initially seen as methods of
coping only precipitated further self-destruction. Pain and distress
oozed from women, whose coping abilities were stretched to the limit.

How a woman is moulded by the social order, its institutions and
ideologies, is embodied in the conventional interpretations of such

behaviours. Explanations of behaviours offered to group members by professionals included laziness, lack of self-motivation, poor education, illiteracy, inertia, personal inadequacy, manipulation and attention-seeking behaviour. Women had also been told that they had a poor understanding of nutrition, were susceptible to media pressure, and were immature. This immaturity consisted of behaving in an infantile manner, being afraid of adulthood and its responsibilities, and having an immature sexuality and an infantile need for security. In addition, lack of self-respect, lack of self-control and a hysterical nature were thrown at women as explanatory statements. Embedded in all these messages to some degree was the assumption that such behaviours were hereditary, an inevitable consequence of being female, and that women were not concerned enough about being attractive to their male partners. There was also a consistent view that women were unable to deal with stress appropriately and were not bothering to take time to relax.

Whatever elements of truth there may be in some of these interpretations, such as attention-seeking behaviour, stress, or not taking time to relax, even these were reinterpreted to the detriment of the woman concerned. The use of arcane language reveals more about professional moralizing than about women's behaviour. Blaming women for their actions, their thoughts, the way they dress, eat, parent, has become a ritualized and stereotyped response, as can be seen in the prejudicial statements made by third-party referees (see Chapter 2). The lack of opportunity to behave in liberating and self-enhancing ways is seen as a woman's fault, and therefore as something she can correct herself, either by acting in ways that are deemed appropriate by others, or by keeping quiet and not complaining.

The establishments that monitor and regulate women's 'health' and their hegemony are prime examples of how identities are distorted, ignored or eliminated. Women are indeed the main targets for legitimized subordination by the medical profession (Dale and Foster, 1986). Our bodies are seen as sources of illness, disease, discomfort, disgust to others, and are prey to the fluctuations of hormones. Partners – indeed children and other family members – readily offered up group members for medical, particularly psychiatric, intervention with the deep-seated faith that this would 'cure' their behaviour. Indeed, social consciousness believes women to be largely in the wrong and to need correcting. Their minds and their reproductive systems need controlling. They are at the mercy of both.

An exploration of the practices of the nineteenth century reveals that 'experts' were railing against 'cerebral women' whose thirst for knowledge and intellectual satisfaction threatened the very existence of humanity. It was maintained that use of the brain caused the ovaries to atrophy and the milk glands to dry up (Ehrenreich and English, 1979). The split between *uterine* and *cerebral* woman highlights that the reproductive role has long been considered the pivotal point of women's psychological and physical structure (Showalter, 1987). In addition, the intellectual, emotional and physical potential of women is measured against the male standard and found to be defective (Broverman et al., 1970).

There is research to show that medical practitioners are society's front-line gatekeepers and decision-makers in reproductive technology (Brody, 1987; Oakley, 1980). When we uncover the subtle aspects of the social control of women in poverty we can see how routine the subjection to impersonal and coercive health care has become. For instance, women's group members lacked knowledge about the side-effects of oral contraceptives; felt that interventionist technology during childbirth was designed more for professional convenience than their own welfare; had experienced unnecessary hysterectomies as a result of cervical cancer, and had been sterilized without their informed consent. In addition, a minority of women had had radical mastectomy operations without being fully aware of the consequences. Also, women in poverty had felt the backlash of lobbying for more liberal abortion laws and had been subjected to the most exploitative medical experiences imaginable (see p. 67). Some group members described how they had been routinely condemned to compulsory pregnancy. Their male partners, whose access to other channels of achievement or prestige had been denied, gained self-esteem and status by producing pregnancy without regard for rearing the offspring. Women had had to defend themselves against the hazards and burdens of excessive child-bearing on the one hand, and infertility and consequent male abandonment on the other. The limitations on women's choices are indeed great:

> I was sterilized straight after Darren was born, my sixth child. Doctors said it'd be better if I had it done all at once, and then my bloke couldn't complain too much. It seemed a good idea at the time 'cos me Mam only had to look after the kids in one go. I wouldn't leave the young uns with him. He wouldn't know one end of a nappy from another. Well, I haven't stopped bleeding since I was sterilized. I keep going to the doctor and I just get tablets.

> I was raped when I was fifteen and I had an abortion afterwards. It was all like a terrible nightmare. And then four months after that my boyfriend had sex with me – I didn't agree to it really and I had another abortion then. I've had all sorts of problems since – lots of pains, y'know. I've had various tests because I might be infertile.

The denial of women's control and autonomy over their health was experienced as a process of mystification of illness definitions, hinging on the separation of mind and body. Such a hegemonic medical culture frames all competing definitions of the world through a process of moral arbitration (Brody, 1987). Group members felt that their doctors sat in moral, paternalistic judgement over them. In addition, women had picked up that as a result of occupational prejudices, their doctors often unwittingly conveyed hope that women patients would become 'better', as well as healthier people. Indeed, doctors decide who has access to family planning, abortion, infertility treatment, or who is recommended for sterilization (Ruzek, 1980). However, these decisions are based on unacknowledged moral or social grounds, especially when a general practitioner doubts the woman's capacity to behave in 'her own best interests'. Such clinical and ethical questions are always answered within the seemingly unproblematic dominant moral code of conduct, which unambiguously grants medical practitioners the permission to use their persuasive power. Bear and care for children, and suffer the tribulations of such responsibilities in isolation and silence, for such is the influence of dominant moral arguments.

Women's identities are built upon the repertoire of social roles they enact and the restricted health-care options available to them. The constraints and forces inherent in the role of family intermediary and negotiator precipitate stress because of limited support. Women's depression illustrates this point; it is the spectre that haunts us, an experience with which all women's group members were able to identify. Women often described diffuse health complaints which lacked specificity, but which symbolized the nature of depression in its broadest sense:

> I just keep feeling sick all the time.
> I get so thoroughly tired during the day and yet when I go to bed I don't sleep.
> I just feel awful most of the time.

In terms of depression, Brown and Harris's (1978) study of working-class women in Camberwell found that a confiding and intimate relationship with a partner, employment outside the home, and fewer than three children still at home offered protection against women's vulnerability to depression after a stressful life event. These factors enhance self-esteem and self-control, which ward off the feelings of generalized hopelessness which characterize depression (Rosenham and Seligman, 1984). They militate against the 'cognitive triad', which Beck et al. (1979) identified as part of the mechanism generating depression: negative thoughts about the Self, about ongoing experiences and about the future. Such negative thoughts conspire with 'errors in logic' to generate despair. Brown and Harris showed that low self-esteem and negative thinking precede the onset of depression and may be considered a causal influence. The perception of a stressful event as threatening to existing coping strategies is therefore dependent upon the content of self-definition. In all of these research studies the point is usually made implicitly or explicitly that the loss of gratification from another is responsible for the connection between loss of an important relationship and depression. Women suffer the loss of confirmation of their relational self-structure. The absence of intimacy is experienced more centrally as a *failure of the Self* (Kaplan, 1984).

Kaplan further asserts that low self-esteem is the result of, and a contributory element in, women's felt responsibility for failures in evolving mutually affirming relationships. Women's sense of self-worth rests so heavily on their ability to make and sustain relationships that the regularity of failure invariably leads to the denial of our own relational worth. Further, the cultural validation of men's pursuit of their own desires exacerbates women's flight from confirmation of their own wishes. Repeated emotional disconnection from others ultimately involves a sense of futility in our actions which gnaws away at the kernel of Self.

This sense of failure inhibits action; this has been explained by Seligman (1975) as 'learned helplessness'. He argues that depression results from the loss of control over the modes of reinforcement for our behaviour. That is, depression occurs if we feel unable to anticipate or predict the consequences of our behaviour, such prediction being necessary if we are to feel able to act to produce change. In the absence of control, we in a sense 'give up' with concomitant feelings of helplessness and futility. We need to examine the impact of this 'loss of control' on women's core self-structure, because it is not only helplessness but self-blame and an overwhelming sense of responsibility that are the key issues here. Responsibility for failures creates a sense of our own destructiveness. Group members at times hated themselves; they were afraid of themselves and afraid of harming others even as they reached out. In addition, some women expressed a sense of personal inauthenticity, epitomized by continually apologizing for everything: spilling the coffee, interrupting, shouting, sitting quietly – in fact, apologizing for their existence. What is striking about these examples is that women felt diminished in self-esteem by minor actions and also did not trust, or even recognize, their own responses. In addition, women experiencing depression are more inhibited in actions which are perceived as destructive and selfish, and more active through behaviours felt to be especially facilitative of others. In the Brown and Harris (1978) study, the only thing that prevented some depressed women from harming themselves or committing suicide was the need to care for their children. Paradoxically, the parenting that makes women vulnerable to depression and interferes with their obtaining help also protects them from suicide.

Chronic and sequential threats to identity (Breakwell, 1986) reduce women's attempts at coping and they may eventually cease trying. Such relentless pressure may act to immobilize a woman's belief that she can achieve anything through her own efforts. Coping strategies which have been used to some effect in the past may be found wanting or may contradict previous coping skills. Attacks on the effectiveness of her actions in one area can generate a perception of the Self as incapable and ineffective. One group member felt her failure in relationships was due to a lifelong feeling of never 'being good enough' for her own mother, who described her as a continual source of disappointment. She could easily recall phrases and statements her mother made about her life-style, all of which echoed back to her childhood. The power of put-downs such as 'Don't listen to her, she's always talking nonsense', or 'You were irresponsible when you got pregnant at fifteen, you didn't take any notice then and you're just as thoughtless now', point to the erosion of self-esteem over time.

Low self-esteem therefore generates core belief systems which revolve around a profound sense of weakness and unworthiness. Some group members feared the retaliation of others' actions so strongly that they felt permanently feeble in mind and body, incapable of developing any source of strength. The belief in their inferiority, that they were closer to matter, earth and animals (Griffin, 1978), and that therefore 'my bloke treats the dog better than me', led them to think that they had no right to make a fuss and disturb the danger which lay behind a superficially benign world.

Self-protection and acts of resistance   One mode of adaptation to deal with a hostile social context is for a woman to build a wall around her identity. Alienation from dominant social norms and values, withdrawal from social contact, slowing down of the level of social activity – all of these were options which group members had previously used as a means of self-protection. At the root of these was *avoidance* and *deflection* – admirable but destructive coping strategies. Denial is a well-documented response to stress (Lazarus and Folkman, 1984). The facts of reality are denied, then their relevance, then their urgency, then the need to act, then the emotions aroused and, finally, the importance of those emotions and their effects on identity. It is as if the mind, having appraised the full horror of the situation, censors the information. There is a fair amount of disbelief in all of this, and women at times deny that their social position is at all stigmatized:

Look, we've got the best deal, really. I want a man to open doors for me, and I wouldn't want to go off to war. All that competitive stuff, it's not for the likes of me.

When women do acknowledge that they have internalized derogatory stereotypes about themselves, they invariably deny that these cause anger, despair or any other emotional reaction. Rejection and dismissal of the emotional and cognitive implications of a hostile social context mean that at its best denial can be used as a tactic to buy psychological time-out before resuming the struggle of life. Unfortunately for a woman's sense of well-being, avoidance and denial can become habitual, encompassing many realms of her life and severely affecting her ability to deal with reality.

Women also described periods of *alienation* which proved frightening and felt as if 'I was going out of my head'. There may be a disturbing sense that one's body has become distorted and that the physical world is so unreal as to be alien. Women described moments of detachment from the Self where they observed themselves as disconnected. This often occurred when expectations about the Self had been violated or when women had failed to act in accordance with firmly held beliefs. Alienation anaesthetizes a woman from pain, but it is not under conscious control and gives a strange sense of other-worldliness:

It was as if I spent all my days wrapped in cling film. All sounds became muffled and I did everything in slow motion. Was this body really mine?

I had these moments when I didn't recognize anything and I didn't dare tell anyone about it. They'd say I was bonkers. I used to watch myself walk down the street, pushing the buggy, going into shops where I didn't know what anything was. I stared at fruit and just couldn't name any of it. I stared at money in my hand, and my palm was hot and sweaty because I didn't know what this money was for. I was desperate and so panic-stricken, but the only thing that brought me back into myself was when I stared at the top of my son's head as he sat in the buggy.

Ironically, this woman's only connection with reality was through her son. For this group member, and for many more, the knowledge of being a 'suspended woman' (Washington, 1981), torn apart by pressure, violence and distress, is readily apparent. Movement into detachment or avoidance provides some respite because it removes aspects of the social context which have generated such responses in the first place.

Women also protect themselves against internal conflict and role stress by limiting the levels of *uncertainty* generated by dominant ideological concepts. One way of achieving this is by 'passing for normal' (Goffman, 1961), where a woman gains access to the 'normality' of male standards by camouflaging her behaviour and intentions. For example, several group members hid bills from their male partners to create the impression that their housekeeping accounts were in order. Rather than attributing the uncertainty surrounding low income to economic injustices, women believed that they were *personally* responsible for the pressures of budgeting and needed to deceive the public world into an image of themselves as impeccable managers of money. Similarly, women would serve up large meals for their menfolk and children, leaving no food for themselves, because of shortage of money:

> I'd rather go without than see them all starve. The local shopkeeper always keeps an account of what I owe. I tell her I'll see her right next time. He shan't know about it.

This is all in the name of creating the cosy, unproblematic nuclear family. Women used such deceptive devices because they hoped for social approval and an enhancement of their self-esteem. Passing for normal had social benefits because it minimized the social consternation to which public acknowledgement of their problems would give rise. Passing for normal has considerable psychological costs, however, because there is the continual fear of discovery and exposure, and any internal conflict still remains. Rather, it emphasizes a disparity between internal and social experiences of the Self.

Women handled chronic uncertainty by playing the game of *compliance*. All group members recognized that they had accepted to differing degrees the behavioural prescriptions associated with femininity, had attempted to live up to these expectations, and had thereby generated no disruption of power hierarchies. Some may say that compliance has pay-offs in that it establishes a clearly defined social status for women. There is no doubt, though, that living up to others' expectations is arduous, especially when the stereotype leads to treatment as a non-person. What is most frightening is that when compliance is prolonged, it has tremendous power to shape experience and affect identity structure:

> I used to go out a lot before I got married, but he's always said he doesn't like me to go out without him. He says I'm too gullible and will trust anybody, whereas he can see right through people, especially men. He gets ever so jealous, y'see. He's only trying to protect me I know. I'm not allowed out very often. It doesn't particularly bother me now. I used to get ever so het up about it but he used to say I looked stupid when I was upset, so I don't bother anymore.

This woman, like so many others, had attempted to cope with existing ideological and social structures by conforming to the restrictions of dominant social and moral codes. She had played the game by a set of rules over which she had no control. Ultimately, women are faced with a double-bind: non-compliance generates social rejection, but so does compliance. What choice did this group member have in a heterosexual relationship fed by inequality and objectification?

Above everything else, we have seen how adherence to masculinist doctrines severely restricts women's behaviour, their ability to take risks and to respond with flexibility to emerging situations. Some of the behaviours that women end up presenting as problems as a result of the above coping strategies are, paradoxically, mechanisms whereby they feel able to gain a little respite and even relaxation. Smoking, for example, despite its increasingly publicized dangers and the risk to personal health, unborn children's health and the health of those around, offers women a momentary escape from everyday rigours. It is no accident that the heaviest smokers are women and working-class. You cannot breathe and smoke at the same time. Smoking fills you with a chemical anaesthetic which numbs the terror of living. Breathing deeply can help to discharge some of the pain, but it is an option not available whilst smoking. The social ramifications of smoking are such that offering another woman a cigarette is not only a gesture of friendship and comfort, but also a means of sharing. Although the dangers of smoking formed a topic of discussion in the groups, women repeatedly indicated that when they had a cigarette lit up, there was far less chance of a row, or of violence occurring, and this increased their nicotine dependency.

Similar explanations were offered for the abuse of alcohol and of prescribed drugs. These provided a distancing from reality that made painful and difficult situations marginally easier to deal with. The dulling of the senses means that otherwise intolerable matters become slightly less so, even if the pain is correspondingly greater once the effects of the substance have worn off. Self-harm is the ultimate form of self-punishment, and yet it is frequently castigated as attention-seeking behaviour by professional groups. Group members' explanations for their self-harm involved the following thought processes:

> Look, I'm desperate, this is the only way I can think of that's going to make you believe me, take notice of me. I don't want to do this, but everything else has failed.

Such forms of resistance act as a wedge between the individual and the dehumanizing effects of an alienating environment, but they push her further into the lack of right to autonomy within the world. Such behaviours are the social expression of a woman's identity, an identity which hinges on self-blame as a means of handling the gap between unfulfilled expectations and the reality of social roles. In such circumstances, coping strategies can take over, moving outside a woman's control and becoming habitual and indiscriminate. Indeed, an act of resistance consists not only of the ability to develop a strategy, but also of the capacity to delimit its sphere of influence. In all this, it is clear why negative reactions to women's resistance take place: they are based in fear, the fear that men experience when they think that women are gaining knowledge about their own uneasy, unstable need to dominate, about the tenuous nature of their power.

A sense of well-being It comes as no surprise that group members defined health as the absence of incapacitating and externally verifiable pathology. There were severe limitations on women's expectations of what it is to be healthy. It was therefore important in group sessions to provide full information and to enable women to make choices over contraception, abortion, childbirth and treatment for breast and uterine cancer. Consideration of women's health issues opens up a whole new approach to health care, namely that group members become active participants. Women who know more about their own bodies, know how to ask questions, can challenge their lack of rights within the medical system.

The effect this has on women's identity is to make connections between mind and body; as a result identity takes on a more rounded, positive shape. The major means of resistance to the accumulated control of the creativity, labour and energy of women by the medical profession comes to be collective action. Through the piecing together of fragments of women's criticism of an environment which continually demeans their relational capabilities, women can be freed from the tendency to place responsibility for their failures on themselves. By using action learning techniques and women's issues material (see Chapter 3) a lessened sense of self-blame leads, in turn, to a point where women can express thoughts about their own emotional and physical well-being. Gradually, it becomes possible to demonstrate how much of their own behaviour which caused them distress, and which they wanted to change, often masked the true depth of their feelings. Most important, women's inner state can be understood without reaching for professional labels of 'dependency', 'neediness' or 'weakness' by stressing women's active relational aspirations. Self-expression gained through the groupwork methods referred to in Chapter 3 allows a woman to recognize herself as a whole being. This is not to suggest that this will cure all ills, rather that she will be left with a stronger sense of her own abilities and worth with which to confront misleading interpretations, acknowledge the roots of her distress, and keep herself healthy.

The discovery of sexuality as positive identity
The third core self-concept which emerged in the group meetings was the potent issue of sexuality, which was most consistently an area of

conflict. From our groupwork experience, we are able to hypothesize that sexuality was perceived initially by women both as *separate* from key aspects of their identity and as *negative* in value. The dialectical interaction between sexuality and self-concept marks the confusion women felt in relation to the internalization of inequality and rigid gender expectations. Women had coped with the distortions and damaging experiences which had accumulated over the years by not acknowledging the conflict between internal and external forces of oppression surrounding sexuality. As a means of altering the negative effects of socialization so that women could reclaim control and personal power, women's group sessions evolved into a consideration of four areas of female sexuality:

(a) body awareness;
(b) the role of reproductive sex and birth control;
(c) heterosexism;
(d) sexuality as self-expression.

By challenging their own and each other's assumptions, attitudes and values surrounding sexuality, women could move from a position of alienation from their bodies and their sexuality, to the point where intimacy and self-expression became a source of strength.

As far as the structural aspects of identity are concerned, women perceived sexuality in separation from their core Self because they had been socialized to avoid seeing themselves as sexual beings. Women's immediate consciousness of themselves as 'asexual' inadvertently conceals the contradictions in social life that determine such beliefs in the first place:

> I haven't really got a sexuality. I don't think I'm very attractive to anyone. My life's just really ordinary, nothing important to talk about.

The colonization and reshaping of sexuality in forms we no longer recognize, the messages we receive about ourselves, our behaviour and expectations are so mixed that we have become detached from spontaneity and a recognition of sexuality as a central part of our being. Women's group members, in keeping with dominant societal beliefs, readily confused the word 'sexuality' with penetrative sex, reproduction and sexual behaviour, and sexual orientation, and made assumptions about this being exclusively heterosexual:

> Sexuality is a source of stress to me. There's just so many high expectations on me from men – I either give them too much sex, and I'm promiscuous, or too little, and I'm frigid.

By exploring the four areas of female sexuality referred to earlier, we can examine the separation of Self from sexuality in greater detail:

Body awareness The disassociation from sexuality is borne out in women's perceptions of their body image as negative ('I'm too fat'; 'I'm too tall'; 'I walk with a stoop to hide myself'; 'I hate my breasts, they're too small'). In addition, group members indicated that they could not understand, control, or manage their own bodies. There are three aspects of women's socialization that contribute to this, namely societal measures of beauty, ageing, and the fragmentation of our bodies.

In terms of attitudes to beauty, women's group members felt unable to conform to the narrowly defined standards of what is beautiful as portrayed by the media, and as a result felt negative about their bodies. Mental health assessments had been made of women's psychological well-being, with judgements based on whether they conformed to a stereotypically 'feminine' appearance. For example, one woman was assessed as emerging from a schizophrenic phase once she started using make-up again; another woman who chose not to wear a bra was thought to be lacking interest in her appearance, to be slovenly and unfeminine. They recognized that within racist societal structures a white skin is valued above a black skin, but they nevertheless felt blotchy, hated their freckles and spots. These negations were compounded by lack of material resources and socio-economic deprivation. Women simply could not afford to succumb to the weight of the cosmetic and fashion industries even if they wanted to, and yet blamed themselves for being 'unattractive'. Younger women in the groups had fallen prey to the masculinist response to beauty through rituals of self-punishment, putting considerable energy into the rounds of dieting and wearing restrictive clothing, such as tight jeans, and 'fashionable' shoes which hurt and pinched. Helping women to cast off the corset of conformity can be a prolonged business.

Older women especially were aware of powerful media images which exhorted them to be young and beautiful through glamour and the attainment of wealth. Indeed, pervasive ageism is so intimately connected with sexist representations because growing older for women is characterized by perceived loss – of beauty, attractiveness, value, and child-bearing ability. Older women's group members recoiled from themselves, by disassociating from the physical signs of ageing – their wrinkles, stretch marks, varicose veins and grey hair:

> I can't look at myself in the mirror. My breasts are sagging, I've got folds of skin which just hang there. My thighs are too fat.
>
> I wear big jumpers because they hide such a lot of me.
>
> I've got a spare tyre around my middle, but I just manage to squeeze into my favourite dress.
>
> I'm losing my figure now I'm getting older.

The armoury of media representations signifies the combined sex-role and age-role apparatus, which group members could handle only through the externalization of the body. Statements such as 'I'm losing my figure now I'm getting older' exist as a supreme example of enforced disengagement from one's physical being.

This alienation is compounded by reductionist principles which fragment our bodies into separate units. These 'parts' then assume greater or lesser degrees of acceptability for display or touch, leaving us with little sense of wholeness. The division of our bodies into erogenous zones serves further to undermine our physical and mental health. Beyond this, women are socialized to believe that their genitals are unclean, should not be touched, and the odour so offensive that it needs to be masked with deodorants.

The role of reproductive sex and birth control   Both the subtle and the blatant assumptions surrounding female sexuality filter into women's perceptions not only of our bodies, but also of our sexual potential. Group members all recollected that as girls and adult women they had learnt that their own sexual perceptions, sensations, impulses were not supposed to arise from themselves, but were to be brought forth by and for men. As adolescents, all members had experienced their physical and sexual stirrings as wrong and dirty. To feel or entertain thoughts about sexual desire had become a source of shame. The loss of personal power associated with female sexuality stems from the message that men will teach us all we need to know about our bodies and that we need an experienced male lover to help us learn. We therefore view our sexuality as being under another's control. Again, a core feature of our lives becomes identified in masculinist terms, taking on its significance in a very specific way, designed to meet men's sexual needs.

Women's loss of power and control over their sexual lives is compounded by the use of female contraception, because group members had little knowledge of the health risks or long-term effects involved:

> I have these Depo Provera injections. The doctor thought it would be better than falling pregnant again.
>
> I had a coil put in me. It was so painful I screamed. The nurse told me I was fussing too much. I bled loads for two days afterwards and I had to go back and have it taken out. It's about time they invented the male pill or something. I felt like a slab of meat at the time.

Through the imparting and sharing of information about women's anatomy and forms of contraception, women can begin to gain control over their bodies and over other aspects of their lives. It is then possible to explore why it is that women define sexuality in such a limiting way.

All women felt they had to be yielding and non-assertive in hetero-sexual relationships, so much so that they had cut themselves off from responsiveness and warmth, telling themselves that their own enjoyment in penetrative sex did not matter:

> I've been so disappointed so many times. I end up wondering what all the fuss is about. He gets his bit of pleasure, but I get more fun out of smoking a fag or eating my favourite bar of chocolate.

The whole notion of foreplay leading up to an orgasmic goal, rather than moving mountains, moved them to a point of desperation and self-blame.

Heterosexism   Embedded in such negations of sexual behaviour are the mechanisms of compulsory heterosexuality, which assume that relationship maturity is possible only through heterosexual union. Rich (1980) declares that heterosexuality is maintained and organized in order to ensure women's physical, economic and emotional dependency on men. Freudian psychology in particular has taught that female intimacy is trifling and sentimental, a prelude only to the adult stage of hetero-relational development. Raymond (1986) has noted that close friendships between women are seen to be 'narcissistic', childish crushes, relics of a bygone time of immaturity, where women have not yet been weaned from the world of women. Added to which, the centrality of reproductive sex takes no account of those women who remain childless or who choose to remain child-free.

The narrowness of such belief systems also means that for women who seek out sexual complementarity from men, emotional fulfilment may be continually thwarted, as many men are not socialized to provide emotionality but are only given permission to be self-centred and goal-oriented. For the majority of group members, the social construction of their sexuality was such that they had almost given up the struggle between dominant societal beliefs and their own perceptions and responses. The bombardment of media images reinforcing such attitudes, the narrow scope for paid employment, the expectations of family and partners, statements made by professionals working with the family – all serve to affirm a woman's role in the heterosexist caring process. A woman's mental health is categorized by many male psychiatrists according to whether she has a man, has had a man, or is attractive enough to be likely to get a man again soon; if not, then her well-being will suffer. Group members often protested about such definitions being seen as the norm but felt torn by the need to gain approval from society.

The ambiguities and conflicting understandings of this balancing act were felt acutely by women. Our upbringing teaches us not to take the initiative sexually but at the same time to be seductive to men. Women therefore frequently found themselves in uncomfortable, potentially dangerous and violent situations for which they were accused of being responsible, when they thought they were acting in socially sanctioned and approved ways. Group members had been assaulted and raped, with little sympathy offered subsequently. This is because supposedly they had not taken more care, had acted provocatively and had only got what they asked for:

> My ex-boyfriend came round when my kids were still at school. I didn't want to see him. Somehow he persuaded me to have him, like, but I didn't want to. I thought, I'd let him have his way with me and then he'd go with no trouble. Afterwards I told him to go 'cos of the kids coming home. I felt ashamed with meself.
> The next day I told this friend about it all and she told me, what else could I expect, he was only behaving like any normal, healthy man. So much for normal, healthy men I thought, but I didn't say.

Through tentatively spoken truths such as these, women can begin to question their perceptions of sexuality and societal views of female provocativeness.

This questioning can only go so far though. The group's ability to unpack the sources of heterosexism thoroughly and to examine the impact of such discrimination on the pscyhe can occur only if the group confronts its homophobia. The existence of egalitarian, fulfilling lesbian relationships represents a significant threat to patriarchal exploitation and subjugation of women (Gartrell, 1984). The fear, hatred and aversion associated with lesbianism is played out in women's group sessions, thereby signifying the internalization of dominant sexual norms. The group therefore needs to explore the effects of homophobia on the lives of lesbian and heterosexual members, as its profound influence impinges upon self-image and our core concepts of Self. We have already discussed the detrimental effects of homophobia on women's friendships (see Chapter 4). If heterosexist assumptions remain unchallenged in the group then lesbian members' self-worth and sense of safety will be eroded further.

Given the socio-political context of compulsory heterosexuality, it is crucial that group members become aware of the personal and cultural ramifications of sexual restrictions. Only by doing this can a woman progressively explore her sexuality in relation to her core self-structure. Figure 5 outlines the major institutions (school, family, medicine, employment) and ideological constructs which group members felt had shaped their personal identity within the context of the social construction of sexuality. Women also described the messages they had received from these institutions about normative sexual behaviour. In this way, the group can begin with the particulars

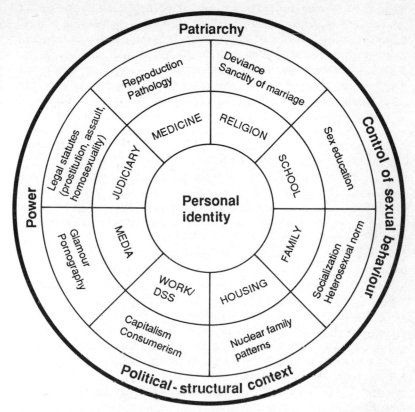

Figure 5 *The social construction of sexuality*

of an individual's experience of constraints on her sexuality and then move out to an exploration of how the particulars are connected to the larger picture. The group can then return to a focus on the personal dimension, which will have undergone modification through such a process of self-discovery. This movement occurs through a woman's insight into the disjunction between women's sexual needs and the capacity of society to fulfil them.

Women realized very quickly that the role and functions of institutions are far from benevolent (see Figure 5). Legislation concerning sexual offences, divorce and custody proceedings, for example, states the ideology which is not only approved, but enforceable (Smart and Sevenhuijsen, 1989). The implementation of legislation decries homosexuality as deviancy and perversion (Crane, 1984) and punishes and controls women's sexuality through legal practices surrounding rape and sexual assault (Kelly, 1988; London

Rape Crisis Centre, 1984). As far as the teachings of family and school are concerned, group members talked about the channelling of their sexuality in childhood. For instance, beliefs abound that masturbation is a source of shame and guilt in which self-stimulation 'sends you blind'. When this is coupled with the pressures to conform experienced at school during adolescence, and religious messages about virginity and the sanctity of marriage, a clear picture emerges of the social control of female sexual behaviour. This is underlined further by the homophobic practices of the medical profession which pathologize women's reproductive capacities and lesbian life-styles. Housing policies reinforce this by giving priority to heterosexual family units. The media presently abound with images of white maternal figures, home-makers and the sexy *femme fatale*. By piecing together the impact of institutional beliefs on women's sexuality, group members can address their concerns about living by the values and interests of corporate capitalism.

The rediscovery of sexuality can be threatening to group members because heterosexism makes it difficult for women to acknowledge, let alone accept, sexual feelings they may have for other women (Boston Women's Health Collective, 1979). It is therefore important that the group focuses on the universality of experiences in their examination of homophobic attitudes and feelings. Through guided discussion, group exercises and the use of audio-visual aids the group can be encouraged to develop positive attitudes towards a wide range of sexual expression and to dispel myths about lesbianism. Kingdon and Bagoon (1983), however, in their description of a ten-session Sexuality Awareness Workshop, recognized that differing levels of awareness amongst women have an impact on group cohesion. Women with limited sexual experiences may withdraw or be embarrassed, for example, and women may express homophobic beliefs out of rigidity and condemnation of differences. In addition, there is the risk that a norm not shared by all members could be established, such as that women should have a range of heterosexual partners before entering a marital relationship. If such norms remain unchallenged, then it is unlikely that lesbian women will risk coming out in the group, for fear of castigation and disapproval. This is particularly the case for women in poverty as class privilege is a major factor affecting coming out choices (Gartrell, 1984).

Sexuality as self-expression   The aim in women's groups must be to awaken women's perceptions of sexuality as a *central* part of Self and identity. Sexuality is bound up with physical and mental health, and also with self-respect and a belief in the right to pleasure and playfulness. The goal should be to broaden out the entire spectrum of what our senses are and to develop an awareness of our capacity for responsiveness and enjoyment (Dickson, 1985). How much more liberating for all of us if we can recognize that our sexuality shapes our every action and reaction, our responsiveness to all stimuli, to music, laughter and people. Sexuality defines our need for connection with others, whether we are seeking comfort for ourselves or offering it to those around us.

Placing sexuality in a socio-political context alters its meaning to the extent that women feel motivated to look at ways of challenging what is happening. They may begin to recognize and make their own connections between media images of women, and their more personal wishes and expectations. As women learnt to separate sexuality from exclusively officially sanctioned sexual behaviour, they could value certain aspects of themselves and of friends. The expression of a female sexuality which primarily seeks to identify our own wants and then begins responding to them in a fulfilling way is a major feature of assertiveness and autonomy. Indeed, assertiveness is easily crushed by assumptions about a woman's wish to engage in conventional heterosexual behaviour. There is a positive correlation here between a growing awareness of sexuality and a woman's self-confidence and positive body image.

Clearly, all relationships contain a greater or lesser degree of the sensual, and this awareness heightened group members' appreciation of each other, increasing their own levels of response in the process. Group members recognized the thoughtful passion, those powerful feelings that fire the continuation of a friendship, and help a woman become her own person (Raymond, 1986). Indeed, Raymond asserts that passion should not be confined to lovers, as it is more fully manifested in the quality of exchanges between intimate friends.

Identity processes

Our exposition of women's core aspects of identity has demonstrated that we cannot segment ourselves into portions, dismantling and examining our identity structure in terms of its form and content. Having specified the substantive composition of identity, we now require an explanation for the development of personal identity across time. Identity continues to be dynamic and ever-changing because it relies on processes which have the capacity to modify its various dimensions and the value attached to them. If we are to have a clearer understanding of the ways in which women's personal identity shifts in relation to social and group change, we must explore *how* it is that a woman actively integrates and accommodates conceptions of Self provided by the social world, shaped as it is by socio-historical reality and cultural heritage.

Fundamental to this process is the use of paradox and contradiction, as already outlined. The contradictions between social roles and the ideologies appended to them are so profound as to require active interpretation by an individual woman. Perception of these social pressures and adaptation to them is necessarily selective, otherwise she would suffer from trying to absorb too much. However, the mere fact that ideologies and institutions are so riddled with conflict and paradox means that a woman is both dependent on social events and also separate from them. Personal identity becomes the permanent residue of the accommodation of each element of social identity and role position (Breakwell, 1986).

We have said that the contradictions inherent in the environment can be dealt with through active *involvement* in the social world, but this has to be coupled with personal *reflection*. A woman can gain self-awareness by coming to understand how others perceive her, by gaining knowledge of the source of contradiction and reflecting upon that knowledge. It is reflexivity that enables a woman to examine internal and external factors impelling her to action (Sherif, 1982). The key element in reflexivity is the act of *recognition*, of *naming* the internal and external aspects of an event. Only then can a woman respond to her own interpretations, as the very act of recognition alters that which is to be perceived:

> When I came to this group, people *listened* to me for the first time in my life. I was so confused, I was speechless and yet here I was in a room where women were saying what I felt. They'd been there as well and they were recognizing my pain. It was like they lifted off the mask and cloak that I wear for the rest of the world. Here, I don't have to be that smiling, good mother who never argues about anything. I can struggle with *me*.

Daring to name or describe an experience is often a risk shied away from. It hurts to give shape to something that lurks at the back of your mind. Naming draws into consciousness and shows up in stark relief the confusion generated by inconsistent interactional possibilities, constrained by social structures.

Oppressive power relations, for example, hold that subordinate groups must *assimilate* into the dominant moral codes and *become* the 'assimilated women' of Washington's (1981) categorization. Through the process of assimilation, women in poverty *absorb* patriarchal definitions and characteristics into their identity structure and *incorporate* such dimensions in a manner which is congruent with masculinist belief systems. Years of socialization into this process mean that adaptation of identity is guided by the consequences of past experiences. The result is that women know men's methods, systems and values more intimately than men need to know patriarchy themselves.

Women's groups, by way of contrast, allow for recognition, those moments of clarity which lead to an identity that incorporates both *being* and *becoming* (Meleis and Rogers, 1987). There is ample space for exploration and integration of new information into existing aspects of identity because women see the importance of self-reflection, coupled with an *evaluation* of the source of oppression. However, a woman will only *adjust* and *reorganize* her existing self-structure when she has assessed the relative salience of the new element (Breakwell, 1986). This involves an appraisal of the meaning and value of existing aspects of identity and an assessment of the relative worth of additions to her personal identity. We must not forget that the assignment of value and worth to a particular dimension of identity is invariably drawn up on a basis established by an unjust and exploitative world. Women's groups can bring into consciousness the realization that all aspects of meaning, value, beliefs and assumptions can be re-examined and overthrown if found wanting or oppressive. There *is* an alternative, more liberating interpretation of events which assigns causes to their rightful place – the social structure. Hence, the process of self-evaluation shifts from concern for largely concrete manifestations of value to focus upon ideologically dictated value. As a result, the content of personal and social identity comes to be valued against different criteria of worth as a woman's awareness develops.

Women's groups therefore challenge the central and salient elements of identity in a way that gives each woman an opportunity to examine the impact of oppressive systems on her psyche. Added to which, the risks of exposing a woman to the threat of new interpretations and explanations of Self-in-society are balanced by collective support.

Identity change

The point at which a woman begins to take hold of her Self and shape it according to her design marks the long, painful and invigorating struggle which change and growth bring in their wake. With the aim of assessing the possibility of and promoting change in women's consciousness and experience, feminist groupwork also recognizes that, paradoxically, identity 'change' is happening all the time. In that sense, it may seem importunate and gratuitous to concentrate on identity development *per se*. However, any change in self-definition and identity springs from a commitment to giving women the *opportunity* to make *informed* choices and decisions. Secondly, we need to make the leap that comes from unconditional women's group support. This is achieved by working with what is *within* women, by not splitting the behavioural and affective, and by conveying the message that each woman is her own resource. Women are scared of taking risks, scared of losing what they have because they fear there will be nothing to replace it. They are unaware of the strengths and capabilities they will discover in themselves if only they had the time to explore.

This section is about changes in that inner world, the facilitation of self-exploration and identity change precipitated by and sustained through the group experience. We have taken a holistic approach to group content and method to demonstrate how personal dimensions are threaded with socio-political explanations. As women recognize paradoxes between received ideas, their personal experience and the differing perceptions of other group members, opportunities for action–reflection–action arise. Group support and confrontation mean that women can refuse to accept *anything* at face value. In this section we want to demonstrate the hidden depths of the links between group and individual identity processes. To achieve this, we will draw out the concepts of reconstruction and re-evaluation which have emerged in relation to our identity themes. Then will come an exploration of the role of self-awareness as a basis for movement away from unconscious repetition of others' interpretations of our behaviour. We will then elaborate strategies which women utilize in coming to terms with the challenges of the group. In doing so we will recognize the central role of self-protection and loss in any identity shift. The key roles of fantasy and creativity in women's developing consciousness will be explored. Finally, we will give credence to the centrality of anger as a creative force in identity change.

Reconstruction and re-evaluation
First of all, we need to reaffirm that the power of the group originates in its strength to reconstrue the situations women find themselves in and to examine the implications these redefinitions have for women's life-styles and identities. We have already outlined in Chapter 3 how information from a wider context is introduced to modify the meaning of group members' positions. How do individual women handle such information in terms of its identity implications?

First, it is highly likely that women will hear explanations for their oppression which they have never heard before. Women's response is initially that of incredulity – that information has been denied to them, that there *is* an alternative way to make sense of such a hostile environment. Such information, when incorporated into existing aspects of identity, is inevitably influenced by and evaluated in accordance with previously internalized value systems. The influence of such values will therefore distort any inferences to be drawn about the Self from this new group experience. When beliefs about identity have been built up through long and arduous socialization they will not be knocked down easily.

Secondly, a feminist perspective gives validation to tentative thoughts which have been there in the past but have got lost in the general malaise. Finding herself in this situation, a woman's cognitions must interact with the process of social influence in the group. Women's group ideology very firmly contradicts the dominant social attribution which places the blame on women's shoulders. The prospect held out by the women's group may be so exhilarating that a woman may leap from self-blame to an external range of factors, which she then uses to explain her difficulties. Responsibility for her oppressed status will be attributed to forces seen as beyond her control, whether this be fate, chance or macro socio-economic processes. Either way, such a quantum leap offers no threat to existing aspects of identity because self-determination is denied. Indeed, if this position is maintained she will feel deskilled and powerless to move out of it.

There are other options which lie somewhere between these two extremes. Out of apprehension, women may devalue the elements of their identity which they see need changing, in an attempt to minimize the threat that change poses. Alternatively, when women feel threatened by a feminist perspective because it challenges a valued existing identity characteristic, they may simply pay more attention to a different element of identity and inflate its value. Hence, the characteristic is no longer allowed to occupy the centre of the identity stage.

This is all made possible because women's groups change the criteria against which women's behaviour and attitudes are judged. The ambivalence of societal responses to caring, for example, stems from the fact that it is judged against financial criteria and inevitably falls short of materialist standards. To counteract this, women's assessment of caring based on welfare and relational criteria is positively connoted throughout all group sessions. The group then has a role in challenging the right of other people to make judgements about a particular aspect of identity. When women were criticized by their menfolk about domestic affairs, all would retort that men could never understand their position because 'they never put themselves in our shoes'.

All these strategies achieve a group atmosphere which gives permission for identity characteristics to be revised, overthrowing the negative values attached by others. It is crucial that this process is undertaken at a woman's own pace in view of the survival mechanisms which she will have evolved over many years and which must not be discarded. The drive towards self-evaluation becomes stronger when women perceive the centrality of a particular opinion, its relevance to their own behaviour, and its importance to other group members.

Self-awareness

We indicated earlier in this chapter that repeated attacks on self-esteem result in the suppression of self-awareness. Women are not given the chance to explore privacy. They exist as public figures in a closed, privatized family environment. As a result, they stop looking outside themselves and lose their powers of awareness. When women *are* given the opportunity to reflect upon their self-knowledge the group reinforces notions of sanity and acceptability, providing a bulwark against the critical, destructive experiences in other areas of life. Experiences that have left their scars – rape, the untimely death of a parent, suicide attempts – become easier to take out and look at.

The process whereby oppression and the hegemonic representation of Self become clearer and more consciously experienced leads to reactions ranging from shock, disbelief, fear and emptiness through to elation and anger. Women are encouraged to acknowledge their pain and the full range of sensations in order to confront and deal with them positively. Concentration on particular senses leads to a fuller appreciation of life rather than the accentuation of how dull and monotonous everything is. Such an emphasis gets away from the distortion of women's caring role and sexuality. Once a woman recognizes the restrictions of her socialization, she is faced with a critical choice, the outcome of which is dependent on the support and responses immediately available. If these are positive, she can use the pivotal moment to turn in a different direction. However, if help is not forthcoming, she will respond with fear to the emptiness in view if she rejects the stereotype and decides that, psychologically, she will stay where she is.

Coming to terms with as much of her Self as she can manage – emotionally, intellectually, physically, spiritually – generates security and confidence. Her perceptive abilities are sharpened, her anger, hopes and desires are reawakened, and she relearns spontaneous expression. Everything stops being bland and third-rate. She begins to generate experiences for herself and discovers that making decisions is possible. Problems are seen more in perspective and each woman learns to cope with situations that demand new strengths of her as they arise.

Acceptance strategies

The encouragement of growth and awareness, helping women to move from stereotyped behaviour towards self-identification, invariably involves pain and distress. *Acceptance* of change can be faltering and may be rejected. At least, if this is the case, a woman will have been given an opportunity to consider a range of options that were previously denied her. Evolution of a self-concept which is drawn from a woman's internal dialogue as well as the process of group questioning is certainly not easy. The group has a responsibility to anticipate some of the setbacks and repercussions which women in transition experience.

Anticipation of a range of consequences of behaviour and attitude change enables a woman to test out or incorporate at least some new information or characteristics into aspects of her identity before trying these out on the world. Am I or could I be adventurous, strong, ambitious and willing to take a stand? What is it that makes me appear cheerful, loyal and apologetic? By anticipating the possible effects of personal development, a woman is not faced with a sudden demand for a disjuncture with her established identity. A sense of continuity can be maintained.

It is clear that women in transition at times *compartmentalize* change by drawing a strict boundary around the addition to the identity structure. The risk of contaminating the rest of their identity is therefore diminished. A group member who successfully organized a few social events continued to behave in the ways she always had outside the group, refusing to modify her view of herself. She was perceived to be well organized and effective in her relations within the group, but at home she felt out of control, in debt, with several loans. At that stage in her life, achievements inside the group were seen only as a drop in the ocean, having a minuscule effect on her self-concept. Compartmentalization can be broken down by incorporating 'home-work' tasks into the life of the group (see Chapter 3), which intertwine inner group experiences with external activities.

Even if a woman feels uneasy with them, her negative self-concepts may prove difficult to jettison, especially when her expressed wants remain unrecognized. Instead of defining herself as resentful or angry, she may therefore acknowledge the precarious nature of her life circumstances, but attribute her reactions to envy (Maguire, 1987) – envy that other women have more privileged life-styles and less tragedy than her own, envy that they can afford a pair of tights and new toys for the children. Recognition of oppression is readily apparent, but she then compromises the implications this holds for her self-perception by suppressing anger in favour of envy. *Compromise* is a strategy which acknowledges the validity of new information but salvages everything possible in terms of continuity of existing aspects of identity. Through the process of attribution, compromise provides a pattern of being and understanding which fudges the true causes of women's disadvantages. It encourages lack of clarity in responses. Aspects of identity continue unscathed, albeit with minor adjustments and modifications, at the expense of *direct* emotional expression.

Common to all these strategies for handling identities in transition is a profound sense of loss and fear, stemming from the strong desire to protect oneself. The hope of a clearer self-definition based in a feminist ideology may be counteracted by the fear of loss of confirmation of existing identity structures. Women can invest tremendous energy in hanging on to the distortions to which their identities have been subjected. What hope do the arguments of the Women's Movement hold for women in poverty? Feminist arguments may be seen as idealistic and unnatural because they fundamentally challenge not only beliefs about the Self in the here and now, but also self-concepts which have crystallized through the legacy of socialization. Many working-class women, brought up with the faculties to survive in harsh circumstances, fear that what they have fought for painfully over the years will be swept away.

Recognition of loss of the Self we know and see in others is also a clear signal that fundamental identity change may be on its way as it symbolizes a woman's adjustment to the learning processes in the group. Hence, a reappraisal of caring, of sexuality, of women's sense of well-being, radically affects our self-esteem, revising the parameters within which identity processes must work. Such changes do not arise the phoenix-like from the ashes; internal dynamics are underpinned by intense emotional responses. Women often described how they would hang on to statements made in the group session, and that these words would reverberate in their heads. Such words would fill them with the warm glow of heightened self-esteem, however transitory this proved to be:

> I left the group last week and I couldn't forget what we talked about, that we don't have to protect men. After all these years, we were saying that we don't have to clean up their emotional nappies all the time. All of what we said thrashed around in my head. It tied me up in knots, it did. And I've seen everything in a different light. All week I've watched women running after men all over the place. They're on to a cushy number that's for sure.
>
> Someone told me last week that they enjoyed my company. I just couldn't believe it, I don't believe it, but I haven't forgotten. It's been with me all the time.

There is no doubt that the rewards of women's group membership in terms of enhanced self-esteem may ultimately outweigh the costs of potential loss of identity characteristics. This process teaches women that their consciousness can be understood directly, rather than filtered through ideologies or stereotypes created by men. They are not passive victims; they are agents, actors, creators of culture and their own identities.

Fantasy and creativity

The unleashing of identity change clearly demonstrates that women can be strategists and performers in relation to the Self. We have mentioned that the process of reconstruction and re-evaluation is painful as well as potentially liberating. During our involvement with women's groups it became clear that a way of easing pain and discomfort is to open up the fantasy and creativity that is lying dormant within women. The discrepancy that exists between the options that society offers to women in poverty and the potential that they find within themselves, as Meyer Spacks (1978) has said, leads women frequently to have complex inner lives of fantasy. Fantasy and creativity are political processes because they provide hope for a present and future defined by women, giving a vision of unity and direction to many working-class women's existence.

In this section, we will build upon the elements of fantasy and creativity identified in Chapter 3, but our focus will be on their links with and effect on personal identity change and growth. Fundamental to this is the creation of a group philosophy which brings out the acceptability of fantasy and its essential role in personal and group development. Fantasies show us a path away from what we are supposed to be, towards what we could be. The expression of our desires breaks down the internalized cycle of oppressive thoughts where we have to be reasonable and rational. Women know a great deal about creation. Group members with children all recognized the hope which comes with childbirth. However, women stop creating themselves. Internalized oppression defines the limits of success and instils a fear of stepping out of line.

In the course of fantasy work, many women alluded to their 'real' and 'unreal' Selves. These were used to explain behaviour which they could not attribute to their abiding self-conception:

> I wasn't myself when I lost my temper yesterday.
> I don't know what came over me when I made that complaint.

Women often decide that their behaviour in these instances is so much at variance with their usual self-image that it must be an aberration. A false separation of 'real' and 'unreal' is created. The 'unreal Self' can accommodate the mix of coping and acceptance strategies discussed earlier, especially those relating to compartmentalization. By defining the 'imaginary Self' as freakish, women fall prey to hierarchical ways of thinking which split humanity and the social world into the false opposites of 'reality' (seen as superior) and 'fantasy' (seen as inferior). Women's groups, however, act as a buffer against such positivism by challenging the divide and rule mentality.

The awakening of creative potential stimulates ideas not only of what we might become, but also of what we are afraid of becoming. Even when these fears are dissipated, there is often a reluctance to act upon the conclusions reached. An additional push to overcome such barriers can be found by recognizing anew the centrality of *play* in the development of responsiveness and emotionality (see Chapter 3). Patriarchy has built a false divide between play and work, childhood and adulthood (Thorne, 1987), reality and fantasy, all of which have major implications for women's identity change:

1 There is an imperative to remember, validate and re-evaluate childhood experiences in recognition of the powerful influence of childhood on the adult woman.
2 Women can recognize anew the child in Self as a means of heightening self-expression and personal identity development.
3 Learning to confront the child in Self faces women who are mothers with jealousy of their own children as the prescriptions on adult behaviour and socialization are fully discerned.

Discovering the hidden child   Part of the ability to break down barriers between real Self and imaginary Self entails an acceptance of the influence of childhood experiences on group members' current behaviour, attitudes and values. The aspects of Self which we choose to hide or have submerged can often be traced to childhood scars. Guided fantasy about childhood invokes memories of forgotten events, feelings, images which can inform our current cyclical responses. Buried within these memories are powerful expectations and prescriptions on behaviour, symbolized most forcefully through the splitting of children into 'good' and 'bad'. Group members recognized very quickly that they were either known as 'the naughty child' or 'the quiet, good one', and the self-fulfilment of these messages echoed through to the present day.

The child in Self   When we are in a position to respond to bitter-sweet memories, the child within us can speak out, recognizing our desires, and can break down 'I should' into 'I want'. Nevertheless, 'should', originating in the distortions as well as the insights of memory, may suffuse the voice of the child within, cloud our wants, and pose obstacles to seeing children clearly. We may not care to value these messages because the hierarchy of parent to child is deeply ingrained. Breaking this down involves challenging notions of linear human development.

Childhood and mothers   The steps which women take to unlock the child in Self can give rise to a whole series of complex responses for those who are mothers. Women have to come to terms with their own childhoods at the same time as they adjust to the ideological and actual connections between themselves and their children. The parallel between children and women is ever present. Frequently women's group members were referred to as infantile by partners, relatives or professionals. It is no small wonder that given the distorting effects of such statements, women yet again turn to their children to define themselves.

The ideological construction that mother and child exist in an isolated dyad was lived out by some members, who found it extremely difficult and painful to separate themselves from their children during group sessions: 'I feel guilty that my child's in the crèche.' Whilst undermining any basis for solidarity between them, any disagreements about mothering stemmed from a common root cause that to a greater or lesser extent all group members felt jealous of their own children. Socialization, the prescriptions on adult behaviour, and the pressures of perfect mothering led women at times to feel enormous pangs of envy in spite of the dreams they had for their own children's future. Many women could not admit to themselves that envy played a part in these relationships. Yet such responses are totally justified and admissible because they provide us with clues about the range of losses which women encounter.

To recapitulate, in this section we have argued that identity change and the process of self-discovery entail constant re-evaluation and reconstruction. Throughout this process, women will check back, reappraising attitudes they have held towards themselves and tracing these to the various roles they fulfil. Certain key factors emerge through this growth:

1 that definition of Self comes from other people and it becomes almost impossible to separate out what is personal thought from what others have instilled;
2 that breaking down women's self-effacement and understatement of achievements has a dramatic effect on personal development;
3 that personal development involves naming, giving ourselves a description. This includes a recognition of the fluid nature of identity change, and the creation of personal space which can prevent catastrophizing responses;
4 that learning to redefine the Self and to have faith and confidence in our abilities is a painful and lengthy process which does not necessarily happen in a linear fashion. Acceptance of change involves anticipation of events, compartmentalization and compromise in order to understand our consciousness;

5   that using women's creativity not only directs our potential, but also enriches our responsiveness, increasing the depths of our emotionality and pushing our energy in positive directions.

We have also indicated how identity change has repercussions which we may want to avoid. Being visible can be dangerous, and yet invisibility eats away at our soul. In order for a woman to recognize herself as an autonomous, self-actualizing person, she has to *act* upon the changes she can see panning out in front of her. Learning to diminish the influence and intensity of guilt is crucial to this process but, equally, there is a need to recognize anger as a motivating force. In the final part of this chapter, anger will rip through the pages as we conclude our examination of identity and its manifestations.

Identity and action: Anger as a motivating force

> I've got this scream inside of me but I can't let it out. The walls of the house would burst open and the neighbours would hear. It's stuck in my throat and I can't breathe.

As women begin to elaborate explanations for events and assign causes which do not involve self-blame, as they come to see the ways in which spontaneity and simplicity in enjoyment have been distorted and denied, then they inevitably get in touch with an affective state which is given a bad press in white Western culture – anger. Women feel angry out of disappointment and betrayal. Anger over giving more than they receive. Anger at the inability to move away from poverty and violence. Anger at the lack of recognition, respect and thoughtfulness they receive. Anger over the loss of happiness that they hoped for. In this society there is a prevailing cultural disapproval of women's anger; it is shunned and maligned. Yet direct anger is an energy force which gives women the strength to sustain changes in their lives. Sen (1984) has urged that gender inequalities should be discussed with 'a bit more rage, a bit more passion, a bit more anger'. Indeed, anger has become a crucial part of feminist analysis. Women have every right to be angry about negligence, and this anger provides us with the commitment to ensure that women can both *be* and *become*.

Action is the social expression of identity. How we act gives others a clue to our identity and, in a sense, identity change will only be crystallized when it is followed by action. Miller (1983a) has stressed repeatedly that there are considerable constraints on the expression of women's anger, and that anger has been encouraged differentially in men and women. At the same time – and this is the distressing paradox – women occupy a subordinate position which constantly generates anger. Any incident of oppression precipitates a range of emotions in women, particularly anger, but these reactions are simultaneously dismissed or pathologized. In the face of punishment, anger is suppressed. Because women's anger is seen as such a threat to the dominant order, its expression provides a powerful recognition of discomfort and the motivation for action. Women's self-esteem can be strengthened when we learn to use an *interactional* expression of anger, rather than the distorting effects of *hierarchical* anger.

Equating anger with aggression   Group members adhered to andro-centric definitions of anger, in that it was equated with aggression. On the occasions when women had witnessed hierarchical aggression, it was men who were the perpetrators – being violent to each other or to women and children. Group members had often tried using the same violent tactics that had been directed against them but, although these had provided short-term relief, little was achieved in the long term. Also, working-class cultural expectations were such that women had 'slanging matches' with neighbours and had sometimes been involved in fights; open quarrels were seen as legitimate. These experiences provided no context in which women could make a direct, honest response and declare how they themselves had been hurt. This is endorsed by the occasions when women had subverted their immediate angry responses by shouting at their children, who themselves occupy subordinate positions. 'Taking it out on the kids' had become a habitual response for handling the anger-evoking conditions of their lives. 'Taking it out on myself' through self-harm or self-criticism were other forms of misdirected anger. Women had found no role models for the constructive use of anger. When they examined important female figures from their own past, they discovered that relatives who were labelled 'angry' (mothers, grandmothers) were in heterosexual relationships in which male partners were considered to be 'under the thumb'. One woman described her mother as a 'good match for my Dad – they just quarrelled all the time'.

Exaggerated perceptions of anger   Miller (1983a) has declared that to the external world any anger is too much anger in women. When asked to talk about 'What I feel in my body when I'm angry', many women described a bottomless well of anger they were afraid to tap. There were descriptions of 'fear of blowing the lid off', 'burning explosion', 'something inside me trying to break out'. The heart thumps, blood pumps around the body, the face goes hot, the throat feels tense and dry, we shake, feel tight across the chest, neck, shoulders, but these sensations are experienced as out of our control. The risk of expressing this anger is great. We wait too long before we act on such a reaction, to the extent that the anger appears exaggerated or we continually apologize and negate our actions. We leap in and shout, end up feeling embarrassed, weep and get ourselves labelled. We do nothing but reinforce the view of ourselves that we are striving to change. This fear that anger will 'leak out' invariably stems from perceptions of anger we have picked up from childhood, where its expression is labelled as immature and dismissed as 'temper tantrums'. In this way, a child's expressive reactivity is equated with naughtiness and wilful behaviour.

Anger does not achieve anything   Anger is believed to be a dangerous, destructive emotion. It is unacceptable, certainly not tolerated by others, and for a great many women expression of anger ends in tears which are experienced as a sign of defeat and 'not coping'. What stops women being angry is a grave concern about the repercussions. Some group members had feedback from others, especially men, that they were frightening and freakish when angry and should 'calm down'. Women fear being labelled aggressive, bitchy, castrating, and hard if they act in accordance with what they suspect *might* be their true nature. The key question 'What am I going to lose?' reverberates around women's heads. Feeling so undermined by others' responses means that women think they will be rejected because the angry response will be *so* horrific. One woman had dreams about murdering her ex-husband by stabbing him repeatedly in the chest. It was difficult enough for her to discuss this dream in the group because she firmly believed people would hate her for it. Being liked is linked so inextricably to the identity themes of caring, well-being and sexuality to which we referred earlier in this chapter. In this cultural and historical epoch there is no assurance that we will be well cared for if we express anger directly. Hence, as Miller (1983a) rightly says, we have an inability to conceive of being caring *simultaneously* with the need for and right to express open anger.

Women have no cause to be angry   Current cultural exigencies mean that the inhibition of women's anger strongly affects our psychological processes. There are numerous ways in which this takes effect:

1   Women often do not *recognize* when they are angry (see p. 136 for a discussion of the importance of recognition in identity). They may behave inconsistently in the face of cultural and interpersonal forces which have stimulated anger. They may live vicariously in the face of instances of maltreatment and systematic subjugation of their needs.

2   If they do not recognize an affective reaction, it may be subsumed under the less stigmatizing heading of envy.

3 Women do not know *how* to be angry.

If there is no cause for anger, then when it happens we can blame anger *itself* for the damaging effects which result rather than societal prescriptions on behaviour.

In the face of such powerful negations of an anger rooted in the mechanisms of patriarchy, what hope is there that women's groups can offer a challenge to this? It is imperative for feminists to confront the brutal misogyny which produces such a warped perception of anger. Feminist definitions of anger propel us into a different, more liberating arena. Let us use Dickson (1982) as a starting point. She moves beyond the superficial layers of resentment and frustration to a deep layer of anger which contains a powerful source of energy. She describes this 'root anger' as a life force which enables us to move forward, giving us a purpose and pushing us to make changes in our lives. It involves direct self-expression, provides the impetus for surviving crises, and encourages us to be creative.

We can help each other to recognize, name and then express angry responses. Handling our own and each other's anger undermines many of our relationships with other women. Indeed, women often believed that if they just said they recognized what they had to do, everything would be all right. The necessity to protect oneself is a reaction which we have mentioned before. It has nothing to do with cowardice, but everything to do with fear. The group is therefore an ideal forum in which to explore fears about anger and its origins, because we need the human resources which support our attempts to be readily available. Anger must be used constructively in the group so that disapproval and dissatisfaction can be expressed without alienating the person whose help is needed.

The positive power of anger becomes contagious and one way of generating this is through role play (see Chapter 3). Role play means that anger can be acknowledged and expressed to some extent before an event takes place. There is no need to fear that the person towards whom you have role-played anger will disappear. The message is to show strength and persistence, but give the other person credit for their ability to rectify the situation. Giving women the chance to sort out their angry feelings allows them to take control of their anger and not to be frightened by the intensity of their responses. They can learn how to use their emotional energy constructively. It can become easier for women to express 'hateful' thoughts and to express ambivalence towards Self – hating and loving the Self at the same time. Women can make statements such as 'I hate my children and would be quite happy not to see them for a while', knowing that they will not be rejected and that the boundaries of the group will remain.

Opportunities to overcome the enormous hurdles surrounding the expression of root anger need to be structured into group sessions. One example is to ask group members to complete the sentence 'I get angry when . . .' (see Chapter 3 on sentence completion exercises) and to read out their responses in a way that demonstrates their anger. Once women begin to catalogue not only the incidents which precipitate their anger, but also the cumulative effect of oppression in which anger has been denied, the power of collective fury takes hold. As each woman shouts out, yells, expresses her statements in whichever way feels right, the intensity increases to moving proportions and the bond between women takes on a profound dimension. There is enormous safety to be found in such knowledge and emotional connection.

None of this process is easy and there are times when women resist, pushing themselves as far away from all this as possible. Learning to express anger means throwing off the chains of suppression and the forces which encourage us to keep our heads down. Many women struggled furiously with direct anger exercises, shouting indignantly, 'I can't do it, I just can't do it.' With verbal and physical encouragement (stroking women's backs, just *being* near), women do overcome these enormous barriers and *do* end up punching and hitting cushions, whilst releasing anger about interpersonal and cultural restrictions. During such exercises, women attack injustice directly, and in the process destroy such messages as always being 'naughty' or the 'tomboy' of childhood.

The enormous relief and sense of exhilaration which follow remain with us far beyond the group session, and the pay-offs are magnified as the weeks go by. It may lead a woman to take direct action within her own life, leaving a relationship, taking up education again. Frequently, this anger may be expressed towards those in authority and in relation to other people's lives. She may feel that she is unworthy of her own campaigning zeal. Nevertheless, the capacity to be angry for ourselves is achievable. The passion, the rage, the anger which Sen (1984) encourages us to recognize become a reality: 'I've never seen women so determined. We've found a way to fight.'

This chapter has addressed a whole range of accumulated inequalities which women bring to group sessions and which relate to their struggle with personal identity. As women find themselves in uncharted territory, they grapple with the challenge of raising questions, finding new answers, new patterns of relating in a milieu which does everything to invalidate their experiences. Through this journey, we have mapped out the centrality of self-definition to women's self-esteem, distinctiveness and sense of continuity in the world. Learning to exercise control and express a whole range of emotions can mobilize identity change to the extent that women feel much more at ease in putting themselves centre stage. The process of self-actualization can seem so daunting and yet the very act of taking risks, testing out new behaviours and responses, can face women with a source of support hitherto unimagined, namely each other. Their survival tactics are positively connoted, their coping strategies are recognized as a source of strength, and they become uplifted by each other's individuality.

6
Making Connections:
The Broader Context

Once group members begin to testify with alacrity to similarities in their inner worlds and experiences of outer events, each woman can begin to draw out the contours of her Self through a process of *inclusion* in group processes, rather than *exclusion*. This group enquiry is not distant from women's daily experiences and comprehension, but is rooted in them and becomes an energizing exercise. In this chapter our reference point shifts to the wider context, away from the internal processes of individual and group functioning to the impact of group energy on the surrounding socio-political environment. It would be foolish to suppose that women's social identity operates in isolation from the complex processes to which we have referred in previous chapters. Individual power, stemming from a positive attitude towards Self, precipitates collectivity. Collective action which involves sub-limation of the Self becomes a training in conformity in the name of a sense of belonging. The last thing a women's group wants to do is provide yet another source of social pressure for women, in which the words may be different but the song remains the same. To that end, this chapter provides a discussion of some of the dilemmas of collective change, the effects on the community, and on workers.

Women facing a multiplicity of caring tasks cannot hope on their own to achieve lasting change. It may be possible to make gains within the context of personal life, gains which objectively appear small, such as a concession not to cook a meal on a particular day, but which have great significance for the woman concerned. For us, the potential for group change and collective action are much greater. Collectivity gives women the reinforcement needed to bring about a change in social identity, on both the private and the public frontiers.

By looking at the connections between group development and social identity change, the structural complexities of the external group context emerge. We will concentrate on the role of damage limitation in feminist groupwork, because there are dangers in exposing women to greater risks in their daily lives and the group has a responsibility for dealing with this. Secondly, we will examine the multidimensional nature of the role of women as workers, who, as the group moves into collective action, are faced with the dilemma of maintaining a professional role and solidarity with the group. Thirdly, we will explore the theme of loss and endings in relation to worker withdrawal from the group, as well as the concomitant notions of hope and strength which emerge when women take over responsibility. Finally, we will summarize and evaluate the central tenets of feminist groupwork, its principles and processes. By reflecting upon and rehearsing the elements we have pursued, we hope to present foundations for the extension and development of this approach.

Social identity, change and the social context

Group development and impact on the community

It is impossible for a group member to know her Self more clearly until she tentatively rehearses new situations outside the group, thus incorporating change into her daily life. No matter how drastic the change in identity, there are dramatic consequences for women who choose to exorcize social myths and reject socially ascribed roles. The affirmation of social identity is indeed much more difficult. The continuity of the group may provide strength to deal with other aspects of identity which are facing ridicule and challenge in the outside world. This clash between salient cultural values of the community and the social values of the group will form the centre of our analysis.

In terms of the relationship between women's groups and surrounding family, friends, community groups, professionals and neighbourhood contacts (see Figure 6), there is no doubt that women's groups are continually in the spotlight and subjected to scrutiny. Women's groups represent a threat to the established order. There are always people in the community who will jump at any sign of failure and help the group on its way to collapse. From group members' point of view, women's cognitions and emotionality are such that it is impossible to split the group off from family, personal and professional lives. Paradoxically, group members' knowledge that they are under scrutiny binds them together against the enemy without. In addition, the development of a strong personal and social identity based in the group provides a challenge to external reality. Indeed, women who strongly identified with the group assumed a politically targeted identity and were able to confront their oppression.

Flowing from the group's recognition and affirmation of individuality, members need to reinforce the diverse ways in which transitions in their social identity occur. Many women feel isolated and shocked when they perceive the normative world-view for what it is, and they reassess social organizations and alter behaviour (see Chapter 5). Whether the larger society is actively hostile or merely unsupportive and indifferent to involvement in the women's group, there is no

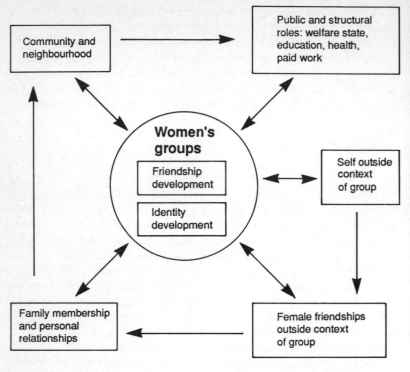

Figure 6   *The impact of group change on private and public relationships*

greater call for group solidarity and sharing than at this point. Whatever the degree of group strength, there still remains the crucial issue of how the women's group relates to the total community. Responding to the tension arising from a personal identity and world-view which society avoids acknowledging or incorporating is a matter of utmost importance.

  Whatever the degree of personal identity change, an unmapped area exists between the internal workings of the group and the pursuit of its principles in a woman's daily life. Out of the expression of doubts and the decision-making of group sessions comes action, and ultimately the consequences of action. Responding to the interplay between societal systems and women's group experience generates a series of choices for group members, and these run in parallel to the personal coping strategies to which we referred in Chapter 5:

  (a) anticipation;
  (b) holding inconsistencies;
  (c) the centrality of dialogue;
  (d) politicization.

Anticipation The group can act as a springboard and safety net for the testing out of ideas, newly learnt behaviours and attitudes. The very fact that a woman can anticipate and rehearse changes in her behaviour within group sessions (see Chapter 3) means that social identity change can be unveiled to the world at large from a background of validation and encouragement. Taking pride and pleasure in the group's strength does not mean that members disregard the distortions of reality within which they have to live, but that at least there is a source of replenishment if confrontation occurs.

Though forced to act as links within the community, women often do not feel part of a neighbourhood (see Chapter 2). The group therefore needs to remain the sounding board for any reappraisals, as a way of providing consistency in the relationships within and outside the group. This process is *cyclical* in two senses. First, reassurance, validation and criticism will be sought and offered within the group (see Chapter 3). Secondly, a particular strategy a woman may have tested out and found worthwhile in a previously problematic situation could be used again, but perhaps she is not aware of it being appropriate in this instance. Here, her co-participants can remind her of her success and prompt her to try it again. She may need immediate support from other group members, perhaps someone going with her to face a difficult situation, or being around immediately after the event. This is a structure that should be available to all participants.

The mind thus opens up to a whole range of possibilities. A woman may become aware of her ability to influence the sphere of family and relationships. In so doing she comes to recognize the ever-shifting patterns that connect her to the relationships within which she exists and the community of which she is a member. She can identify *herself* as one of those links.

Holding inconsistencies Members' behaviour within and outside the group demonstrates that many working-class women do hold inconsistent attitudes, or attitudes which contradict behaviour. The fact that the philosophy and behaviours of women's groups may be incompatible with everything else in women's lives is something which group members *do* live with. Indeed, we have outlined repeatedly the ways in which contradiction and flexibility are part and parcel of women's identities (see Chapter 5), and are a motivating force to action. Women may become *aware* of the part they play in unconsciously perpetuating the treadmill of existence and the sense of the daily round but may decide not to *act* on that knowledge in the social arena. To compartmentalize in this way removes any facility for recognition of inconsistencies. Hence, the world becomes both alien and familiar.

The effects of being a member of competing self-help groups with disparate ideologies have been explored by Lieberman and Bond (1978) in their review of outcome measures in self-help groups. They found lower levels of disruptive dissonance amongst women attending both consciousness-raising and traditional psychotherapy groups than had previously been expected. Women who attended both groups experienced an increase in self-esteem and a decrease in targeted problems, which surprised the researchers. Obviously, the surprise is more a reflection of psychology's need for order than it is of women's abilities to move between diverse groups with ever-changing goals and values.

The centrality of dialogue   Women can use group solidarity as a source of social influence. Openness to dialogue with those outside the group is essential, even if this involves, as Huws (1982) notes, the risk of having one's own mind changed and not changing someone else's. Having influence as a group provides a role model for other women and is a direct method of rocking the boat without subverting individual or group identity in the process.

Politicization   Tackling issues outside the confines of the group is a matter of considerable weight. It can occur only when a woman generalizes from her membership of the group to an appraisal of her role in other social groups, measuring her experiences in terms of oppression, discrimination and violence. Then comes the realization that she is part and parcel of a continual state of socio-political evolution. Her fear of the unknown, her realization of the enormity of the task at hand and her feelings of potential empowerment simultaneously become greater. This is the essence of politicization harnessed by solidarity. It transcends mere clannishness because its whole is greater than all its parts.

Women surprise themselves when they have an impact on the bureaucratic decision-making process by confronting and challenging agencies which attempt to control their lives. They may demand a supervised crossing place for their school-age children, a more efficient recall system for cervical smears, more sympathetic pregnancy or abortion counselling, or council action on substandard housing. The impetus necessary to carry through such ideas and take responsibility for different elements of organization emerges out of the group's commitment to sharing. A group member can take over where another woman leaves off. Comfort is provided in the face of resistance and disappointment; delighted support emerges in moments of success.

What is significant about these options is that they reflect a holistic approach to collective practice in that the relative salience of particular choices for each group member and for the group as a whole will fluctuate. In terms of the relationship between the group and its social context, if we turn to Figure 6 we can see that there are fluctuations in the significance of any one set of relationships for any individual woman. This mirrors the movement in relationships within the group. The very fact that women's groups exist in an ambiguous, conflictual and competitive environment means that social identity can allow for the expression of inconsistencies and doubt.

We are demonstrating here that each woman functions within her own personal space and that at times there may be little movement within this. Growth may be linear ('progress' as charted by herself), or cyclical ('progress' that takes place in relation to specific events, and that appears to diminish once these have passed). Each woman exists within her personal 'space bubble' through the context of the group and the wider relationships of family, community and state (Figure 6). A growing awareness of these relationships, their complexity and interplay, can initially engender feelings of powerlessness. Conversely, the impetus for change based in personal frustration, commitment, anger and need can generate knowledge of the means whereby power can be gained and taken.

The problematic nature of social change and action

There are dangers of a disjunction developing between the potential for fulfilment and the structural inequalities by which women are surrounded. When women return to their daily lives they are thrown back on to their own resources and therefore need to act as instruments of both resistance and acceptance. On the one hand, the development of a collective approach means that women end up believing that they *can* do something about their situation, that they *can* take responsibility for action rather than resignedly accepting circumstances as they are. On the other hand, social action and change are set against negative forces represented by any of the groups in Figure 6. We cannot neglect the influence of faltering community services, social, economic and environmental, which squeeze the quality of life of working-class women in similar circumstances to group members. Potential and growth can thus prove contradictory and change can occur in many different directions simultaneously.

The moment change begins to be measured against any absolute, whether within women's personal lives or within the community, the likelihood of failure being seen to have occurred is greatly increased. Women set themselves standards that take into account other people's views and expectations. Their wishes for improvements within their own community are also likely to be measured against information they get about what happens elsewhere. These processes of social influence which impinge upon group activities will be our reference point now.

In this section our realm of enquiry will be the constellation of factors which influences women's decision-making in respect of social change in the personal and professional spheres. The implications of personal and social change whilst occupying a position of economic and social dependence are great. Nevertheless, group members rebelled against social constraints because they had nothing to lose by challenging situations which generated their anger.

The public sphere of influence   Group action in the social arena exposes women to the risk of assimilation into dominant social belief systems as a result of the tight hold of power differentials. To be effective in controlling social change the group has to talk through strategies for action, develop tactics and views which are presented steadfastly and with unanimity. With this comes an understanding of the purpose of organizations, how they develop and the connections between them. By so doing, the group upsets the established norms and rules of communication and creates an imbalance in the smooth functioning of the social system. At the same time, it is important that women's groups reach out to other groups which share common aims and philosophy, in order to respond to solidarity. Identification with other groups increases the likelihood of influencing the environment. For instance, over a period of time the rural group built up a network of relationships with other women's groups in the area, some of which were issue-based, concentrating on health, whilst others had a campaigning focus. This network enabled group members to revise their perceptions of the relative power of sections of the population, to increase their reference points and sources of validation. Widening horizons proved to be an especially significant part of social change because it enabled the groups to share information, skills and talents and, most important, to use each other as role models. The excitement of sharing news about community matters meant that group members' achievements were measured against those of other women who had the same ideological base. What this highlights is that women are able to take on significant roles as decision-makers *in spite of* the severe limitations imposed on them by the environment.

What are the constraints women encounter and ingeniously surmount? How do they cope with the distress associated with being a group member? The overwhelming constraint stems from a public sphere which can only handle challenges to its structure and value base by interpreting women's group action as deviant. Innovations and originality are not seen as expressions of 'positive behaviour' but as the idiosyncrasies of a few individuals who can be seen as 'over the top' and dismissed. The social conflict which women's groups generate does not necessarily have immediate effects because it challenges deeply held values of dominant systems. The public sphere may respond by retrenchment, rigidity and ridicule of group practices in an attempt to subvert its influence and assimilate the group into the mainstream flow. However, one of the women's group's main tactics is to avoid assimilation (see Chapter 5) and integration by maintaining an *adaptability* to the social forces external to the group. Women therefore have an active role to play in the dynamic relationship of opposition or co-operation with public relationships outside the group.

There are specific ways in which this dynamism takes effect for women's groups located in areas of poverty and deprivation. First, it has been noted repeatedly on the community work front that women have been conspicuous in issue-based community action (Curno et al., 1982; Mayo, 1977) and that working-class women respond to problems that affect them *directly*, as opposed to the use of middle-class abstract ideals of self-fulfilment (R. Davis, 1988; Reinharz, 1983). The rider to this is that women are more likely to become activists *on behalf of others* facing similar problems (Mayo, 1977). Women's group knowledge grows out of members' direct experience of local issues. Their action in the community is based on *direct* and *honest* communication which cocks a snook at the more sophisticated, manipulative and devious forms of white, middle-class, liberal discourse.

Secondly, the motivation for social change is that women are fighting *for other women*, and this proves to be a major turning point for group members who habitually act on behalf of families and children. Women in poverty have no legitimate socially granted power to determine their own fate economically, socially or politically. Yet through membership of the group, women can bring about anything that is within their grasp by placing each other centre stage.

We will use a few examples to illustrate the discovery of the skills to influence a course of events. One group participant, for instance, dissatisfied with the work her solicitor was doing in relation to the access arrangements for her son to his father, appeared at the lawyer's office without an appointment and refused to leave until matters had been organized to her satisfaction, berating the lawyer all the time. The solicitor herself phoned one of the group co-workers, as she was aware of the existence and nature of the group, to explain that although she appreciated the need for increased self-assertion, she herself had a busy practice to deal with and could not respond instantly to each demand for action.

A further example of dealing with 'public' matters is that of one participant who was faced with eviction for rent arrears. She knew that the council officers were at fault and that her entitlement to housing benefit had not been sorted out. She demanded legal representation and a proper check of the records, including her claim form, in an assertive manner. She met considerable resistance but remained undaunted, and ultimately was proved correct. Although she was scared throughout this experience, she was carried through it by an inalienable knowledge of being right. When recounting the episode in a group session, she said that the strength and self-confidence gained from attending the group had given her the faith in herself that she had needed to survive. Had such an experience happened earlier, she would not have had the confidence or courage to contradict what was being said. Her conviction of the accuracy of her interpretation of events would have begun to waver in the face of opposition.

Over time, groups can establish an information bank of strategies for handling such public relationships and can create a catalogue of incidents where women have stood their ground. For example:

- dealing with the general practitioner who is persistently cagey about a suspected chronic illness;
- dealing with the police officer who comes to investigate a burgled meter and implies strongly that the burglary is home-grown;
- dealing with the headteacher who refuses to accept that your child is being intimidated for having one parent;
- dealing with post office staff who refuse payments on the grounds that the name on the benefit book is wrong;
- dealing with council engineers who take days to come to do repairs;
- dealing with housing officials who seem unwilling to accept the need for a move;
- dealing with probation officers who put little credence in statements about ending a relationship;
- dealing with engineers who seem unprepared to accept that the owner of a machine knows what she is talking about.

The common link between all these examples is that women learn to take responsibility for their own actions, making statements in such a way that the other person realizes their seriousness. Beginning a sentence with 'I' locates the power and responsibility and does not immediately suggest criticism. Women stop saying, 'You haven't done this job properly'; 'You said you would come at 10a.m.'; 'You haven't given me enough money'. Instead, to say 'I am unhappy with this piece of work'; 'I was expecting you earlier than this'; 'I understood that I was entitled to more', still gives the other person a chance and shows that 'I' value 'myself' as a person with some importance. All group members began to recognize the centrality of the right to *ask*. It takes courage to achieve this. Women have the undeniable right to question what has previously been taken for granted.

The private sphere of influence   Just as public institutions can react to women's group practices with retrenchment and negativism, so too the responses of family, friends and relatives can be equally damaging in intent. On the personal level, women enter into areas of great risk when they attempt to effect change within more intimate areas of their lives. What happens to women's family life when they become involved in the group? In terms of heterosexual relationships, how successful are group members in pressing their demands and how do men react to this assault on their integrity? What are the implications for women's friendships and how do lesbian women handle the choice to come out, made as a result of group influence?

Women often make wide-reaching demands and, whatever the action in which they get involved, it always modifies, sometimes transforms, personal relationships at home. When women are in a struggle with other women that is not just for themselves, they are prepared to take on the menfolk in a way they would not otherwise do. These changing relationships and the emotional effects always show up in women's actions. Even though there are benefits on a long-term basis, in the short-term it costs women a great deal to shift their priorities. The anxiety, doubt and determination involved are carried by women into sessions; they add to the feelings expressed there and also account for the spasmodic nature of women's struggle. Women's involvement in activity for themselves means that they become the sort of women that men do not like because they are solving problems themselves rather than waiting until the men come home.

In Chapter 4 when we discussed the role of friendship development amongst women, we referred to the difficulty men have in listening to and respecting women's talk, let alone women's conversations with each other. The intransigence of male family members stems from their disbelief that group members refuse to define the value of what they are doing in terms of its relationship to men. Some men became very hurt and defensive that individual male differences were getting lost in over-generalization. They protested that they were different, that the group was finding them guilty of sexism and heterosexism on the basis of spurious evidence. In all of this, the underlying query that lurks at the back of men's minds is: 'What can women be doing with each other that is really constructive?' In its extreme form, this query leads to the tactic of *avoidance*, in which male partners pretend that the threat does not exist, and attempt to control women through the conspiracy of silence. One participant recounted how her cohabitee had forbidden her to discuss the activities of the women's group: 'I don't want you to talk about it in this house.' Men find it extremely difficult to understand that the women's group priority is to learn about ourselves.

There is a sense in which women's low expectations in some heterosexual relationships serve to minimize risk anyway. The struggle against the inertia that dogs their efforts to reject habitual patterns of male–female relations means that many women fall back upon the old cop-out: 'Why should I be an adult when I can get away with being a child?' On these occasions, the struggles are personal because it is hard to fight any enemy that influences your thoughts. Significantly, women who instigated changes in heterosexual relationships experienced considerable levels of anxiety because they feared the loss of rewards which go with sex-role behaviours. One woman secured her partner's agreement and participation in housework by going on 'strike' and only cooking meals for herself and the children. She found that she had anxiety attacks when the time came for him to do his share. She realized that having stepped out of sex-role behaviours, she feared the loss of benefits involved. The realization of what she was feeling and why made her more angry at first, as she felt trapped by her intellectual rejection of a belief system that she could not disengage from emotionally. The reasons for her ambivalence about changing the relationship also lay in her expressed uncertainty about her achievement: 'Could I have done it without him?' This reflects not only a distrust of her own power and a fear of change, but also a loss of a certain degree of power inside the prison.

What is significant about the demands that were met with a reluctant, but ultimately favourable, reception is that women found they could be assertive one day and nurturing the next and that this was a measure of their individuality, not manipulation or deviousness. The courage of women's convictions also brought disappointments, however, in that fundamentally men did not *understand* women's emotionality. They did not have a conception of what women were trying to talk about with them.

There were many occasions when women were faced with outright conflict because they dared to challenge accepted norms. Changes which *did* seriously threaten male dominance or which affected the direct material interests of the family were fought vigorously, sometimes by invoking the power of the state in the guise of welfare agencies. Family members felt a compulsion to act against the requirements and pressures of the women's group. This entailed refusing to do what the group member wished or even doing the opposite in a given situation. It did not take long before familiar expressions emerged to describe group members' activities – 'bloody-mindedness'; 'trouble-seeking'; 'pigheaded'; 'getting too much will-power'; 'too wilful for your own good'. Such antagonism represents a hedge against the despair which patriarchy experiences when faced with an assertive group of women. Men refuse to change because they do not see the need for it.

Men's rejection and refusals can become generalized and vicious, expressed through indignation, derision or outright hostility. With men who did not confer much on women by way of life value, when women tried to act more independently they were punished for it. One male partner eventually refused to allow his wife to go to group sessions, and to be certain that she was aware of the lengths to which he was prepared to go, he locked her in the house during women's group mornings, hit her, and refused to give her money. Through her own ingenuity and courage, she did manage to attend sessions on a sporadic basis by climbing out of the kitchen window. However, she felt on tenterhooks during the sessions as she had to be home by a certain time to avoid his wrath if he was to discover her escape plan.

The power of oppression was felt by one group member whose growing self-awareness and determination led her to enrol for 'A' level courses at the local college. Her strength was far-reaching in that she managed her studies in between holding down two jobs as a factory worker and serving behind a bar. As a lone parent with two young school-age children, her responsibilities weighed heavily. When her ex-husband discovered that she was pursuing her education he began to follow her to college, wait outside the gates and generally harass her. She then received a visit from a child protection worker, who was responding to an anonymous call that she was neglecting her children and leaving them unattended whilst she engaged in her own 'selfish' pursuits. Whilst these allegations were ill-founded, the incident demonstrates that some men will flex muscles of repression, portraying women as anti-social and stubborn, in order to hang on to their own rigidities. Such remorseless protection of the status quo causes the entrenchment of their identity.

Some group members took a radical approach to the repressive measures meted out to them by leaving damaging relationships. They had the courage to walk out of the door, taking their children with them and seeking temporary refuge until their own accommodation could be guaranteed. There were also instances where, pushed beyond all limits of endurance, women did literally hit back, much to the shock and amazement of their partners who for once, getting the tiniest taste of their own medicine, would stop being so violent for a while.

When repressive measures fail, a final resort which men use is to agree to minor changes or to assimilate feminist views in an attempt to water them down and reassert control. Some women brought back stories of how their male partners thought their demands were 'only a whim', that they would make concessions but hope that the fire would die down. L felt uncertain about her cohabitee's commitment to her, to the extent that she did not trust his behaviour, but always found herself giving in to his demands and his charm. He lived the life of a single person, never telling her where he was going, spending days, sometimes weeks, away from home, bringing other women to the house and spending the bulk of the family's Income Support on himself. Whenever L had tried to challenge him about his lack of concern for her, he had shouted that she was trying to possess and suffocate him. It was his life and he could do what he wanted.

During one of his absences from home, L changed the locks on the external doors and when he returned home a few days later, she refused to let him in. She told him that until he involved her in the daily arrangements of his life, then she was not prepared to be treated like his 'lackey' any longer. This was a big risk for her to take. The house was a joint council tenancy and she knew that he had every right to enter the premises. The group's underlying principles had given her the space to analyse his repeated statements about her neediness, dependency and hysteria. She now believed in her emotionality and felt that he was too afraid to know how to handle it. Nevertheless, for the moment he was part of her consciousness and her physical life and she wanted to put the relationship to the test to see whether there was a strong enough basis on which to instigate changes.

When he came back to the house the next day, L told him that she was not happy with their life-style, that she expected honesty because this was the only way she could trust him. She wanted him to let her know his daily whereabouts, so that she could make plans accordingly. After much protest, he agreed to this and began to leave her notes indicating where he was and when he would return. L later told the group that he had given in to her demands, but that fundamentally she still felt controlled and dissatisfied because he hoped she would lose her resolve so that 'things could get back to normal'. She subsequently heard that he had told some of his drinking mates of *his* decision to keep L informed of his whereabouts because she was going through a difficult patch.

For this cohabitee, and other men, there is a recognition of what will be lost through change, but little comprehension of any gains to be made. It is not just a simple issue of individual choice in the sense that men are trading in their licence to control. All group members, including L, recognized men's claims of 'independent action' when in reality their ideas and behaviours were supported by their womenfolk, thus revealing the importance male partners placed on maintaining full authority within their family. That change might be stimulated from outside is seen by some men as weakening male legitimacy. By incorporating women's group understandings but taking credit for originating the change, male partners relegitimate control of their social world and simultaneously reduce discontent. It is clearly in their own self-interest to do this, and whilst men's responsiveness may improve, the fundamental power imbalances remain.

This is especially the case when we examine men's interpretations of the expression of direct anger (see Chapter 5). A common complaint about women's groups is that they *make* women angry. Women indicated that the group did not 'make' them angry, it helped them to discover that they already *were*. The most difficult consequence of experiencing anger, as discussed in Chapter 5, is facing up to the decision as to what you are going to do about it. Acting out of anger means entering uncharted territory, where there are plenty of signs around saying 'Danger', 'Travel at your own risk'. Some men responded to the expression of anger with shock and hostility, feeling humiliated and hurt. Dealing with an emotion directly is threatening to their identity; men end up feeling isolated and unsupported, and respond competitively through their attempts to reassert their role as 'managers' of these 'damaged goods'.

There are some men, though, who hail the changes as innovative and desirable. Some women did find it possible to begin reasoning with their partners in ways that previously they thought would have no effect. The difference this time was that the women's assertive arguments were seen to be irresistible. They would have to be listened to and grudgingly acted upon. One woman, for example, tired of acting as mediator between her son and her partner and not wanting to lose either of them, made it clear to them after only a few group sessions that if they had any disagreements in future, then they would have to sort them out for themselves and not rely on her to smooth things over. Even if this meant the two males not speaking to each other, she was not going to relay messages nor encourage them to interact. If they argued then it was their task to try to rectify this and find a better understanding. In the past, whenever she had disagreed with or stood up to her partner, he had reacted violently towards her. This time things were different; she made it clear that she wanted their relationship to continue but his bullying to stop, and for him to take responsibility for his actions in connection with her son. For the first time ever he heard her out, acknowledged that his behaviour had been reactive, and agreed to adapt. As a result, she felt much more relaxed and able to get on with her daily tasks without fear of interruption. Her son and her partner knew they had to sort themselves out quickly or live in an atmosphere of tension and silence, which neither wanted.

We have already recognized that a woman's ability to influence the people around her and gauge the effects on her of others' expectations depends upon the degree of elasticity within her network of primary relationships (Peck, 1986). Lack of elasticity pushes a woman into weighing the impact of any changes against the possible loss of relationships which form part of her self-definition (Gilligan, 1982). It creates a situation where a woman is forced either to live through her relationships, or to attempt to change these and risk the concomitant 'loss of Self' we described in Chapter 5. The major difference here is that, given the group's support, women face the exhilaration of doing something for themselves, especially when they have reached the end of their tether and have nothing left to lose.

The other difference is that changing interactions affect not only heterosexual relationships, but also relations with other family members. The more women said to themselves and those around them, 'This is me and this time I'm defining the limits', the more criticism they received. However, they found that holding their ground ultimately commanded respect and that once the other family members became familiar with the idea, they adjusted their demands. The following are examples of immediate, obvious changes:

• One woman began relating to her children in a way hitherto unobserved. She became affectionate towards them, and insisted on taking more responsibility for defining their life-style, thereby giving less space to her mother and ex-mother-in-law, who had both tried to usurp her role.

• One woman began to see herself as kind and helpful, and as attractive and worthy of respect, as opposed to being a passing fancy. She felt more relaxed and came to see the freedom of her life-style, rather than viewing it as oppressive. She learnt to say NO when she felt put upon and not to feel deprived as a result.

• Another woman developed the ability to stick to convictions about the upbringing of children, to define where responsibility lay and to make this clear to others. This woman said quite clearly, 'I'm a good mother.' She shocked her own parents with the force of her arguments, but they listened.

• Some women came to realize that other people suffer too. It is important to give others the space to talk, to confess how confused and unhappy they are. Conversations and relationships take on more colour and a deeper significance. It becomes possible to give more and to reap the benefits of greater trust.

• Some gained the courage to compliment friends and relatives, men especially, without any hidden motives. Everyone who did this remarked on how surprised the recipients of the compliments were, but how much pleasure they themselves derived from giving. They found that if they were complimented, they no longer assumed that those giving positive feedback were being devious.

• One woman learnt to stand ground in ending a relationship where before she had capitulated several times. This woman underwent massive changes in her life-style and was clearly sustained by group solidarity in the face of comments from others that she was unfeeling and bad; she was then able to stick to her newly-formed principles and withstand pressure from outside. She also made friends whilst going through these changes – a capacity she truly thought she had lost.

- Another woman changed her physical appearance quite dramatically, altering her hairstyle and wearing brightly coloured clothes. She also began to see herself as gregarious, enterprising and possibly a good mother. She learnt to hold her ground with her ex-husband. She recognized the qualities she had rather than wishing she was different.

One of the most significant effects of the existence of women's groups in any locality is that they facilitate the revision of the relative power of women – as friends, as neighbours and as extended family members. How deeply felt and permanent were the women's changed attitudes towards other women? All women found a genuine enjoyment in each other's company, a stimulation and excitement in each other's ideas and observations of experiences. In many respects, however, it is easier for women to deal with public relationships and relations with men because those ideas and exchanges are all 'out there' somewhere. It is neither so safe nor so comfortable to deal with feelings about other women in the here and now. Self-esteem and self-image are enhanced in direct proportion to the increasing visibility of and openness about women's friendships. The common link across all group members was that eventually women recognized the depths of warmth, ease and closeness to be derived from female friendship. The consistency of the affective dimensions of friendship is supported by Rose and Roades (1987), who found similarities across feminist and non-feminist groups in terms of the satisfaction and esteem gained from female friendships.

Negotiating time alone with friends demonstrates the lengths to which women are prepared to go to maintain these relationships. Friendship requires timing because circumstances in a woman's life may militate against the forming of a close friendship at a particular point. Meaningful choices have to be made which require a certain thoughtfulness. Such was the harsh climate in which group members led their lives that for their own protection they needed to make discerning judgements about what form a friendship should take. This ensured survival of the relationship which was held up as a positive example for all the masculinist critics who were ready to knock it down.

Group members also began to take more care in choosing their friends in terms of which qualities they valued and what commitments they were willing to make. Women learnt to their cost that friendship cannot be aroused all at once; it needs to be sustained over time. With women so bereft of emotional support, any sign of closeness and intimacy was initially seized upon and squeezed dry, or rebuffed and ridiculed. This see-saw effect can have a devastating effect on the maintenance of friendship. Women are either overenthusiastic about or draw away from investing in the relationship. At times, members of the group went through short periods where they felt great intimacy and closeness because it was safe to disclose and discuss their innermost feelings. Often, these short-lived experiences would be followed by apparently aimless activity. Friendship was then written off. The lesson for group members was that affectionate friendships can break down the taming of women because the ability to arouse and influence each other is continually rekindled. However, these affective exchanges may seem so new that women need to pace their friendships, and to temper intimacy with thoughtfulness and respect for each other.

An appraisal of friendships within and outside the group gives members the chance to recognize their affinity with and struggles for women. The realization of the links between feminist politics and female friendship means that women quickly develop a sense of affiliation with women outside the group, leading to feelings of a community of women which transcends the physical confines of the group experience: 'It's as though the history of women's struggles is here with us in this room.'

The care and thoughtfulness which develop in female relationships can help to deal with the constraints of secrecy felt acutely by lesbian group members. They may, for instance, express pride in their ability to side-step questions about their personal lives and deny that this dishonesty has any negative impact on their associations with friends and family members. Eventually, lesbian women acknowledge how painful it is to make their relationships invisible, how terrified they feel when asked about their personal lives, and how this requires tremendous expenditure of energy. The risks involved in coming out in terms of personal and economic loss can prove overwhelming to women in poverty, who face loss of low-paid jobs, their homes, their children, if their lesbianism becomes known (Rights of Women, 1986). In terms of exploring options, the group can help a woman to plan future changes which will allow her fewer restrictions whilst recognizing the harsh realities of her socio-economic position.

In such circumstances it is important to evaluate the long-term psycho-social consequences of secrecy and pretended heterosexuality through the toll on psychic energy. The longer a group member has feigned heterosexuality, the greater her guilt will be when she informs those around her of past deceptions. The group can assist a woman with the timing and setting of coming out so that she undertakes this from a position of as much strength and pride in her lesbian identity as possible. Acknowledging her lesbian status proudly, affirmatively and directly not only bolsters a woman's self-esteem, but also makes it clear that she feels good about her life. This is an important communication, since she should not put herself in a defensive position.

In all of this, it is crucial that lesbian group members protect themselves from unnecessary vulnerability by presenting their lesbianism in a directly factual manner in interactions with people who are relatively inconsequential in their lives. In this way, there is no invitation to detailed or intimate discussion. No lesbian group member felt able to come out at work, however, because they were occupationally insecure and felt exploited enough through their labour. The decision to conceal their sexual identity was accompanied by an internalization of the negative attitudes which they assumed others would express if their lesbianism was acknowledged. In contrast, on the occasions when lesbian members *were* honest in communication, they came away with an ability to externalize rather than internalize the anger felt in response to homophobia.

What is also important is that heterosexual group members can provide active support to and form an alliance with lesbian members, in order to resist the tyranny of heterosexism. All group members need to learn that heterosexism is *their* problem. By doing so, group members can enjoy a greater sense of personal freedom about their sexuality than has been experienced previously.

'Time out' for connections   If we peel back the layers of dilemmas with which group members are faced when considering the relationship between group experience and social context, the core of these refers to self-perception as outlined in Chapter 5. For instance, there can be no assumption that each group member will feel equally committed to attend or participate in all group meetings and take part in group action all of the time. There has to be a recognition and acceptance of different states of mind at different times and of the impact of family and household responsibilities. Of equal weight is the effect of fear, self-doubt and uncertainty relating to the process and progress of change that a woman may experience. The desire to change brings with it a degree of responsibility to carry out a particular course of action. What other choices are available to women as they grapple with this range of dilemmas? Not attending the group for a number of sessions is one option, perhaps to test out new ideas in the outside world, perhaps to reappraise all that has been discussed and to make decisions about its sense and suitability. 'Time out' can offer a sense of perspective on what is happening within the context of one's own experience. It may

well signify a radical change in direction for that particular woman. Having reached a critical point in her life, she may want to make major decisions, try acting on them, and then return to the group for reappraisal.

We want to explore the experiences of one woman, to look at the intricacies, tensions and positive developments which occurred through the direct relationship between the women's group and its social context. C was a young white woman who needed to decide between life as a single person with an eighteen-month-old child, and the option of stating and maintaining her own rights in the face of threats and incidents of violence from her partner. C took time out from the group to test out whether in reality she could stand up to this man, to confront him with the consequences of his behaviour.

What she learnt from participation in the group was to think of her own needs and capabilities in a different way, to begin with herself in the centre. Stemming from this was the need to recognize and make compromises in her expectations, and not to see this as failure, but rather as a validation of her ability to think laterally. None of this could happen without pain and disappointment, setbacks and exhaustion. Personal and social change can lead to a new situation where enough elements of life are improved to compensate for whatever else has been lost in the process. The energy expended in maintaining a relationship that is ultimately detrimental both to a woman and her child can be redirected in forming new friendships, doing work on her home, joining a keep-fit class.

During several weeks of struggle, C also had to question her several roles. As a parent, and the person needing to maintain a home for the child, she rightly felt it was appropriate to keep the tenancy of the house. As a daughter, she knew that her parents hoped she would be able to make the best of a bad job, both for her sake and for the child's, so that there would be the appearance of stability in the relationship. Informing them of her decision to give her partner an ultimatum to move out, she thought they would view as her giving up, letting them down and breaking up the family. As a member of the local community, C also felt that her neighbours, many of whom were aware of the violence and drunkenness that she had to endure, would criticize her for similar reasons.

In the end, her fears proved largely unfounded. Her partner eventually left. He was struck by her calm and resolve in telling him what she felt. Whatever disappointment her parents may have felt in her choice of partner, they were pleased that she was finally taking the initiative towards a better life for herself. As far as neighbours were concerned, she found she could live without those who were critical of her behaviour as there were enough other people who rallied round to help. Indeed, C felt much more a part of the community and of her local street than had ever been the case hitherto.

On her return to the group, she presented an account of the preceding few weeks rendered with a mixture of pride and self-esteem, but also the awareness that she had not wanted to return without a 'success story' to relate. It was difficult to assess whether she would have returned if her hopes and aspirations had not been met, because she believed that the group would have seen her as a failure. Nevertheless, C's history demonstrates the evidence of dynamic interaction, as women gradually see the ways in which they might change certain aspects of their lives for the better. The energy they discover and acknowledge within themselves from attending the group can lead to a positive, liberating redirection of personal resources.

Damage limitation   This sense of accountability to the group and perceptions of failure are particularly relevant when we examine the anxiety-provoking and not necessarily liberating aspects of social identity change. In a particular woman's life, for example, the power and validity of the group may be side-stepped or temporarily overruled by a life crisis, such as domestic violence, bereavement, eviction or prosecution. This inevitably throws off balance any belief in self-motivation which is encouraged and sustained by the group. Demands on women's time and energy may mean that the pursuit of these changes has to be postponed. Whatever her circumstances, there is only so much that any one woman can do at any one time, and frequently there will be conflicting priorities to be faced. As one group member said: 'I can't leave today. I haven't done the ironing.'

The very nature of participation in the group encourages risk-taking, some of which is bound to lead to danger and disappointment. As workers, to what extent do we have jurisdiction over damage limitation? We cannot prevent or avoid some damage occurring and it is not right, let alone realistic, for us to assume that this is possible. To the extent that damage limitation exists, it needs to involve workers and group members in:

1   a full discussion with any woman planning to take direct action of the provision she might have to make to deal with the implications of her plans;
2   ensuring that she has been given accurate, up-to-date information relating to her circumstances, or that she knows where to get it;
3   a discussion about what sort of back-up system we are able to provide.

We have to give encouragement to whatever decision a woman makes and help her see the ramifications of either path without her feeling under more pressure. We can predict, to a certain degree, the reactions of a woman and significant others to a particular set of changes and events, and offer warnings about this, but we cannot predict their possible range of actions.

Although charting the history of the groups highlights fluctuations in individual women's commitment and participation, it can still be shown very clearly that groupwork can be a source of power in a community, connecting women with the background to their lives. Socio-economic and psycho-social influences become more apparent and significant, so that this new-found knowledge can be used to make decisions at a community level.

Women as professional workers

The special poignancy of groupwork and its place in the initiation of social change is by no means restricted to group members. As workers, we are also located within the network of mutual and conflicting interests depicted in Figure 6. This faces us with a personal dilemma. On the one hand, we identify with the group as women, on the other, as participants in the change process that leads to social action. Workers face a daunting choice. There comes a point in the group's life when we can maintain either a professional role in connection with the agency, or solidarity with the group in its endeavours. Either way, the notion of professionalism is called into question. Whilst this personal questioning and critique of occupational culture take place, workers continue to operate as major change agents within the group itself.

In so many ways the experiences of women workers in groups are inextricably bound up with the despair and aspirations of group members. There are also times when we can perceive disharmony. In Chapter 1 we recognized that the core identity of 'woman' is overlaid by writer and worker roles and that this is a potential area of discord. We explored the ways in which economic and material differences and inequalities affect not only structural relations, but also the very fabric of our identity. We demonstrated how the groupwork process raises our awareness of strengths and weaknesses, convictions and fears. As our use of language changes (see Chapter 3), and we learn to learn anew, our eyes are opened wider, our senses are sharpened, and we begin to question the rigidities of professionalism.

As feminists, we are forced to confront a whole host of misgivings about professional codes of conduct. Struggles for power characterize most human social experience. For workers given or seeking the responsibility to provide services, the exercise of professional discretion and judgement involves the use of power over women who turn to us for help. We cannot hide from the fact that society has generated powerful images of omnicompetent professionals soothing, curing and removing the hurt, pain and problems of living. As Illich et al. (1977) indicate, professionals claim areas of work as their own and selfishly protect them until their expertise is recognized. In asserting secret knowledge which they alone control, they have a special, incommunicable authority to determine what women need. These images are so deeply engrained in our culture that women are as eager in their expectations of painless solutions as we are willing to take on the responsibility of providing them.

What are the damaging effects of wholesale belief in professional solutions? An expansion of professional propaganda has occurred at the expense of our own self-awareness and personal competence. Because of the mystique of professionalism, we are not allowed to *be* ourselves. There are many forces at work which perceive a rejection of the professional mould as heresy. Organizational culture is a profound illustration of this. The oppressive position in which women are placed in patriarchal agencies is reinforced by the expectations of us, which are so much higher than of men. On the one hand, we are expected to conform to professional and agency codes of conduct which bear little resemblance to our experience. On the other hand, we have to be more intelligent, more efficient, more malleable than our male colleagues. The getting by, the complacency, that men are permitted, is never allowed us. Behaviour which is tolerated from men damages us and others all the time. Double standards definitely prevail.

Women working in male-dominated organizations, where stereotypical views of sex roles abound, are forever fighting for survival. Life is one eternal compromise, with personal identity and integrity under threat. We live in constant pain and anger. Confronting the many misrepresentations of ourselves and our behaviour drains our energy. Comfortable mediocrity has become the norm in such organizations. Our emotionality is denied. Expressing direct anger is liberating, but it takes commitment and energy; we each of us only have so much in our grasp, and can easily become burnt out.

Exploitation occurs in every aspect of our professional lives, so much so that we internalize the mixed messages with which we are presented. The expectations of others become part of our psyche so that merely 'being good enough' is not enough for us. We set ourselves up to be perfect. The way we become sucked into the organizational ethos is symbolized by our use of language. In order to be understood, we adopt dominant discourse, which has a detrimental effect on our thought processes. We are never on the same wavelength as those with whom we are conversing. Faced with a discourse based on paternalism and benevolence, we speak to male colleagues as if they were children. However, we are not replicating the patterns of interaction found between mother and child. We may take care of men, bailing them out on a regular basis, but we do not possess the same level of power which is intrinsic to a parent–child relationship. Surrounded by compromise and dishonesty, any direct communication becomes diluted. Male managers dump their mistakes on women workers with expectations that they will pick up the pieces. Coping with these multiple demands carries enormous personal costs and few rewards. We do not trust the system and those who work within it. The conservative impulse of organizations clashes with our radical belief systems. It is like swimming against the tide. Ultimately, we feel inhumane and inhuman in our work environment because patriarchy denies our humanity.

So do we play the rules of the game for all they are worth? However much we feel weighed down by male policies and behaviour, the ability to carry on the struggle in such an environment gives us enormous determination. Each time we experience oppression, we dust ourselves down and deal with its stultifying effects. We become irritants for organizational change, systematically chipping away at patriarchy's foundations. Our outrage at organizational practices which further oppress women users of services provides us with the emotional strength to break out of the downward spiral of being a victim. Playing such a role in organizations reduces our manoeuvrability. We can use our personal power by exposing ourselves to the demands, sufferings and joys of women's group members. In doing so we are likely to be attacked as acting 'unprofessionally' or 'unethically'. For us, our professionalism is expressed by the extent to which we can acknowledge how we feel and take responsibility for our actions. We can strive to use our knowledge and experience to assist women in their discovery of group solutions to problems of living. This is a far cry from the professional who manages feelings, failing to acknowledge the effect of their behaviour on others. Knowledge and experience are withheld as a means of subjugation and domination in the client–worker encounter.

Issues of professionalism are awakened when we examine the complexities of workers' relationships with group members. As part of the simultaneous pulls towards closeness and differentiation (see Chapter 5), group members may want the worker to be the perfectly responsive carer. There is a constant tension between these two dichotomies, however, the expression of which is dependent on the worker's own history and life experiences. For example, the worker may sometimes be intrusive in her caring, becoming the self-sacrificing nurturer who expects group members to 'improve' in return. When this does not happen, she will feel uncared for and unappreciated. Such martyrdom is familiar in our family histories, but we know from experience that we expect compensation by way of guilt or nurturance in return. Alternatively, the worker may be the distant, competent mother, giving the group autonomy which inevitably exposes its vulnerabilities. She will feel frustrated by members' demands for care, especially as the professional code requires the repression of her own needy self. The more uncared for we feel in our own lives, the more difficult it will be for us to respond sensitively to our clients' requests for care.

Professional ethics involve balancing the fears and longings of group members with the worker's role as an agent of social control. As workers, we often do not acknowledge our ambivalence about closeness and separation because we may wish to maintain group relationships and thus be unprepared to recognize members' growth, which could lead to our withdrawal from the group. We may also resent members' helplessness because it places excessive demands on us. Both of these conditions – moving away and moving towards – can stimulate anger in workers which has more to do with our own personal issues than with group relations. We may end up feeling vulnerable, which is likely to increase our self-protective reactions. To facilitate our growth as workers, however, we have to harness our vulnerability to the need to get angry about our professional culture. This culture smothers us with layers of insensitivity, separating our recognition of pain and nurturance from the realization that this pain is happening to us. So when we blame group members for not making 'correct' decisions, we are telling them that they are not good or worthy of love. We are also fooling ourselves that we can make professional discriminations and moral judgements.

How can feminist groupworkers deconstruct this form of professionalism? First, at every stage of the group's life the worker must respect the personal integrity of members and must not impose her own personal preferences. Yet we have seen that groupwork practice is laden with beliefs about its value, power and efficacy; otherwise it could not be offered or accepted. The worker's relationship with members is indeed a major instrument for promoting change and neutrality would only manifest itself as indifference. The resolution of this paradox requires the worker to be clear about the possibilities available, and to use this as a basis for discussion and negotiation. Individuals can make choices for themselves and must assume responsibility for this. We can be involved in learning, giving, receiving, without trying to convert or convince.

Secondly, there has to be a willingness to allow blurring of demarcation lines between roles during the process of working with the group. Thirdly, we need to believe that conscientization, dialogue and education can take place anywhere, as long as there is a ground plan which can evolve at varying rates and in differing ways. Fourthly, as workers we must receive support as well as give it. A feminist approach places enormous demands on us. Developing ways of giving ourselves adequate care and seeking out validation is a priority. This provides us with a more honest concept of 'well-being'.

Fifthly, in the course of responding to group change, it is inevitable that at times we will make mistakes and feel helpless. Confusion, anger and pain frequently arise but these can be used to positive ends if we learn to be compassionate with ourselves. Mistakes can be seen as a source of creativity and an opportunity to learn. Forgiving the Self is a crucial lesson because then we can discover the power of our own vulnerabilities. We do not have to be hard on ourselves. As one group member said, 'You're in no position to help me if you don't look after yourself.'

All of this requires us to expose the messiness of our emotions so that we do not always flee to rationality and order. Emotional rawness means that the professional front is lowered, that we can be vulnerable and use this within the group. By doing this are we taking up valuable group time? An illusion such as this protects us from knowledge of our own helplessness, arising out of discrimination in the workplace. Guilt becomes our hiding place. Guilt means that we can acknowledge our privileges but we cocoon ourselves against the misery of many working-class women's lives. Before we can accept the totality of their oppression and not feel guilty about it, we must accept the wholeness of ourselves.

The changes we need to make in our professional practice can emerge only through change in our experience. As we begin to do things differently, so we begin to feel the benefits of these changes. No one can underestimate the sense of relief and exhilaration when we are honest in our modes of communication, honest with ourselves and each other.

Even if women workers on occasion *want* to retreat to the relative safety of traditional professionalism, we cannot ignore the impact of the group, which reflects back workers' behaviour in such a way that is impossible to ignore. Group members do not perceive us simply as workers; in part we are created by a process of prescription and ascription. Whatever solidarity and empathy we can offer, there always remains the distancing effect of our legal status and responsibilities with regard to them and, where applicable, their children. Once women begin to recognize the system within which workers function they make demands on us, of our potential role in providing them with better, more appropriate services for their dependants. In an established group, members will challenge workers' right to continued group membership in view of what could be seen as our divided loyalties.

How do the above principles concerning professionalism influence our practice? Complete honesty is needed about the likelihood of change and what our degree of influence might be. This invariably leads us to situations where we are working against our employing agency. Facing up to this issue and demonstrating our willingness to participate is a measure of our commitment to the group and its need to take change beyond its own confines.

In this way, egalitarianism becomes a reality, with women taking responsibility from workers as they see fit, dictating our role in discussion and organization. Acting thus can be generalized to situations outside the group because practising on workers makes external challenges more easy to grasp. It would be counter-productive if, despite all that members had been able to realize and discuss about their oppressed position, women still felt unable to challenge the workers and take this consciousness outside. Such a contradiction would lay workers open to the charge of wanting to maintain the status quo, not providing any shift in ideology.

As workers, we are faced with the structural absurdity of trying to break down the constraints of a hierarchical system by setting up a group of this nature for women and by assuring them of our deep commitment to change and to altering established hierarchies. We are trying to work within the masculinist system, but also to stand outside it, to demonstrate that such a system *can* and *should* encompass a diversity of approaches. It is possible to beat the system and survive it. All this is implicit and explicit in feminist groupwork. Whilst this process continues, we still have to remind ourselves and the women participants that we are prey to professional and bureaucratic constraints over which we can have only so much influence. What are we trying to do? Show the human face of bureaucracy, but say at the same time that it can make only occasional appearances?

The reflection of ourselves as workers is even more apparent when members shift boundaries and blur distinctions between the professional and the personal. We were faced with the sobering, growing realization of the appalling experiences women live through and survive. Yet, despite this, the traditional boundary between work and leisure proved to be a false divide. Women learnt together and carried out their discussions when they met each other in the course of their daily lives. This extension of purposeful activity proved to be especially poignant when, as previously highlighted, women were prepared to support each other through distressing, intensely disturbing events at any time of the day or night. Members often commented that they passed each other's houses and looked to see if everything was all right. In contrast, professional activity often gets hooked on a particularly narrow course of action which blocks out the view of the whole.

The evaluation process means that we are accountable to women. Co-workers need to evaluate themselves and each other, and get feedback from members about their performance. We can become more conscious of how a particular behaviour, attitude or feeling manifests itself through the group process. Can we recognize the connections between feelings and behaviour? What happens as the situation develops? What is it like afterwards? Feedback from others creates a more detailed picture of what we are doing and may suggest options and possibilities. By seeking out constructive criticism, workers give women permission to comment on aspects of our practice. An awareness of dissatisfaction can begin to open up possibilities for change. We can visualize ourselves performing in a certain way and attune ourselves to this. Acknowledgement of feelings which will hinder our progress is also part of responding positively to the group. Fear, embarrassment, shame can create barriers, so it is crucial to reconnect with the original vision. We can move forward by building on our positive abilities and, once this is achieved, reward ourselves for the discovery of inner strength and commitment.

Evaluation of the co-working relationship is an integral part of feminist groupwork. It helps us to review our initial expectations, to identify how far our original hopes and fears have materialized and what we have learnt in the process. We must be honest in our appreciation of the co-working partnership so that we can build upon this and strive for greater openness. The ability to praise or criticize our co-worker without fear of rejection can give us the impetus to test out improvements in our practice, because we know that direct feedback will be readily available. By the end of the group, co-workers should be clear about members' views of their involvement and what facilitated or impeded their learning.

The whole question of the role of women workers is enmeshed within the group and its social context. It is an academic exercise to pull apart the various strands of professionalism and evaluation, in that there are a multitude of converging patterns which become interchangeable. Whatever the circumstances, the business of being a worker in a women's group is a continual challenge, a source of stimulation and vision.

Loss and empowerment

'I don't want the group to end.'

Our journey in this chapter has taken us through the troughs and heights of social identity change and shifts in workers' use of professional and personal power. The aspirations of workers and group members alike are based on issues of power. A group of this nature can only go some way towards rectifying the structural imbalances that shape working-class women's lives. Yet by demonstrating to women the strengths they have and the pride they can feel, the group acts as a catalyst for empowerment. The imperatives for women to take power for themselves are, first, the rights and dignity of each of us and, secondly, the demands of worker effectiveness. If our professional power does limit or prevent women from taking positive action, it challenges our legitimacy. There has to be a point where workers withdraw from the groups. Despite the losses involved, worker withdrawal gives credence to women's abilities to take responsibility for the future of any self-directing group.

Using direct power through worker withdrawal   In Chapter 4 we looked at ways of translating the philosophy of empowerment into an easily understood language, reshaped through changes in workers' behaviour and attitudes. Skills can be shared as long as we do not slip into condescension, and if we address members' reluctance to acknowledge and use their instrumental skills. We also examined women's use of indirect power in their daily domestic lives, and a more positive, direct power in the group which draws on an understanding of the mechanisms of prejudice. Despite all these struggles surrounding empowerment, the negative consequences of the group's achievements come home to roost when workers discuss their withdrawal. No matter how far group members have found the empowerment of each other to be a valuable and gratifying activity, the moment women take power for themselves it is seen as selfish and destructive. We fear that our use of power will lead to abandonment which threatens the core identity concept of the Caring Self (Chapter 5). Loss of workers reinforces the belief that when we are openly powerful, we will end up alone.

These misconceptions can be broken down when the group confronts the definitions of power which collide in members' heads. Women link the concept of power with the ability to augment one's own authority or influence, and also to control and limit others (Miller, 1982). Group members were absolutely right to fear the use of power as it has been generally conceptualized and used. There were enough examples of this harsh reality from women's daily lives.

An exhilarating use of direct power, by way of contrast, involves change, even in an individual thought or emotion, and an ability to create movement (Miller, 1982). In the group, women became accustomed to using their individual influence for the collective good, and encompassing this strand within the notion of power. Finding ways of interacting in the group and with significant others so that we can enhance others' power whilst simultaneously increasing our own is crucial. Positive energy sources can be found in each other. Recognizing skills, being innovatory, and having an ability to communicate are all valuable sources to be tapped. However, women had virtually no legitimate power through resource control and formal authority. What they had in abundance was emotional power and an affirmation of their cultural strength.

One way in which group members can act powerfully is by sharing and developing skills and knowledge which are important to the functioning of the group once workers have withdrawn. Individuals can devise a framework which adapts with flexibility to the changing structure of the group. Mutuality (Chapter 4) is still central to this process. No one has all the answers and everyone has problems in handling endings. As decisions are made about the group's plans, future structure and campaigns, so it becomes necessary for a picture to emerge of who will do what. Problem-solving of this kind is heavily dependent on the level of trust, openness and recognition afforded to each member's strengths and limitations. A group member may, for instance, panic in emergencies and would therefore feel exposed when dealing with council officials. However, she may have handled a new participant's distress with sensitivity and may therefore be more willing to introduce new members to the group in the future. In terms of how group sessions are to be organized whilst planning its future, it may be appropriate for one person on a given day to make a note of all that is discussed, and of who has decided to do what. Beyond this, the traditionalist assumption that there needs to be a chairperson can be resisted.

Each person can either offer skills that she is happy to use in the service of the group, or decide that she wants to take on something new and challenging, testing out the limits of her abilities in a way she has never had the chance to exploit. There will be participants who either do not feel confident enough to offer work in a planning session, or who have too many commitments already and on whom it would be unfair to exert more pressure. Women must be given space to say these things and not feel obliged to act with equal enthusiasm. Some will function best working alongside others in a joint enterprise, some will perform tasks handed to them by other people, with appropriate information provided. Ultimately, these women may feel able to take on more tasks with a measure of power, control and independence.

Certain women will have access to different aspects of information depending on their individual life experiences and they may choose to use these to promote whatever 'their' task is. Women may seek out the role of expert in a particular field and gain validation from others in achieving this. The consequences of such an approach are that:

1   An increase in self-confidence and/or interest in a particular field
    can precipitate a decision to take it further. For example, some
    women returned to part-time education, having played truant to a
    great extent throughout adolescence, or left school relatively young
    because of early pregnancy.
2   It can demonstrate to other women that they too could follow the
    example of one of their number and concentrate on developing
    their knowledge.

Empowerment such as this gives women a purpose. Some women
will risk planning certain aspects of their lives in advance, in order to
create and sustain the rewards gained from group participation. For
instance, one group member had been described as slovenly and
lacking in motivation by professionals and family members alike and,
probably in defiance of these accusations, had always kept her curtains
drawn with the lights on in the house to keep the world at bay. This
pattern had taken its toll of her physical and psychological well-being,
not least in the size of the electricity bill. Far from passively accepting a
social position based on the definitions of others, this woman engaged
in constructing her own active position in the group. This was
awakened when discussions were under way about the group taking on
a self-directing status.

For her, the *acknowledgement* of her skills (to deflect members'
pessimism, quietly to seek order within the chaos of a whole host of
ideas), and the *reputation* she accrued as a result of being a women's
group member, were regarded as valuable commodities. She took
great pleasure in shaking people's perceptions of her as idle, feckless,
'rough' and 'unrespectable'. In the past, she had fallen heavily at the
obstacles of economic dependence and inferior status, with little
chance of improvement, but through the group she rose to establish a
position which gave her at least a toehold in the public domain. She no
longer wanted to be bottom of the pile.

Workers must tread carefully through the quicksand surrounding
their intentions when transferring the responsibility of group function
from workers to members. Feminist groupworkers usually adopt a
facilitative role, leaving women free to participate in learning and
growth of their own choice. Any lack of achievement in terms of
transfer of skills and knowledge could be interpreted as due to a failure
on the women's part to capitalize on the opportunities in the group by
choosing to perceive their future solely as wives, partners, mothers,
unskilled workers, and so on. However, women do not choose to
have less education, less skilled jobs and lower pay than white men.
Women can only choose from the range of options presented to them,
and if these are circumscribed by stereotyping, sexism and gender

differentiation, then in effect there is no choice. Few options are available based on a recognition of the differential talents and interests of the individual women we have described so far.

The problems in achieving a smooth transfer of the group to the sole power of its members are exacerbated by inadequate transport and child-care facilities, health-endangering housing, inaccessible health care and insurmountable poverty. This is a strong enough justification for insisting that workers must take an interventionist role where appropriate. Women can be encouraged to develop and specify goals and values for the self-directing group and identify means by which these might be achieved. As a result, they can be helped to examine the ways in which group conditions will alter and how new objectives must be introduced and checked at regular intervals.

When parting is such sweet sorrow   Workers must ensure that endings are not abrupt and arbitrary. Developing a finely tuned sense of accountability must be seen as a prerequisite for the achievement of this. Otherwise, the group's ending will be perceived as just another one in a series of inevitable losses over which there is no control. Reminders can be given throughout the duration of the group of its time-limited nature. A specific period can be set aside to look at the notion of loss and endings, to begin to incorporate their effect into the fabric of everyday experience. Thus, it is possible not to dismiss or diminish but at least to mitigate the impact of the group's changing shape. As a result, some women may be able to see previous changes as events that provided scope for self-actualizing and liberating behaviour.

Within the context of the variety of losses which women experience it may appear natural that the group should have an ending. The group is a fixed but ever-moving point in women's lives, and workers must play a transitional role in its life. As discussed in Chapter 4, the 'spirit' of the group lives on beyond its physical existence, but this does not mean that participants can use it in the same way as a reference point. The ending of something good can be put to positive use. If there *is* a sense of loss, this is placed in perspective and is not seen as overwhelming.

As the majority of women said they found the groups stimulating and beneficial, it can be assumed that they wanted sessions to continue. The changed sense of purpose and identity was not going to be given up easily, if at all. Although timetables are set out from the start, these are often quite arbitrary and say a great deal about workers' organizational agendas. Also, they cannot take into account a woman's emotional and psychological attachment to the group, nor the fact that this outlives by far the actual length of time that she remains involved. The contradictions which the group has to face during this period may seem insurmountable. The level of interdependency formed in relationships may, for instance, be much stronger than any individual member could imagine, and the group may founder over how to deal with this.

Nevertheless, the group has to end as we know it, because *we* have to move on, perhaps to different jobs, perhaps because funding has run out, perhaps because we can no longer convince our managers of the value of what we are doing. Such was the wish for the groups *not* to collapse that women continued under their own steam. This desire for continuity is a measure of how women feel and behave once officially sanctioned group meetings have ended. First, women can cement and sustain friendships made within the group, offering each other help and support. Secondly, the group can continue to meet with its own organization and focus, holding sessions in private houses and recruiting sisters, cousins and friends from the area. In such circumstances, women meet in defiance of the wishes of male partners who see themselves as having humoured 'their' women by allowing them to attend the group in the knowledge that it was time-limited. The continuation of meetings is an indication of the degree of strength, self-confidence and autonomy felt by the women concerned.

The growth of a self-directing group symbolizes the ending of one stage and the beginning of another. It implies a positive evolution in which loss and endings become the bridge towards personal responsibility and collective development. As workers, we cease to be the givers, the providers, and even if we continue our enabling role, this becomes more and more egalitarian. Endings should not be framed in such a way as to preclude further creativity, further exploration of behaviour, further dialogue under new and unforeseen circumstances. The cycle of endings and beginnings goes on throughout our lifetimes, and as women adjust to group change so the same themes and issues are likely to re-emerge later on. The patterns of growth never end.

The difficulties women may have with partings can be expressed by withdrawing from pain, by leaving a session early or just not turning up one day. This leaves them feeling in control of relationships. Alternatively, they may attack what feels painful, complaining that the group is useless anyway and it is 'all a load of rubbish'. Some women may attempt to merge with the workers, clinging on for as long as possible and seeking approval from them. Some women will wait for the worker to say when the moment of separation is imminent. The contemplation of goodbyes will bring a multitude of responses but ultimately we cannot ignore the pain of parting itself. It helps if each group member can identify something of the other person which she can take with her. She may be able to 'internalize' another person, so that when faced with new situations she thinks 'What would X say?'

An image of the group can feel like an internal guide, a part of the Self that watches what is going on from a slight distance. This will enable her to tolerate ambiguity. After the group has been in existence for a while, individual members stop expecting a total and dramatic transformation into a completely different person.

From the workers' point of view, there is a great deal to confront around the time of parting. Disappointed and blaming ourselves for things that have not been achieved, we may fear that without our help members will 'slip back'. Are responses such as these a sign of our lack of trust and faith in group members? Why do we feel that we are the only people who can offer the group help? Our worries and anxieties hide the depths of our feelings, for the group is just as much a part of our lives as it is of group members' lives. Each of us must face up to the loss of containment which the group provides, the loss of unconditional acceptance and intimacy, the loss of structured time for the Self.

Once partings are faced, then it is so much easier for group members to anticipate the future. The apparent opposites of loss and gain mean that a member may be embarking on a new phase of the journey with a sense of independence. Endings signify a rite of passage in which we reclaim and accept hidden parts of ourselves and the last session is the final ritual for reviewing the group and summarizing the insights gained. We can mark our pleasure in the group's past existence by having a farewell party, a trip out during which we can reminisce and be nostalgic. One women's group gave each co-worker a bowl of daffodil bulbs, which have subsequently been planted in the garden of one of the authors. Each year the golden blooms multiply in numbers, as if to signify the strength of solidarity, and to celebrate rebirth and renewal.

With the benefit of hindsight: Evaluating the whole   Time spent in developing a thoughtful ending raises the need for workers to adopt a consciously evaluative attitude to the feminist approach. This is our responsibility because the harsh economic and political climate is biting even harder and we are bombarded on all sides by calls for justification of our existence. Evaluation is necessary for managerial purposes, but it is not enough to restrict ourselves narrowly to areas of achievement and limitation, and to the provision of feedback on progress. Evaluation needs to be measured in individual personal terms, according to the degree of stability, change and enhancement of circumstances brought about by group participation. Each woman needs to see the changes taking place in her awareness and abilities to act (see Chapter 3). If we are specific in our search for meaning, then changes and limitations will be discerned more speedily. Regular recapping of events and charting of the changes that have occurred enable each woman to look at how she would have dealt with a series of issues previously, what she would have said, how she would have reacted, and what her behaviour is like now.

We constantly need to improve the quality of our feminist practice and to be mindful of the myriad variables which affect the group experience. The nature and degree of members' difficulties, their social situations, and the extent to which they accept the rationale of the group all affect outcome. Workers' personal and interactional styles are also significant. Giving thought to these variables and analysing their development in the group can help to highlight those qualities which are necessary, if not sufficient, for feminist groupwork. Evaluation should not be relegated to the position of postscript, a retrospective and anecdotal look at the group. It is an integral part of groupwork which can be carried out using the methods described in Chapter 3. Direct observation, questionnaires, self-assessment, rating scales and women's statements can all be used as long as the purpose is clear and we gain information that is closely linked to our original questions.

In our groups there were obvious practical improvements in members' life-styles without drastic negative consequences. Everyone stated how much more polarized life had become; they were able to acknowledge the misery that certain events brought but the good was clearer and easier to value and enjoy. The women learnt that within the group setting it was safe to say anything; they witnessed differences of opinion which did not result in relationship breakdown; they learnt that they had the right to ask, to speak; that they did not have to wait until the time was right, because how do you decide when that moment has come? They learnt to recognize and value their qualities. They realized that giving everything of themselves did not necessarily lead to reciprocation and that it was for them to set the limits. Once they were more clearly defined, others responded to them more positively.

However painful and liberating the process of endings and evaluation proves to be, women's group members can explore their own potential in order to achieve a level of dignity and self-respect. What follows are women's affirmative statements about the role of the group in their lives:

I never realized I had so much inside me.

This has changed me – I'll never be the same again.

It used to be 'Him first, then the kids, and if there was anything left – perhaps me'. Now I can just about make myself put me first some of the time.

It's been wonderful to talk about all those dreadful things that happened years ago, and not be made to feel it was my fault.

I hope you younger women will learn from my experience, my mistakes –
leave while you can, while you've got some life left to live.

I put the valium down the loo and started doing yoga. It was the best day of
my life.

Connecting strands: Women's groups past, present and future

We began this book with an exploration of the impact of isolation on
women's lives and the destruction and dismissal of certain working-
class life-styles by the culture of white dominance. The ways in which
interdependence and support networks are despised in favour of an
ever more individualistic and entrepreneurial society reinforce the
fragmentation of women's psyche. Consciously or subconsciously the
hierarchies of dominant institutions exist to keep women apart
because fundamentally there is a fear of the power of women together.
Whatever the variations in individual circumstance, detail and
consequences, the repercussions of separation and isolation are felt by
workers and women alike. For women in poverty, the enormous
struggle to survive compels them to adopt the most individualistic
strategies which, they are informed by dominant cultural messages, are
the only possible ways to respond. Yet these are completely at odds
with the traditions of collective action which have developed within
working-class communities, both in the workplace and at home
(Jones, 1983). Indeed, through our practice we have seen how
negatively so many women view themselves, how hard they find it to
accept positive aspects of themselves, how confused they are by media
and professional messages.

For women workers, the damaging effects of white masculinist
organizational structures bite so hard that women feel they have to be
better and work harder than men to achieve recognition. Painfully we
learnt that to lose our sense of direction or to become overwhelmed by
the pressures of a patriarchal environment only left us with one option:
we had to hang on to the fundamental right to *be*.

More than ever we are convinced of the value of groupwork as a
vehicle for change in an era when we have fewer material resources to
offer than before and when the conventional view of women is being
reinforced in the face of feminist statements. The patterns of isolation
can be broken down irrevocably by the strength and decisiveness of
women together. The prevailing ideology will not take this lying down.
Change on a woman-centred, feminist basis is seen as too great a
challenge and has to be resisted. This presents women's groups with
something of a moral victory because patriarchy loses its legitimacy
through its own unjust actions.

As a way of drawing together the threads of our writing, we want to present an overview of the differing elements of feminist groupwork and its overarching purpose in breaking down these crumbling walls of injustice. Feminist groupwork provides:

1 A basis for reassessing social structures and contradictions by presenting an alternative linguistic and conceptual code. Rather than putting the blame for societal ills on women's shoulders, feminist ideology reshapes personal experience within a socio-political framework.

2 A balance between group structure, planning and spontaneity which avoids rigidly prescribed patterns. These provide the necessary boundaries within which safety, warmth and compassion can flourish.

3 As much variety of activity as possible within itself in order to draw out women's potential, as limits on this are artificial.

4 A basis for the development of group identity through the validation of the relational elements of group process and dynamics. An atmosphere of mutual identification and influence emerges out of the growth of trust and reciprocity. This is made possible through open self-disclosure and positive feedback. Women's groups also need conflict of growth to enhance individual and collective learning. Group conflict and contradictions are necessary conditions for the establishment of alliances between women based on a recognition of each other's differences.

5 A forum for the appraisal of structural power relations and processes within the group which are necessary for members to have control and be empowered. Teasing out patterns of interaction between members based on stereotyping and prejudice can be used to break down group roles, such as scapegoat or clown. The realization that group processes involve the negotiation of power can begin to free women from the victim role.

6 A basis for self-exploration and personal identity change. Paradox and contradiction in women's groups facilitate the awakening of women's self-definition based around caring, a sense of well-being and sexuality. In such circumstances, personal identity develops through a process of recognition, of naming, reflection and then re-evaluation. Enhanced self-awareness brings with it an increase in self-esteem and a sense of continuity in the world.

7 A basis for understanding female psychology which draws upon cognitive, emotional, behavioural and spiritual elements, placing these within a structural context.

   (a) Women's groups reinforce members' struggles to organize their thoughts and to frame these constructively so that even if validation fluctuates there is a positive baseline to which to return.

(b)   Women's groups give permission for the expression of a range of emotions, however intense and messy. It is possible for women to be sad, happy, angry or confused and for these not to become fixed points in an individual's identity. Anger is awakened as a key motivating force in social action.

(c)   Women's groups recognize the extent to which behaviour is reinterpreted and misconstrued and how it is possible to free women from this.

8   An approach to evaluation which concentrates on individual development and group process, and avoids looking at whether the group has 'succeeded' or 'failed' in hierarchical terms. Rather than having a specifically labelled goal to aim for which everyone stands or falls by, it is for each woman to draw her own conclusions about her self-awareness and capacity for change as enabled by the group.

9   Models of female behaviour based in strength, confidence and a sense of personal worth which have a profound impact on the personal and public spheres. Family and friends must adjust to women's new-found certainty. The stereotypical responses of professionals and institutions are shaken, causing disruption to their ideological pursuits.

Feminist groupwork delabels, deconstructs boundaries, expands a sense of personal vision and makes the connections between these and wider socio-economic forces. The changes in women's personal lives have irreversible repercussions. Sustaining social change in the face of resistance and ridicule is nurtured by the bedrock of the group. Feminist groupwork breaks down the destructiveness of individualism.

This approach is adaptable. Its fundamental principles and practices are transferable to work with women from all walks of life. Undoubtedly the details, the particular concerns will be different across diverse cultural situations, but the shape remains the same. Whatever the differences between women based on sexuality, class, age, disability, race, ethnicity and religion, groupwork with women has a wide application.

Women's groups call everything that is familiar and predictable into question. This generates anger, confusion and resentment on all sides and we run the risk of leaving these tensions unresolved. Critics have said disparagingly that we cannot do anything radical to change the lives of women in poverty, so why raise their hopes? We know that we have a responsibility to raise hopes. Feminist groupwork facilitates a sense of belonging, a sense of grounding within the context of certain events and societal structures. This leads to an appraisal of how events occur, of how history gets made, and of which issues assume importance within a woman's biography. By developing a vision of how things can be different, women's groups have a dramatic impact across historical and cultural divisions. How can we ignore the importance of the following group member's statement?

> I feel proud to hold my head up and say 'Look at me, there are things I can do with my life.'

Our protests free women's creative potential from the stifling fog of woman-hatred. Feminist groupwork gives women permission to value their intuition, bringing their submerged imaginativeness to the surface.

Every time this happens, the world does not remain the same.

References

Allen, H. (1987) *Justice Unbalanced: Gender, Psychiatry and Judicial Decisions*. Milton Keynes: Open University Press.

Anderson, R. (1975) Leisure: An inappropriate concept for women? Canberra: Australian Government Publishing Service. Quoted in Egar and Sarkissian (1985). p.123.

Arendt, H. (1978) *The Life of the Mind*. New York: Harcourt Brace Jovanovich.

Barker, H. (1986) Recapturing sisterhood: A critical look at 'process' in feminist organising and community work. *Critical Social Policy* 16, 80–90.

Barratt, M. (1980) *Women's Oppression Today*. London: Verso.

Beck, A.T. and Greenberg, R.L. (1974) Cognitive therapy with depressed women. In V. Franks and V. Burtle (eds) *Women in Therapy*. New York: Brunner/Mazel.

Beck, A.T., Rush, A.J., Shaw, B.F. and Emery, G. (1979) *Cognitive Therapy of Depression*. New York: Guilford.

Bell, C. and Roberts, H. (eds) (1984) *Social Researching: Politics, Problems, Practice*. London: Routledge & Kegan Paul.

Borkowski, M., Murch, M. and Walker, V. (1983) *Marital Violence: The Community Response*. London: Tavistock.

Boston Women's Health Collective (1979) *Our Bodies Ourselves: A Health Book by and for Women*. Harmondsworth: Penguin.

Bowles, G. and Klein, R.D. (eds) (1983) *Theories of Women's Studies*. London: Routledge & Kegan Paul.

Bradshaw, J. (1972) The concept of social need. *New Society* 19 (496), 640–3.

Brandes, D. and Phillips, H. (1977) *Gamesters' Handbook: 140 Games for Teachers and Group Leaders*. London: Hutchinson.

Breakwell, G. (1986) *Coping with Threatened Identities*. London: Methuen.

Brodsky, A. (1973) The consciousness-raising group as a model for therapy with women. *Psychotherapy: Theory, Research and Practice* 10 (1) Spring, 24–9.

Brody, E.B. (1987) New reproductive technologies and women's rights: Framing the ethical questions. *Health Care for Women International* 8 (4), 277–86.

Brook, E. and Davis, A. (1985) *Women, the Family and Social Work*. London: Tavistock.

Broverman, I., Broverman, D., Clarkson, F., Rosenkrantz, P. and Vogel, S. (1970) Sex-role stereotypes and clinical judgements of mental health. *Journal of Consulting and Clinical Psychology* 34, 1–7.

Brown, G. and Harris, T. (1978) *Social Origins of Depression: A Study of Psychiatric Disorder in Women*. London: Tavistock.

Brown, R. and Williams, J. (1984) Group identification: The same thing to all people? *Human Relations* 37 (7), 547–64.

Bryan, B., Dadzie, S. and Scafe, S. (1985) *The Heart of the Race: Black Women's Lives in Britain*. London: Virago.

Butler, P.E. (1981) *Self Assertion for Women*. San Francisco: Harper & Row.

Caplan, P.T. (1983) Between women: Lowering the barriers. In Robbins and Siegal (1983). pp. 51–66.

Carby, H. (1982) White women listen! Black feminism and the boundaries of sisterhood. In Centre for Contemporary Cultural Studies, Birmingham, *The Empire Strikes Back, Race and Racism in 70's Britain*. London: Hutchinson. pp. 212–35.

Carew-Jones, M. and Watson, H. (1985) *Making the Break*. Harmondsworth: Penguin.

Chesler, P. (1972) *Women and Madness*. New York: Avon.

City of Leicester Teachers' Association (NUT) (1987) *Outlaws in the Classroom: Lesbians and Gays in the School System*. Leicester: CLTA (NUT).

Cockburn, C. (1978) *The Local State*. London: Pluto Press.

Crane, P. (1984) *Gays and the Law*. London: Pluto Press.

Curno, A., Lamming, A., Leach, L., Stiles, J., Ward, V. and Ziff, T. (eds) (1982) *Women in Collective Action*. London: Association of Community Workers.

Dale, J. and Foster, P. (1986) Welfare professionals and the control of women. In *Feminists and State Welfare*, Radical Social Policy Series. London: Routledge & Kegan Paul. pp. 81–104.

Daly, M. (1973) *Beyond God the Father: Towards a Philosophy of Woman's Liberation*. Boston: Beacon Press.

Daly, M. (1978) *Gyn/Ecology*. London: Women's Press.

David, M. (1986) Morality and maternity. *Critical Social Policy* 16, 40–56.

Davidson, S. and Packard, R. (1981) The therapeutic value of friendship between women. *Psychology of Women Quarterly* 5, 495–510.

Davies, W. (1982) A women's group – A case study to think about. In Curno et al. (1982). pp. 103–12.

Davis, A. (1982) *Women, Race and Class*. London: Women's Press.

Davis, R. (1988) Learning from working class women. *Community Development Journal* 23 (2), 110–16.

Dex, S. and Phillipson, C. (1986) Older women in the labour market. *Critical Social Policy* 15, 79–83.

Dickson, A. (1982) *A Woman in Your Own Right: Assertiveness and You*. London: Quartet.

Dickson, A. (1985) *The Mirror Within: A New Look at Sexuality*. London: Quartet.

Donnelly, A. (1986) *Feminist Social Work with a Women's Group*. Social Work Monographs 41, University of East Anglia, Norwich.

Doyal, L. and Gough, I. (1984) A theory of human needs. *Critical Social Policy* 10, 6–38.

Du Bois, B. (1983) Passionate scholarship: Notes on values, knowing and method in feminist social science. In G. Bowles and R.D. Klein (eds) *Theories of Women's Studies*. London: Routledge & Kegan Paul.

Eastman, P.C. (1973) Consciousness-raising as a resocialization process for women. *Smith College Studies in Social Work* 43 (3), 153–83.

Eckenstein, L. (1963) *Women under Monasticism*. New York: Russell & Russell.

Egar, R. and Sarkissian, W. (1985) Coping with the suburban nightmare: Developing community supports in Australia. *Sociological Focus* 18 (2), 119–25.

Ehrenreich, B. and English, D. (1979) *For Her Own Good: 150 Years of the Experts' Advice to Women*. London: Pluto Press.

Eichenbaum, L. and Orbach, S. (1987) Separation and intimacy: Crucial practice issues in working with women in therapy. In S. Ernst and M. Maguire (eds) *Living with the Sphinx: Papers from the Women's Therapy Centre*. London: Women's Press. pp. 49–67.

Ellis, E. and Nichols, M.P. (1979) A comparative study of feminist and traditional group assertiveness training with women. *Psychotherapy: Theory, Research and Practice* 16 (4), 467–74.

Erikson, E.H. (1950) *Childhood and Society*. New York: Norton.

Erikson, E.H. (1970) *Identity through the Life Cycle*. 2nd edn. New York: Norton.

Ernst, S. and Goodison, L. (1981) *In Our Own Hands: A Book of Self-Help Therapy*. London: Women's Press.

Faderman, L. (1985) *Surpassing the Love of Men. Romantic Friendship and Love between Women from the Renaissance to the Present*. London: Women's Press.

Ferree, M.M. (1983) The women's movement in the working class. *Sex Roles* 9 (4), 493–505.

Finch, J. (1983) Dividing the rough and the respectable: Working-class women and pre-school playgroups. In E. Gamarnikov, D. Morgan, J. Purvis and D. Taylorson (eds), *The Public and the Private*. London: Heinemann. pp. 106–17.

Finch, J. (1984) It's great to have someone to talk to! The ethics and politics of interviewing women. In C. Bell and H. Roberts (eds) *Social Researching: Politics, Problems, Practice*. London: Routledge & Kegan Paul. pp. 70–87.

Finch, J. and Groves, D. (1983) *A Labour of Love: Women, Work and Caring*. London: Routledge & Kegan Paul.

Firestone, S. (1972) *The Dialectic of Sex*. London: Paladin.

Freeman, J. (1984) The tyranny of structurelessness. In *Untying the Knot*. Dark Star Press and Rebel Press.

Freire, P. (1970) *Pedagogy of the Oppressed*. New York: Seabury Press.

Friedan, B. (1963) *The Feminine Mystique*. New York: Dell.

Gartrell, N. (1984) Issues in psychotherapy with lesbian women, *Work in Progress Series* 83–04. Wellesley, Mass: Stone Center for Developmental Services and Studies.

George, V. and Wilding, P. (1976) *Ideology and Social Welfare*. London: Routledge & Kegan Paul.

Gilligan, C. (1982) *In a Different Voice: Psychological Theory and Women's Development*. Boston: Cambridge University Press.

Glendinning, C. and Millar, J. (1987) *Women and Poverty in Britain*. Brighton: Wheatsheaf.

Goffman, E. (1961) *Asylums*. Harmondsworth: Penguin.

Goodenow, C. (1985) Women's friendships and their association with psychological well-being. Paper presented at the meeting of the American Psychology Association. Los Angeles, Calif. Quoted in Rose and Roades (1987).

Graham, H. (1984) Surveying through stories. In C. Bell and H. Roberts (eds) *Social Researching: Politics, Problems, Practice*. London: Routledge & Kegan Paul. pp. 104–24.

Griffin, S. (1978) *Woman and Nature: The Roaring Inside Her*. London: Women's Press.

Hancock, B. (1986) Changed lives: The power of community work and second chance education. In P. Flynn, C. Johnson, S. Lieberman, H. Armstrong (eds) *You're Learning All the Time: Women, Education and Community Work*. Nottingham: Spokesman. pp. 80–98.

Hearn, J., Sheppard, D.L., Tancred-Sherriff, P. and Burrell, G. (eds) (1989) *The Sexuality of Organization*. London: Sage.

Highet, G. (1986) Gender and education: A study of the ideology and practice of community based women's education as observed in three groups operating within the city of Glasgow. *Studies in the Education of Adults* 18 (2), 118–29.

Hillery, G.A. (1955) Definitions of community. *Rural Sociology* 20 (2), 111–23.

Hooks, B. (1982) *Ain't I a Woman: Black Women and Feminism*. London: Pluto Press.

Houston, G. (1987) *The Red Book of Groups and How to Lead Them Better*. 2nd edn. London: Rochester Foundation.

Hutter, B. and Williams, G. (eds) (1981) *Controlling Women: The Normal and the Deviant*. London: Croom Helm.

Huws, G.M. (1982) The conscientization of women: A rite of self-initiation with the flavour of a religious conversion process. *Women's Studies International Forum* 5 (5), 401–10.

Hyde, C. (1986) Experiences of women activists: Implications for community organizing theory and practice. *Journal of Sociology and Social Welfare* 13 (3), 545–62.

Illich, I. (1976) *Limits to Medicine: Medical Nemesis, the Expropriation of Health*, 2nd edn. London: Marion Boyars.

Illich, I., Zola, I.K., McKnight, J., Caplan, J. and Shaiken, H. (1977)*Disabling Professions*. London: Marion Boyars.

Itzin, C. (1987) Head, hand, heart – and the writing of wrongs. In L. Sanders (ed.) *Glancing Fires: An Investigation into Women's Creativity*. London: Women's Press. pp. 108–18.

Jackson, J. (1980) Commentary: Racism and sexism. *Chattanooga Times*, 4 Aug., p. A6. Quoted in Reid (1984), pp. 247–55.

Jones, C. (1983) *State Social Work and the Working Class*. London: Macmillan.

Jones, C. and Mahoney, P. (1989) *Learning Our Lines: Sexuality and Social Control in Education*. London: Women's Press.

Joseph, G. and Lewis, J. (1981) *Common Differences: Conflicts in Black and White Feminist Perspectives*. New York: Anchor Press.

Kaplan, A.G. (1984) The 'Self-in-relation': Implications for depression in women, *Work in Progress Series* 14. Wellesley, Mass.: Stone Center for Developmental Services and Studies.

Kaplan, A.G., Brooks, B., McComb, A.L., Shapiro, E.R. and Sodano, A. (1983) Women and anger in psychotherapy. In Robbins and Siegal (1983). pp. 29–40.

Kelly, L. (1988) *Surviving Sexual Violence*. Cambridge: Polity Press.

Kenner, S. (1985) *No Time for Women*. London: Pandora Press.

Kingdon, M.A. and Bagoon, S.R. (1983) Sexuality Awareness Workshop for Women. *Journal for Specialists in Group Work* 8 (1): 17–23.

Kirk, S. (1983) The role of politics in feminist counseling. In Robbins and Siegal (1983). pp. 179–89.

Klein, R.D. (1983) How to do what we want to do: Thoughts about feminist methodology. In Bowles and Klein (1983).

Lazarus, R.S. and Folkman, S. (1984) *Stress, Appraisal and Coping*. New York: Springer.

Leicester City Council (1983) Survey. Quoted in Leicestershire Racism Awareness Consortium, *Information Pack on Some British Cultures*. Leicester: LRAC.

Lewis, J. (1981) Women, lost and found: The impact of feminism on history. In Spender (1981). 55–72.

Lewis, J. and Meredith, B. (1988) *Daughters Who Care; Daughters Caring for Mothers at Home*. London: Routledge & Kegan Paul.

Lieberman, M.A. and Bond, G.R. (1978) Self-help groups: Problems of measuring outcome. *Small Group Behaviour* 9 (2), 221–41.

Liebmann, M. (1989) *Art Therapy for Groups: A Handbook of Themes, Games and Exercises*. London: Routledge & Kegan Paul.

Loeffler, D. and Fiedler, L. (1979) Woman – a sense of identity: A counseling intervention to facilitate personal growth in women. *Journal of Counseling Psychology* 26 (1), 51–7.

London Rape Crisis Centre (1984) *Sexual Violence*. London: Women's Press.

Long, S. (1984) Early integration in groups: 'A group to join, and a group to create'. *Human Relations* 37 (4), 311–32.

Longres, J.F. and McLeod, E. (1980) Consciousness-raising and social work practice. *Journal of Social Casework* 61 (5), 267–76.

Lovell, T. (1980) *Pictures of Reality: Aesthetics, Politics and Pleasure*. London: BFI.

Lury, C. (1987) *The Difference of Women's Writing: Essays on the Use of Personal Experience*, Studies in Sexual Politics 15. Manchester: Manchester University Sociology Department.

MacDonald, B. and Rich, C. (1984) *Look Me the Eye: Old Women, Ageing and Ageism.* London: Women's Press.

Maguire, M. (1987) Casting the evil eye – Women and envy. In S. Ernst and M. Maguire (eds) *Living with the Sphinx: Papers from the Women's Therapy Centre.* London: Women's Press. pp. 117–52.

Marchant, H. and Wearing, B. (eds) (1986) *Gender Reclaimed: Women in Social Work.* Sydney: Hale & Iremonger.

Mavor, E. (1971) *The Ladies of Llangollen.* Harmondsworth: Penguin.

Mayo, M. (ed.) (1977) *Women in the Community.* London: Routledge & Kegan Paul.

Meeker, B.F. (1983) Cooperative orientation, trust and reciprocity. *Human Relations* 37 (3), 225–43.

Meleis, A.I. and Rogers, S. (1987) Women in transition: Being versus becoming or being and becoming. *Health Care for Women International* 8 (4), 199–217.

Meyer Spacks, P. (1978) *The Female Imagination: A Literary and Psychological Investigation of Women's Writing.* London: Allen and Unwin.

Miller, J.B. (1976) *Toward a New Psychology of Women.* Boston, Mass.: Beacon Press.

Miller, J.B. (1982) Colloquium: Women and power, *Work in Progress Series* 82–01. Wellesley, Mass.: Stone Center for Developmental Services and Studies.

Miller, J.B. (1983a) The construction of anger in women and men, *Work in Progress Series* 83–01. Wellesley, Mass.: Stone Center for Developmental Services and Studies.

Miller, J.B. (1983b) The necessity of conflict. In Robbins and Siegal (1983). pp. 3–9.

Miller, J.B. (1984) The development of women's sense of self, *Work in Progress Series* 12. Wellesley, Mass.: Stone Center for Developmental Services and Studies.

Millett, K. (1971) *Sexual Politics.* New York: Avon.

Morgan G. and Ramirez, R. (1983) Action learning: A holographic metaphor for guiding social change. *Human Relations* 27 (1), 1–28.

Morley, D. and Warpole, K. (eds) (1982) *The Republic of Letters. Working Class Writing and Local Publishing.* London: Comedia.

Mullender, A. and Ward, D. (1985) Towards an alternative model of social groupwork. *British Journal of Social Work* 15 (2), 155–72.

Nairne, K. and Smith, G. (1984) *Dealing with Depression.* London: Women's Press Handbook Series.

Noddings, N. (1984) *Caring: A Feminine Approach to Ethics and Moral Education.* Berkeley, Calif,: University of California Press.

Oakley, A. (1980) *Women Confined.* Oxford: Robertson.

Oakley, A. (1981) *Subject Women.* London: Fontana.

Ogilvie, D.M. (1987) Life satisfaction and identity structure in late middle-aged men and women. *Psychology and Ageing* 2 (3), 217–24.

Packwood, M. (1983) The colonel's lady and Judy O'Grady: Class in the Women's Liberation Movement. *Trouble and Strife* 1.

Pahl, J. (ed.) (1985) *Private Violence and Public Policy: The Needs of Battered Women and the Response of the Public Services.* London: Routledge & Kegan Paul.

Peck, T.A. (1986) Women's self-definition in adulthood: From a different model? *Psychology of Women Quarterly* 10 (3), 274–84.

Penfold, P.S. and Walker, G.A. (1984) *Women and the Psychiatric Paradox.* Milton Keynes: Open University Press.

Pheterson, G. (1986) Alliances between women: Overcoming internalized oppression and internalized domination. *Signs: Journal of Women in Culture and Society* 12 (1), 146–60.

Phillips, A. (1987) *Divided Loyalties: Dilemmas of Sex and Class.* London: Virago.

Plath, S. (1963) *The Bell Jar.* London: Faber.

Preston-Shoot, M. (1987) *Effective Groupwork*, BASW/Practical Social Work Series. London: Macmillan.

Raymond, J. (1986) *A Passion for Friends: Toward a Philosophy of Female Affection*. London: Women's Press.

Reid, P.T. (1984) Feminism versus minority group identity: Not for black women only. *Sex Roles* 10 (3/4), 247–55.

Reinharz, S. (1983) Women as competent community builders: The other side of the coin. *Issues in Mental Health Nursing* 5 (1–4), 19–43.

Rendel, M. (1978) The death of leadership or educating people to lead themselves. *Women's Studies International Quarterly* 1 (4), 313–25.

Rich, A. (1976) *Of Woman Born*. New York: Bantam.

Rich, A. (1979) *On Lies, Secrets and Silence: Selected Prose 1966–1978*. London: Virago.

Rich, A. (1980) Compulsory heterosexuality and lesbian existence. *Signs* 5 (4), 631–60.

Rights of Women Lesbian Custody Group (1986) *Lesbian Mothers' Legal Handbook*. London: Women's Press Handbook Series.

Robbins, J.H. (1983) Complex triangles: Uncovering sexist bias in relationship counseling. In Robbins and Siegal (1983). pp. 159–69.

Robbins, J.H. and Siegal, R.J. (eds) (1983) *Women Changing Therapy* – New Assessments: Values and Strategies in Feminist Therapy. Special issue of *Women and Therapy: A Feminist Quarterly* 2 (2/3).

Roberts, H. (ed.) (1981) *Doing Feminist Research*. London: Routledge & Kegan Paul.

Robinson, C.R. (1983) Black women: A tradition of self-reliant strength. In Robbins and Siegal (1983). pp. 135–44.

Rose, S. (1985) Same and Cross-sex friendships and the psychology of homosexuality. *Sex Roles* 12 (1–2), 63–74.

Rose, S. and Roades, L. (1987) Feminism and women's friendships. *Psychology of Women Quarterly* 11 (2), 243–54.

Rosenham, D.L. and Seligman, M.E.P. (1984) *Abnormal Psychology*. New York: Norton.

Rowbotham, S. (1973) *Hidden from History*. London: Pluto Press.

Rowbotham, S. (1974) *Women's Consciousness, Man's World*. Harmondsworth: Penguin.

Rowbotham, S. (1979) The Women's Movement and organising for socialism. In S. Rowbotham, L. Segal and H. Wainwright (eds) *Beyond the Fragments: Feminism and the Making of Socialism*. London: Newcastle Socialist Centre and Islington Community Press. pp. 9–87.

Rowbotham, S. (1983) Women, power and consciousness: Discussion in the Women's Liberation Movement in Britain, 1969–81. In S. Rowbotham, *Dreams and Dilemmas: Collective Writings*. London: Virago. pp. 136–60.

Ruzek, S.B. (1980) Medical response to women's health activities: Conflict, accommodation and cooptation. *Research in the Sociology of Health Care* 1, 335–54.

Sayers, J. (1986) *Sexual Contradictions: Psychology, Psychoanalysis, and Feminism*. London: Tavistock.

Scott, H. (1984) *Working Your Way to the Bottom: The Feminisation of Poverty*. London: Pandora Press.

Scott, M. (1989) *A Cognitive–Behavioural Approach to Clients' Problems*, Tavistock Library of Social Work Practice. London: Tavistock/Routledge.

Seligman, M.E.P. (1975) *Helplessness*. San Francisco: W.H. Freeman.

Sen, A.M. (1984) Food battles: Conflicts in the access to food. *Food and Nutrition* 10 (1): 81–9.

Sherif, C.W. (1982) Needed concepts in the study of gender identity. *Psychology of Women Quarterly* 6, 375–98.

Showalter, E. (1987) *The Female Malady: Women, Madness and English Culture, 1830–1980*. London: Virago.

Smart, C. and Sevenhuijsen, S. (eds) (1989) *Child Custody and The Politics of Gender*. Sociology of Law and Crime Series. London: Routledge & Kegan Paul.

Smith, G. (1980) *Social Need*. London: Routledge & Kegan Paul.

Spender, D. (1980) *Man Made Language*. London: Routledge & Kegan Paul.

Spender, D. (ed.) (1981) *Men's Studies Modified: The Impact of Feminism on the Academic Disciplines*, Athene Series. Oxford: Pergamon Press.

Spender, D. (1982a) *Invisible Women: The Schooling Scandal*. London: Writers and Readers.

Spender, D. (1982b) *Women of Ideas*. London: Routledge & Kegan Paul.

Spender, D. and Sarah, E. (eds) (1980) *Learning to Lose – Sexism and Education*. London: Women's Press.

Spitzer, S. (1973) Towards a Marxian theory of deviance. *Social Problems* 22 (5), 638–51.

Stanley, L. and Wise, S. (1983) *Breaking Out: Feminist Consciousness and Feminist Research*. London: Routledge & Kegan Paul.

Swanson-Kauffman, K.M. (1987) Overview of the balancing act: Having it all. *Health Care for Women International* 8 (2–3), 101–7.

Thompson, J.L. (1983) *Learning Liberation*. London: Croom Helm.

Thorne, B. (1987) Re-visioning women and social change: Where are the children? *Gender and Society* 1 (1), 85–109.

Unger, R.K. (1983) Through the looking glass: No wonderland yet! (the reciprocal relationship between methodology and models of reality). *Psychology of Women Quarterly* 8, 9–32.

Urwin, C. (1984) Power relations and the emergence of language. In J. Henriques, W. Hollway, C. Urwin, C. Venn and V. Walkerdine, *Changing the Subject: Psychology, Social Regulation and Subjectivity*. London: Methuen. pp. 264–322.

Walker, B.M. (1981) Psychology and feminism – If you can't beat them, join them. In Spender (1981). pp. 111–24.

Washington, M.H. (1981) Teaching black-eyed Susans an approach to the study of black women writers. In P. Scott, B. Smith and G. Hull (eds) *Some Of Us are Brave*. Old Westbury: Feminist Press.

Wilkinson, S. (1986) Sighting possibilities: Diversity and commonality in feminist research. In S. Wilkinson (ed.) *Feminist Social Psychology: Developing Theory and Practice*. Milton Keynes: Open University Press. pp. 7–24.

Williams, J.A. (1984) Gender and intergroup behaviour: Towards an integration. *British Journal of Social Psychology* 23 (4), 311–16.

Willis, P. (1977) *Learning to Labour*. Farnborough: Saxon House.

Wilson, E. (1977) *Women and the Welfare State*. London: Tavistock.

Woods, N.F. (1987) Women's lives: Pressure and pleasure, conflict and support. *Health Care for Women International* 8 (2–3), 109–19.

Index